14.95

EDINBURGH
EDUCATION AND SOCIETY
SERIES

General Editor: Colin Bell

OH, DEAR ME

Oh, dear me, the mill's gaen fest,
   The puir wee shifters canna get a rest,
Shiftin' bobbins, coorse and fine,
   They fairly mak' ye work for your ten and nine.

Oh, dear me, I wish the day was done,
   Runnin' up and doon the Pass is no nae fun;
Shiftin', piecin', spinning' warp, weft and twine,
   Tae feed and cled my bairnie affen ten and nine.

Oh, dear me, the warld's ill-divided,
   Them that work the hardest are aye wi' least provided,
But I maun bide contented, dark days or fine,
   But there's no much pleasure livin' affen ten and nine.

MARY BROOKSBANK

The World is Ill Divided

Women's work in Scotland
in the nineteenth and early twentieth centuries

edited by
Eleanor Gordon
and
Esther Breitenbach

EDINBURGH UNIVERSITY PRESS

© Edinburgh University Press 1990
22 George Square, Edinburgh

Distributed in North America
by Columbia University Press
New York

Set in Linotron Palatino
by Koinonia Ltd, Bury, and
printed in Great Britain by
Page Bros Ltd, Norwich

British Library Cataloguing
    in Publication Data
The world is ill divided: women's
    work in Scotland in the nineteenth
    and early twentieth centuries. –
    (Edinburgh education and society
    series).
1. Scotland. Women. Employment,
    history
I. Gordon, Eleanor II. Breitenbach,
    Esther III. Series
331.409411

ISBN 0 7486 0116 3

The publisher acknowledges subsidy from
the Scottish Arts Council towards
the publication of this volume

CONTENTS

CONTRIBUTORS

Alice J. Albert
Alice J. Albert is a Canadian of Scottish descent. She lived for several years in Glasgow, where she carried out research into women's work in the late nineteenth century. She is a graduate of The University of Strathclyde, and now lives in British Columbia, Canada.

Wendy Alexander
Wendy Alexander is a graduate of the Universities of Glasgow and Warwick. She has worked as a political researcher, and as the editor of a journal on local economic development. She is currently a researcher with the Labour Party in Scotland.

Esther Breitenbach
Esther Breitenbach was a founding member of the *Scottish Women's Liberation Journal* and its successor, *Msprint*, and contributed regularly to these publications. She is the author of *Women Workers in Scotland* (Pressgang, 1982), and has contributed articles on women in Scotland to *Feminist Review, Cencrastus, Radical Scotland*, and the *Scottish Government Yearbook*.

Callum G. Brown
Callum G. Brown is a graduate of the University of St Andrew's and Glasgow, and is a Lecturer in Urban History in the Department of History at the University of Strathclyde.

Eleanor Gordon
Eleanor Gordon has taught in higher education in Scotland for some years and is currently a Research Fellow in the Department of Economic History at the University of Glasgow. She is the author of a number of articles on women and work, and of *Women and the Labour Movement in Scotland*. (Oxford University Press, 1990). She is a member of the committee and of the editorial collective of the Scottish Labour History Society

Lynn Jamieson

Lynn Jamieson holds a Ph. D. from the University of Edinburgh on 'The Development of the Modern Family: the Case of Urban Scotland in the Early Twentieth Century. ' She is a Lecturer in the Department of Sociology at the University of Edinburgh, and has contributed articles to *Sociology* and to *Labour and Love*, edited by Jane Lewis (Blackwell, 1986).

Linda Mahood

Linda Mahood was born in Western Canada and is a graduate of the Universities of Saskatchewan and Glasgow. She has done research on the sociology of the family, and is author of a book on women and prostitution in Scotland. (Routledge & Kegan Paul, 1990).

Siân Reynolds

Siân Reynolds studied at the University of Oxford and Sussex, and obtained a doctorate in history at the University of Paris. She was a Lecturer at the University of Sussex from 1974–89. She has lived in Edinburgh since 1980, and is currently a Lecturer in the French Department at the University of Edinburgh. She has translated a number of books by French historians and written articles on French history. She edited *Women, State and Revolution: essays on power and gender in Europe* (Harvester, 1986) and is the author of *Britannica's Typesetters: Women Compositors in Edwardian Edinburgh*, (Edinburgh University Press, 1989).

Barbara W. Robertson

Barbara W. Robertson received an Honours degree in Sociology from the University of Edinburgh as a mature student in 1969. She is the author of 'The Border Farm Worker' in *Essays in Scottish Labour History*, edited by Ian MacDougall (John Donald, 1978).

James J. Smyth

James J. Smyth is a graduate of the University of Glasgow, and was awarded a Ph. D. by the University of Edinburgh in 1987. He has worked on the Social Change and Economic Life Initiative, Research Centre for Social Sciences, University of Edinburgh. He is currently a Research Fellow in the Department of Economic and Social History. He is the author of *Labour and Democracy* (Edinburgh University Press, forthcoming).

Jayne D. Stephenson

Jayne D. Stephenson is a graduate of Lancashire Polytechnic in Preston, and is the Local History Officer for Stirling District Council and the Smith Museum, Stirling.

INTRODUCTION

The 1980s witnessed a flourishing of research and interest in women's history, accompanied by a proliferation of publications in the field. Unfortunately, in terms of the latter there has not been such a rich yield in Scotland. In 1983 the Glasgow Women's Studies Group produced *Uncharted Lives: Extracts from Scottish Women's Experience, 1850–1982* (Pressgang), one of the first volumes of essays on Scottish women's experience written from a broadly feminist perspective; in the Introduction, it was noted 'how very little published material there was which concerned women in Scotland and how much there could be'. Sadly, several years on, the situation is much the same. There is certainly not the same volume of research into nineteenth and twentieth-century women's history in Scotland as there is in England. But what is more significant is the enormous disjuncture between research and interest on the one hand and published material on the other which arises from the ethnocentrism on one side of the border, and male prejudices on the other. It is to be hoped that the example set by the Edinburgh University Press in publishing women's history will be followed by others.

We hope that the publication of this collection might fulfil a number of objectives. First, we hope that it will contribute to the present knowledge of the history of the people of Scotland, for despite the increase in publications on Scottish social and labour history in recent years, the experience of women has to a large extent been ignored. A comprehensive historical survey of women's work in Scotland is still a project that awaits its historian. Nonetheless, the essays contained in this volume cover the major sectors of women's employment for much of the period concerned: agriculture, domestic service and textiles. Thus the essays must both broaden and enrich our understanding of our antecedents, through the description and interpretation of women's experience, and through the exploration of both regional and cultural differences within Scotland, though without attempting to elucidate or define the distinctiveness of Scottish women's experience.

Our understanding of the past grows through the examination of specific historical contexts which illuminate the configuration of forces that bring about change. Thus our second objective is to integrate the history of Scottish women's work into the broader canvas of women's history in such a way as to shed light on current debates in women's history. Therefore the essays explore key issues and themes which have emerged in recent research, discussing and illustrating them in the light of evidence which has been collected in Scotland. The essays are written from a variety of perspectives, but have in common a preoccupation with the sexual division of labour, with how this division has changed over time and place, and with how it has shaped women's lives.

Some contributions are case studies of particular occupations and industries and explore particular debates on gender divisions within the workplace; others do not focus on any particular industry or occupation but examine broader themes in the history of women's work. Most of the essays are concerned with working-class women, although one contribution deals with professional women. All contributions relate to waged work, although some take into account those women who for official purposes may not have been recorded as working.

Overall, the essays provide confirmation of the persistence of gender divisions in the world of work, the circumscribed choices available to women, and the tightly prescribed boundaries of women's sphere. However, they also provide evidence that despite the persistence of these divisions, the boundaries of women's work have not been fixed, and that even within these boundaries women made choices and perceived themselves as having some control over their fates.

It has become a commonplace to refer to the existence of two separate labour markets, one for women and one for men, with women concentrated in certain well-defined sectors of the economy and occupying a subordinate position within the workplace in terms of authority, skill and pay. The pattern of women's work in Scotland between 1850 and 1940 to a great extent confirms this view. Whilst there had been some widening of the sphere of women's employment, until the Second World War forty per cent of working women were concentrated in only three sectors of the economy. This horizontal division of labour was paralleled by women's low pay in relation to men. At the turn of the century the average pay for women was only forty-two per cent of men's average pay and in the inter-war years women still only earned between fifty and sixty per cent of the average male wage.

The consequence of this degree of occupational segregation was, of course, to seriously constrain women's choice of employment. James Smyth's essay on young women textile workers in Fife underlines the limited range of jobs available to them and the restrictions placed upon their choice by both their sex and the local economy. He also examines the forms of control that governed their working and non-working lives. In the workplace, young women were subject to the often arbitrary authority of male foremen, and although these girls earned an independent wage, they were still expected to submit to the authority of their parents well into their adult life. For some women, decisions about employment were taken by others, usually parents, and earnings were handed over to relatives. Perhaps the most extreme case of this powerlessness was that of the women bondagers of the south-east farming regions, whose experience is documented in Barbara Robertson's essay. These women, when they were relatives of the male farm servant whose task it was to provide the female out-workers, had no control over when they worked or where they worked, and their earnings were appropriated by their closest male relative for the benefit of the family economy.

Contemporary discussions of women's employment were often couched in moral terms; middle-class observers and trade unionists, each for their own purposes, were anxious to emphasise the moral dangers that lay in store for women who entered paid employment. Consequently there was much debate around the question of 'suitable' work for women, that is, work compatible with women's culturally prescribed role. The moral fervour which surrounded these debates often masked less lofty concerns, such as the desire of trade unionists to exclude cheap female labour from their trades. Whatever the sincerity of these pronouncements on the 'unsexing' effects on women of particular kinds of work, the consequences, as Linda Mahood's study of the Magdalene Institutions demonstrates, were that the boundaries of women's work were policed by men and that women's behaviour was also morally regulated.

It would be flying in the face of the evidence to deny the powerful social and cultural constraints on women's employment, and the obstacles erected by certain groups of male workers in order to prevent women from entering into their trades or to deny them training in particular aspects of work. Much feminist scholarship has made us only too aware of the role of trade unions and professional associations in restricting women's employment opportunities.[1] Indeed, two of the contributions in the present volume deal with this question. There is clearly much evidence to support the standard account of women's employment history which emphasises their subordination in the labour market and their lack of authority, status and control. However, within this broad and rather bleak canvas there lurks a more complex reality. The boundaries of women's work have frequently shifted (admittedly, not always to the advantage of women), and women themselves have often played a significant role in pushing these boundaries back. Wendy Alexander's essay reminds us of the early struggles of women to become accepted into the medical profession; Siân Reynolds' traces the efforts of women compositors to maintain a foothold in the Edinburgh printing trade. Therefore, in contrast to the dominant image of women workers as passive victims buffeted by the dictates of others and unable to exert control over their lives, many of the essays collected here stress the choices which were available to women and challenge the notion that women workers were passive and compliant.

Wendy Alexander argues against the received view that women doctors were driven abroad to missionary work because they were excluded from mainstream medicine, and stresses the element of positive choice in their career paths. She raises the question of whether women *chose* to enter female specialisms such as gynaecology and obstetrics, electing to work in areas that involved working with women patients, though she also demonstrates that women were effectively barred by male prejudice and male medical interests from having a free choice.

But not only professional women exercised choice in their working lives. Many working-class women, even those in jobs classified as unskilled and at the lowest rung of the jobs hierarchy, selected their occupations from a range of possibilities and often regarded them positively. By the turn of the twentieth century it had become relatively difficult to recruit domestic servants. The received view attributes this fact to the growth of better-paid and less demeaning employment alternatives for women. However, Lynn Jamieson suggests that domestic service was a heterogeneous category encompassing a variety of jobs ranging from dairy maid, housemaid and laundry maid to children's nurse; she argues that even for some urban women, who are usually regarded as the least favourably disposed to domestic service, these jobs held certain attractions and were preferred to factory, shop or office work.

Similarly, Jayne Stephenson and Callum Brown, in documenting the views of women themselves conclude that what is missing from the literature is, 'the view of working-class women with employment choices: women with decisions to make regarding their own careers, with perceptions of a hierarchy of skills and job-status, and with employment ambitions. '

There is a constellation of views on women's work which has crystallised into an orthodoxy. Typically it has been argued that waged labour for women ended with marriage, that work was something to be tholed until that time, and that because women, preferring domestic life, worked only when economic circumstances dictated, work was an arid and negative experience, lacking the compensating skills and status of much of men's work. However, there is increasing evidence, gleaned from oral history and, often, from the reinterpretation of existing sources, that this is a simplistic characterisation of women's work experience.

The majority of women undoubtedly ceased full-time and permanent work when they married. However, the 1911 census figure that recorded only 5. 3 per cent of married women working in Scotland does not reflect the true levels of women's employment at that time; rather, it reveals the deficiencies of the census itself, which tended to omit casual, part-time and seasonal work, that is, the kind of work likely to be undertaken by married women. When other sources are used to supplement official census figures, it becomes clear that work was a common, if intermittent, experience for married women. As Alice Albert demonstrates in her essay on 'sweated' Glasgow home-workers, the precarious nature of working-class male employment meant that married women's earnings were often central to the family income, and, on occasion, the *sole* source of income. It is also important to remember that women's experience was not homogeneous and that it was differentiated by class, culture and region. In Dundee, where according to official figures almost one-quarter of married women worked full-time, women who did not work were regarded as lazy.

Even amongst the middle-classes, who most closely adhered to the ideal of domesticity and where male earnings were likely to be sufficient to support a family, the conventional picture is flawed. Wendy Alexander dispels the myth that women doctors abandoned their careers after marriage and that they were less committed to the practice of medicine than their male counterparts.

A reassessment of the evidence would suggest that whilst full-time, permanent work was dominated by single women, it did not exclude married women who were also likely to have experience of casual and part-time work. Women were therefore not cocooned in a separate domestic world and the experience of men and women did not neatly correspond to the public/private division which was such an important element of bourgeois ideology.

Another received notion is that work was a negative experience for women, unleavened by any intrinsic job satisfaction; in the case of married women the experience of waged labour is usually referred to as a double burden. It would be fanciful to suppose that work was none of these things when, particularly in the period we are dealing with, the hours were long, the pay low and the work usually arduous. And yet men's work, which was not so very different, is often written about positively, stressing its enriching aspects and its importance to self-esteem.

A number of essays in this collection focus on this neglected aspect of women's working lives, illustrating the value women often placed on their work, the pride they took in performing it and the companionship they derived from it. It would be a mistake to assume that because women's work was usually regarded as being at the lower end of the skills-and-status hierarchy that women themselves evaluated their work negatively. Siân Reynolds' piece begins with a quotation from an Edinburgh woman compositor whose attitude to work is uncharacteristically enthusiastic for any worker, male of female. Even where the labour involved was routine or repetitious, women have often derived considerable pleasure and support from the camaraderie of the workplace. Oral testimonies of working women frequently recall the friendly atmosphere of the workplace, the exchange of banter, the communal singing, or simply the idle chatter that accompanied their work.

Women's work has become synonymous with 'unskilled' work, even in the accounts of feminist historians. Yet Anne Phillips and Barbara Taylor have convincingly argued that 'skill' is a social construct which is 'saturated with male bias', or to put it more simply, that skilled work is work which men do.[2] Siân Reynolds's essay on the printing trades shows how shifting definitions of skill ensured that women's work was always excluded from this classification regardless of actual job content.

The essays in this volume confirm the deep-rootedness of the sexual division of labour in Scotland as elsewhere. They also demonstrate that whilst the boundaries of this division may change over time, in general the division itself does not. From time to time, due to technological innovation or to the availability of labour, what was previously men's work becomes women's, but this does not happen through an equal participation by men and women, but through a redefinition of the sexual segregation of the labour market. Women have often played an active role in redefining these boundaries, in an attempt to gain a share of the labour market where the work involved has been perceived to be more challenging, satisfying, and remunerative. But even work which has been regarded as unskilled and monotonous could be a source of satisfaction and pride for women, thus reminding us that prevailing definitions, often carrying a male bias, require re-evaluation.

The present collection can only hope to fill in some of the gaps in our understanding of the history of Scottish women. Our third objective, then, is to encourage more interest and research and, most crucially, to stimulate further publications.

NOTES
1   See the collected essays in Angela V. John, *Unequal Opportunities: Women's Employment in England, 1850-1914* (Oxford, Basil Blackwell, 1986); and E. Gordon, *Women and the Labour Movement in Scotland, 1850-1914* (Oxford University Press, 1990), forthcoming.
2   Anne Phillips and Barbara Taylor, 'Sex and Skill: Notes Towards a Feminist Economics', *Feminist Review* no. 6 (1980).

1

THE VIEW FROM THE WORKPLACE:
WOMEN'S MEMORIES OF WORK
IN STIRLING *c.*1910–*c.*1950

JAYNE D. STEPHENSON AND CALLUM G. BROWN

It has become commonplace in the writing of women's history to state that work has played a distinctive and *diminished* role in the lives of working-class women. At a simple level, women's paid work in urban and industrial society has been distinguished from men's in that it has been mostly a temporary and economically necessitated interlude to a dominating domesticity in, successively, the parental and marital homes. But, at another level, women's experience of work has often been portrayed as distinctively oppressive and negative, and of less personal value than men's experience. Using the transcripts of eighty 'whole-life' interviews in the Stirling Women's Oral History Archive, this chapter explores the positive and life-enhancing experiences which women recall from their periods of employment.[1]

HISTORIANS' VIEWS OF WOMEN'S WORK

Historians' understanding of women's work has been tremendously influenced by the concept of 'separate spheres', according to which men and women are perceived as inhabiting different 'worlds': men the public world of work; women the confined, private world of home and family. With the industrialisation and urbanisation of Britain in the late eighteenth and nineteenth centuries, a 'domestic ideology' which disapproved of working women, and which located feminine virtues in domestic and familial duties, was raised to a position of great power in middle-class life. But whilst the evidence for this domestic ideology in the Victorian bourgeoisie is strong, the extent to which this ideology was dominant in proletarian lives is a matter for dispute. What is being challenged here is the view that working-class women derived their identity from domestic life and regarded work as a negative or peripheral experience.

The latter strain of thinking permeates much of the literature on British women's history, particularly works using first-hand accounts of the early twentieth century. In their introduction to a recent collection of essays based on the oral testimony of women's work, Leonore Davidoff and Belinda Westover write: 'Women do not experience their lives in compartments of home, work and leisure but mesh employment with domestic commitments. In this way their work fits around their lives, unlike the pattern regarded as normal because it applies to men.'[2] The leading oral historian of British women's history, Elizabeth Roberts, has concluded that domestic ideology grew stronger among working-class women in the century after 1840, culminating in 'a full flowering' during the inter-war period. She continues: 'Unmarried women could be expected to work for wages outside the home but this was regarded by women, and by others, as simply a useful way of filling in time until marriage.' Roberts regards work after marriage, which varied greatly from place to place within Britain (and indeed within Scotland), as having had negative motivations: 'They appear to have worked because of financial necessity and their ambition was to stop work and to be at home; *they saw their liberation as away from full-time work and towards domesticity.*'[3]

In this way, historians have come round to seeing domestic ideology as confining women not only because of external pressure from employers, husbands and peers, but because women themselves did not want to work. In her study of early shorthand typists in London, Teresa Davy concluded that 'on the whole, women accepted their domestic role and employment was only sought in times of domestic hardship.'[4] Roberts again: 'Working-class women found themselves in a difficult position. Financially they were forced to work.'[5] Historians stress that women tended to occupy unskilled, low-paid, low-status jobs.[6] Sexual segregation at work forced women to occupy a set of jobs discrete from that of men – jobs predominantly classified as unskilled or semi-skilled. This has led to the view that female employment was very much undifferentiated in comparison with male employment; in other words variations in working-class women's skills are underplayed. Felicity Hunt summarises the London bookbinding and printing trades of the late nineteenth century: 'Status based upon skill and craft-based labour organisation proved to be the key factors for the male workforce. ' In contrast, she says, 'the women held very similar positions throughout the trades as they were restricted to well-defined categories of "women's work", which lacked both skilled status and adequate wages.'[7]

The issue of skill differentiation in women's work, and thus of the existence of a hierarchy of occupations for women, tends to be overlooked. There is a ready acceptance that women's jobs classified as unskilled or semi-skilled were really deserving of those descriptions. But as two recent writers have pointed out, 'the classification of women's jobs as unskilled and men's jobs as skilled or semi-skilled frequently bears little relation to the actual amount of training or ability required for them.'[8] Jenny Morris has shown how in the Victorian tailoring trades employers split up the work process into many different parts to enable the employment of supposedly semi-skilled and unskilled female labour on low wages.[9] Yet, where this kind of development occurred in women's jobs, the work undertaken was usually composed of the same skills, using the same equipment, and was merely split up among many workers. The skills were redistributed amongst women, but not lost. Indeed, very similar developments in the shipbuilding industry at the same period amongst male workers were taken to represent a recomposition of craft skills rather than a diminution of them.

Even with increasing numbers of women in the labour market during the first half of the century, continuity rather than change is emphasised. Penny Summerfield summarises the inter-war period thus: 'The findings of oral historians are that their family was still dominant in working women's lives. Often girls did not decide for themselves about their careers but relatives and family friends secured openings and provided training and a young women's wage was not automatically her own.'[10] Women appear in the literature as not only exploited but submissive, being put to work when the family economy so dictated, and being confined to family duties in the home for the rest of the time.

Whilst economic need was a powerful determinant of career decisions (as the Stirling evidence will show), and whilst women occupied a subordinate position in the labour market in relation to men, what is missing is the view of working-class women with employment choices: women with decisions to make with regard to their own careers, with perceptions of a hierarchy of skills and job-status, and with employment ambitions. As Eleanor Gordon has said in her study of Dundee jute workers, dependency and low wages 'did not mean that women workers defined themselves solely in relation to their domestic role or that their responses to their work roles were conditioned only by their domestic responsibilities'.[11] Equally, there tends to be little consideration of working-class women enjoying their work, gaining from it a sense of independence from domesticity, an opportunity for self-development, and a popular culture of personal friendships, peer-companionship and leisure pastimes. Diana Gittins has already drawn attention to the way in which oral-history testimony from women frequently indicates a far greater source of memory, pride and life-significance residing in work rather than in family or leisure. She said of those women who had worked full-time: 'Accounts of their work were detailed and elaborate, while responses to questions concerning family life were far less so.'[12] The exploration of this theme through the Stirling material is the purpose of the present chapter.

THE RESPONDENTS

The eighty women in the Stirling Archive were born between 1894 and 1926, with 1909 the mean year of birth (making 1923 the mean year of entry into the labour market). All but one had undertaken paid or self-employed work during their lives. The range of respondents' occupations, as illustrated in the table, represents a reasonable cross-section of the occupied female labour force as recorded in the 1921 Scottish census. However, the

TABLE. Occupational Structure of Respondents, and of occupied female population Stirling and Scotland in 1921

(Numbers)	Stirling Archive Respondents (80) %	Stirling Census 1921 (3 022) %	Scotland Census 1921 (636 092) %
Domestic Service	33.8	22.1	26.4
Textiles	22.5	11.6	14.5
Retailing	15.0	14.9	13.7
Clerical	15.0	10.0	10.7
Military & Munitions	8.8*	0.	0.1
Metal, Wood, Rubber Working	6.3	3.0	2.3
Teaching	6.3	5.2	3.8
Agricultural and Mining	5.0†	1.6	4.4
Laundry Work	3.8	2.1	1.7
Textile Goods	3.8	8.2	8.5
Food, Drink, Tobacco making	2.5	1.0	3.5
Waitressing	2.5	1.0	2.5
Transport, Posts	2.5	2.4	1.8
Others	15.0	16.9	6.1
TOTALS	142.8	100.0	100.0

*Wartime work, 1915–18 and 1939–45. †Including wartime work, 1915–20.
Sources: Census of Scotland, 1921: vol 1, prt 34, County of Stirling, table 23; and vol 3, tables B, 12 and 14.

figures are not directly comparable: column 1 records the *multiple* occupations which individual respondents held during their lives, whilst columns 2 and 3 record the *single* occupations held by women at one date. The greatest imbalances in column 1 arise with domestic service and textile millwork. Textile jobs recorded in the Stirling census of 1921 were low in number – in part, at least, because of the depression in that year. And domestic service, as discussed later, was a type of job held by a significant number of women in their mid-teens before passing on to other jobs. Of the eighty respondents, 56 per cent had experience of only one type of work, 35 per cent had experienced two types, and 6 per cent had undertaken three or more types of work.

All but one of the respondents had married. Marriage bars operated in certain occupations (notably domestic service), but though the majority gave up their jobs after marriage, approximately half returned to work later for some period, mostly on a casual, part-time or short-term basis. Characteristically, work after marriage was in retailing, clerical jobs, 'charring' ('daily helper') and laundry work. The testimony in this chapter relates to work both before and after marriage.

LEAVING SCHOOL

Women's attitudes to employment were, for the most part, initially formed when they reached the minimum school-leaving age – which, for the majority of the respondents, was fourteen years. A variety of pressures came to bear on them at that point: pressure from parents, teachers and headmasters; the pressure of family economic necessity; and the girls' own career aspirations.

The desire to remain at school to obtain qualifications was expressed by nearly half the respondents. But for all but a handful of the eighty interviewees, 'staying on' was impossible. When asked if she would have stayed on longer at school if she had the opportunity, Mrs L .1 (born 1919)[13] replied: 'You didnae have money, hen; you had to get out and get a job,' Mrs W. 2 (1916) said she would have liked to remain at school, but instead stayed on at night school studying domestic science 'cause we knew we'd be going into domestic service. ' For those brought up in the countryside, as Mrs T.1 (1906) observed, part-time education did not even exist.

The case of Mrs O. 2 (1899) illustrates the plight of the gifted girl in a poor family. The eldest of five children, her mother was a weaver and her father a lorryman. She wanted to go on to secondary education at the High School, and won a bursary of five pounds. But this sum was insufficient:

> I won the bursary twice. I won it the first time and then the next time I happened to be first again and the headmaster wanted me to follow on to the High School, you see. But no, mother said five pounds wouldnae keep me. You see, you'd to get tennis [equipment] and all these different things, and a uniform and [she would] look at all the books you had to buy and everything else and she said, 'Oh no,' she says, 'I havenae got it. '

So instead Mrs O. 2 went to the lower-status 'higher grade school' where 'We got cookery lessons ... And then in the winter time you were shown how to wash different things, you know: woollens and cottons and all these different things. ' Two years later, she won the dux prize and the headmaster came to her again: 'when I left school at fourteen I lifted the dux prize, but oh, he came to me and pleaded with me. I said, "Oh no," I said, "it's no use, I've got to go to work." ... Oh I was disappointed, very disappointed, 'cause I wanted away to get a better education. '

The predicament of widows' daughters was even more acute. Mrs C.3 (1913) recalled: 'I couldn't stay longer [at school] because my father was dead, my mother was trying to keep the home together. There was no money, so I just had to go out. All girls were – everybody – expected to go and get a job. If jobs were scarce you took anything. ' Lack of income not only prevented continuing in full-time education, but also thwarted career ambitions. Mrs Q.2 (1912), the daughter of a plumber and gas-fitter, needed qualifications. 'I was wanting to be a nurse, but they [her parents] couldnae afford to put me through for that. It would have meant a lot of sacrifices, you know, and they couldnae afford it. '

Clearly, working-class girls were in a position similar to that of many boys when they reached school-leaving age. The family needed, and parents expected, the extra income which a fourteen-year-old could generate through employment. But, unlike boys, proletarian teenage girls expected in certain circumstances to be required to give up education before they were of school-leaving age. If the mother was ill, infirm or dead, the eldest girl was invariably required to act as the surrogate. This applied in cases where the father was alive, or where both parents were dead. Compulsory education, introduced in Scotland in 1873, disrupted this traditional female role, but the education system still made allowance for it. Until at least the 1920s, the school authorities in Stirlingshire would grant an exemption to a twelve-year-old girl to leave school to assist in the parental home if she was the eldest fit female in the family. The same factor prevented continuation at school. Mrs P.2 (1911) recalls:

> I had to leave because by that time my mother wasn't very well, and I had to go home, to stay at home. And the headmaster wanted me to go on to Stirling High School, but father went up to speak to the headmaster, and he said, 'No, I can't give my permission for [her] to go on to Stirling, because she's needed at home. Her mother's not very well. ' So I had to stay at home, to sort of help in the house.

The issue of whether daughters should stay at school also divided some parents. Mrs I. 3 (1904) was asked by her mother to leave school at fourteen to work for the family's income while the father was fighting in the First World War. His return in 1918 caused domestic friction:

> When he came home, I had started work, and he was very angry at this. And very angry that my mother had not done something to keep me at school, which was a great big row. I always remember that, for I thought she was quite right. She had – I could see her point of view – she had four children: others to keep dressed, fed and clothed, everything done for them that they needed with the one wage. Which wasn't a wage, it was just an army allowance from 1916. And as soon as I was fourteen, I was so glad to be able to leave school so that I could contribute toward the income of the house. And help to dress myself, and buy myself a pair of shoes or a new ribbon, or a new frock, or a new coat, which you seldom got – was a new coat. And I could not in any way stop the work.

The desire of university-qualified headteachers for their pupils to pursue academic qualifications was sometimes contradicted by pupil-teachers promoting more petty-bourgeois ambitions. Mrs N.2 (1906) recalled of her teacher: 'she asked us all what we wanted to be, you know, when we left school. And I told her I wanted to be a tailoress. Oh, and she laughed, she thought it was a silly joke. She says, "I would like you to go into an office and learn the shorthand and book-keeping. " And I laughed, and I said to her "Oh, I dinnae want that". I would have eventually got out and went as a tailoress. ' As it turned out, Mrs N.2 became an apprentice tailoress on leaving school: 'I was quite happy in it, you know. That's what I'd wanted and I got it. '

Such differences over careers between pupils, parents, teachers and headteachers revealed the different perceptions of occupational hierarchies for young women. A clear gulf existed between the middle-class teaching profession and working-class families over what constituted 'respectable' jobs. In the proletarian framework, economic necessity legitimised manual work. But what is apparent from the Stirling material is the greater willingness of mothers compared with fathers to allow their daughters to forego educational opportunities. Daughters could see the logic of a mother's position, yet were often more receptive to the occupational utility of education. Two autobiographers, Flora Thompson and Winifred Foley, found that their parents thought book-reading 'unrespectable' because of its apparent 'idleness', whilst their schools and Sunday schools encouraged it.[14]

In any event, all but five of the eighty respondents left school before or at the minimum age. They obtained their first jobs through family connections ('being spoken for'), domestic servants registers, or through the newspapers. Advertisements were the main source for work in retailing. Mrs N.3 (1910) recalled: 'All the young folk used to go down the Craigs before the papers got into the shops. You were quicker if you went down to the [*Stirling*] *Observer* office and just got a paper there. You didn't wait, and then you got the jobs and you could go quicker than if you waited till they were in the paper shops.' The range of occupations that women considered for their first job varied. Proximity of the parental home to textile or manufacturing mills provided obvious and, indeed, anticipated job opportunities. Work in retailing was another common option, for which there was expectation of moving to live with a shopkeeper or in lodgings. But by far the most common starting-point was domestic service.

DOMESTIC SERVICE

It was noted above how the 1921 census did not, and could not, record the full proportion of women who had been employed in domestic service. A position in service, usually as general maid, was an extremely common first job for working-class girls. Including those in hotel service or working as domestic cleaners (living-out servants), 31 of the 80 respondents (or 38.8 per cent) had tried this type of employment at some point in their lives. Of these, 16 women (20 per cent) moved to other jobs during their working lives. Amongst the 34 with experience of more than one occupation, 15 had tried domestic service.

This suggests a high turnover in domestic servants, and one resulting from dissatisfaction with the job – a phenomenon noted by many historians in other parts of Great Britain.[15] Popularly portrayed as 'the most respectable' working-class female occupation,[16] it is clear that during the early twentieth century women saw diminishing status in domestic service as alternatives appeared.[17] Though the sample is extremely small, the Stirling testimony gives some support to this. On the one hand, 14 out of 40 respondents entering the labour market in 1908–23 tried domestic service, as opposed to 17 out of 40 entering in 1924–40. Yet, of the 16 women who moved from domestic service to other jobs, the vast majority – 11 – entered the labour market after 1923.

Girls propelled into domestic service at the age of fourteen were frequently unprepared for the length of the working day and month, for the homesickness and solitude of living alone in a house with no peers, for the low pay and poor conditions, for the formidable formality that prevailed and for the demeaning attitude that was taken toward them. Whether as daily help (living-out domestic servant) or as domestic servant (living-in), there were few jobs in which the reality and sensation of exploitation was so great.

Mrs W.1 (1913), for example, did not last long in domestic service: 'The first day I was there I was sent into this big room to clean the grate. I hadn't a clue about cleaning grates; I had never done a thing like that in my life before. And I got to clean the knives. One of those machines which you stuck the knife in and wound the handle. Three days was more than enough. My sister had to go back and collect my aprons and things which I left. [Laugh] I see the young man to this day that I used to work for. He's an old man now.'

Mrs X.3 (1906) had a similar experience. In her mid-teens she got a position as a general maid in a house in Dunblane and was paid ten shillings a week. She lasted a month: 'About the back of seven in the morning you would be shouted to and you would be at their beck and call 'til about eight or nine at night ... I didnae wait very long, I don't mind telling you.' Like many women in the 1910s and 1920s,[18] she preferred instead to be a charlady at a shilling an hour, which she remained for most of her life. Mrs L.1 (1919) recalled similar sentiments: 'When you went into service, you were at their beck and call all the time. You had your half-day at each weekend, you know. And when I used to come home it used to break my heart 'cause I was going back. I didnae like it.'

Like many, Mrs D.2 (1907) preferred retail work to service: 'I didnae like it much so I moved on – to better things I hope. I went to the grocer shop as a message girl, that was ten shillings a week.' Mrs Q.1 (1900) left school two months before the outbreak of the First World War, and went into service as a general maid. She was paid one pound a month as the only servant: 'I was in service with a vet and I left it because they [her friends] were getting more money than what I got in service. When you went to service your pay was one pound a month and you had your uniform to keep up off that ... I didn't like it, I didn't like it and I come back home and got a job in the pit ... I seen the manager at Fallin [colliery]. I got a job on the tables ... picking the stones out of the coal before it went into the wagons'.

The exploitation varied according to the type of household service. Lower middle-class families tended to pay less, to have only one servant (making the volume of work greater), and to obtain their workers through less reputable 'servants registries' or agencies. Service in farmhouses and lodging-houses was even harder, and was often the last resort. Mrs A.3 (1913) described her position of general maid on a farm outside Stirling: 'it was slavery – slavery for very little money'. Mrs L.2 (1912) was paid 12s 6d as an assistant block printer in a textile mill, but was forced into service when the mill closed. For four years, she worked as a live-in general maid (i.e. the only servant) to a lady who took in boarders. For 7s 6d per week, she worked from 5 a.m. until 10 a.m., with Sunday afternoons off. She left for work in a private household for £3 a month where she worked another four years until her marriage.

Over half of those respondents who tried domestic service disliked it and moved on to other types of work. Mrs H.3 (1902) was careful to avoid service. She applied for unemployment benefit in the 1920s: '... they wanted me to go into service, and I said "No". I says: "That's not my work, and I'm not going into it". And, oh, they were going to stop my broo money [unemployment benefit] – it was very little then.'

However, some women moved up the ladder of service and found enjoyment in the status which a 'good house' brought. After a short period in factory work in Glasgow, Mrs U.3 (1913) started at the poor end of domestic service.

> Thirty shillings monthly you were paid. So, and you had to provide your uniform and fortunately my mother was good at sewing so it didn't cost her so much. Well, from then, I had to pay two-and-six [to the registry] for that job, but as I was only there a fortnight my aunt says, "You're not paying a ha'penny. " Then comes the minister ... his daughter said to my mother, "You'll take her to a decent registry office".

She was sent to an old-fashioned registry office – 'a Miss Glass, she was like something out of Victorian times: black, all black and a black band' – who got her a position as between-maid to a titled lady in Kelvinside. The head housemaid there put her in touch with someone who needed a fourth housemaid in a large house in Helensburgh, 'and that was me started on the ladder up'. That ladder, as Mrs U.3 made clear, operated not out of the registries but through personal introduction: 'We were all great letter writers to keep in touch in service. '

SHOPWORK

After domestic service, retail work was the next most popular first job. For many it was merely a stepping-stone to something better, though some stayed in the work for life. The first job for Mrs D.3 (1908) was as a sales assistant in a paint and wallpaper shop for eight shillings a week: 'I liked it alright, but when I got something better that was the main thing'. She stayed a year until she was offered the position of assistant in a baker's in Alloa, but on a day trip to Kippen the grocer heard she was looking for a job and offered a position: 'So, I just jumped at this and told the other company that I wouldn't be, that I had found something more suitable. So I was there forty years. I loved my job. ' Similarly, Mrs N.3 (1910) started as a message girl with a large fruiterer, confectioner and florist at the age of fourteen, and worked her way up to be manageress by the age of twenty-seven.

What is striking is the extent to which respondents perceived retailing as a skilled job. A lengthy informal apprenticeship had to be served, involving progression from unskilled to skilled work. After working part-time at school as a messenger for the Co-operative, Mrs Z. 2 (1905) obtained a position in the Co-operative Drapery as a shop assistant:

> For the first good few months I was only allowed to dust: dust the shelves and tidy the boxes and sort the papers, you know. I'd take it off the reams and fold it up and put it nice so that they could use the paper and string – y'know, the old string, take the knots out of old string and make it usable again; and sweep the floor and wash the looking glasses ... And then go messages, deliver accounts, things like that.

She worked two years at unskilled work before progressing. 'You were dying to serve customers ... but it was your job. You were being trained.' The training was varied: 'You were taught how to make parcels, sort up parcels. I was taught how to alter, shorten coats or skirts ... You were taught how to turn up hems, all these sort of things ... We were taught to show the full stock of what we had. ' The technical skills of alterations were combined with emphasis on training in personal service, and considerable pride came from the quality of that service.

Mrs H. 3 (1902) wanted to enter shopwork on leaving school in 1916 but was unable to find a position immediately. After several months' piece-work polishing chairs in a chairworks (at 9d per dozen chairs), she became a grocer's assistant at 7s a week. She progressed quickly from shop to shop, chasing higher wages based on the skills and experience she built up. As a shop assistant she felt a 'Jenny o' all thing'. She recalls her experience in her second shop, in a miner's village:

> And you had to start on a Monday morning, and the first thing you got was ... a great big round ... of tobacco. And the miners always bought that thick black tobacco, and some of them chewed it down the pit. And you had all that to make up into ounces, and you daren't have a lot of wee bits, for the men wouldn't take it. You had to learn to be kind of accurate at cutting that ... Well, you'd that to do, then you started on to butter, and you'd all your butter to make up. You had your sugar, flour, oatmeal, tea, all these things to make up. There are no grocers now; they don't know what it is to be a grocer.

With such skills she sought new positions. She told her brother: '"whenever I move", I says, "I make a good move, I get a big pay". '

Employment as a shop assistant, as all the respondents who worked in that sphere make clear, had many attractions. In contrast to some jobs, there were considerable skills to be learned. On one level, these were the skills of personal service – of knowing how to 'show' goods to customers, and how to converse with and serve customers with the care and attention that would ensure sales. On another level, there were technical skills. In the grocery, bakery, confectionery and florist trades, the skills were those which have in recent decades been diminished and overtaken by factory preparation: ranging from learning how to make wreaths, bouquets and buttonholes to cutting tobacco and packaging food. Such skills were sought after by shop owners and managers. Retail jobs were generally advertised in newspapers, and written application was often required. Much more than in factory or domestic service, there was a high degree of mobility evident from the Stirling testimony. The women who worked in retailing changed employer voluntarily much more frequently than any other occupational group, and were likely (like domestic servants) to move some distance.

Moreover, shop-assistant work was generally held in high regard, especially in comparison with domestic service. For one thing, the cash pay was better – up to twice what a maid could earn, with payment coming weekly rather than monthly or half-yearly. Even if meals and lodging were not included, there was no requirement as in service to pay for one's own elaborate uniform. The conditions of service were also better. The hours were distinctly shorter (usually from 8 a. m. or 9 a. m. to 6 p. m. , compared to 6 a. m. to 9 or 10 p. m. in service): shop employees could take Sundays off and half day on Saturdays (the superior shops) or half-day on a weekday (the inferior shops) whereas most servants only had Sunday afternoon off. The respondents make clear that there was less of a sense of being 'ordered about' in retailing than in domestic service. Servants were subjected to a great deal of formality: 'You had to go through all this formality … , it was all formality' (Mrs T.1 (1906). Work in a shop might entail formality when customers were present, but things might be more relaxed the rest of the time. And in any event, meeting customers was widely regarded as the appeal of the job.

An illustration of where retailing fitted into the hierarchy of women's occupations can be found in the following two cases. Mrs E. 3 (1923) started her working life in the bottling works of a brewery, where she was made to wear thick clogs with iron fitments to protect against broken glass, a 'great big massive blue and white overall', a 'thing on your hair' and a rubber apron on top. She left that work for a job in Woolworth's where the pay was good – almost double that in the brewery. And it brought status: ' A lot of them at work in the brewery did that. They left there, I don't know how, and we went to Woolworth's. We must have thought we were toffs for leaving the brewery and going to work in Woolworth's. ' But Mrs A. 1

(1911) recalls Woolworth's differently; as a source of good money as a part-time worker, but of low status in comparison to her full-time work as a block printer in a textile mill: 'Working in Woolworth's was nothing 'cause they could put you anywhere, and I only took the job in Woolworth's for the sake of the extra five bob.' In the mill the work was skilled – 'an intricate job at the designs ... whereas in Woolworth's you were only another shirt'.

MANUFACTURING

Some retailing jobs for women crossed the boundary into craft work with its attendant status. Mrs T. 2 (1899) long held an ambition to be a milliner:

A   Someone had said to my mother when I was wee, on a wet day, I'd rake out any of my mother's old hats. And I said I wanted to be a trimmer, I was too young to understand millinery then. But my mother says on a wet day, I would sit for hours trimming a hat this way and that way. And she says I went out with some of them.

Q   How did you learn your job? Were you given training?

A   Yes, I got the handsome sum of half-a-crown a week.

Q   So it was a kind of apprenticeship you went through?

A   Yes. And it was a classy shop.

Millinery and drapery were occupations which attracted many young girls. They were jobs reserved for women, 'feminine' in character, and skilled both technically (in sewing and stitching for instance) and aestheti-cally. The skill of a dressmaker, for instance, was highly prized, though none of the Stirling respondents became dressmakers. However, after her three days in domestic service, Mrs W. 1 (1913) become a tailoress. She followed her sister into a tailoring firm in the midst of the Slump in 1932–3. She was occupied in learning the business for four and half years:

I was learning how to make the vests and trousers. By the time I was finished I could make a pair of trousers in a day. The boss cut all the bits out for you and said: "There you are Jeannie, get on with that. " Now, at that time we got the contract for the Fire Brigade. Now it was big heavy blue trousers – lovely stuff, lovely material, and he made the jackets and I made the vests and the trousers.

She gained considerable pride in learning the trade. She recalls working on Saturday mornings until Stirling's town fire siren went off at midday: 'and that was the time for down tools for all tradesmen ... Whenever this thing burst through the town – finished. ' However, her career was abruptly ended in 1937: 'I almost finished my training when the ready-mades came in. The tailors were finished, the small tailors anyway ... The work finished off, so I had to go and look for another job. Now, I went up to a job in the Centre Chambers that sold material for tailors; so I knew what I was selling there. '

Though for the most part lacking the status of apprenticed work, and lacking aesthetic appeal, mill-working contained a hierarchy of skill to which many of the respondents alluded. Stirling was ringed with large carpet and textile mills – in Bannockburn, in Cambusbarron, in the centre of Stirling itself, and further afield in the Hillfoots. Although commuting to work by train was common in the villages around Stirling, the situation of most of these mills in satellite communities ensured a significant degree of recruitment through family connection and tradition. Mrs H. 2 (1900) followed a set career path to a local carpet factory when she left school. She worked from the age of fourteen until she got married at twenty-one: 'There were four of us worked in the mill at the same time – four sisters. The older sister, and when she got married the other one had to keep the house, you see, that's how it worked. When one got married, the other had to keep the house and when she got married the other had to keep the house and the other – the other one had to keep the house 'til we was all out of the mill then.' Mrs H. 1 (1907) worked in the same factory, and her family followed a similar process: 'my other sister Cathy, she went to the factory in Templeton's; then of course I followed suit and I went when I was thirteen. Then Cathy left to get married. Ina – that's the other one – she went to the factory as well.'

The women who worked in the textile and carpet mills remember clearly the skills involved in their jobs, even when those jobs might not have been classed as 'skilled'. Mrs A. 1 (1911) worked as a fabric block printer in a shed with sixteen girls working two to a table. At each eighteen-yard table they printed designs on material sixty-four yards long:

> Before you put it on the table you had ... a barrow at the side of the table and you put paste on it – just flour and water. And you spread that on the table. Then you spread your material on and then put that barrow away and got your barrow with the colours, whatever colours. You had a code on the end of whatever design you were doing. It was quite an intricate job at the designs ...
>
> See, there were only two of you at the table, and you went down the row printing this. Some of the prints werenae very big, some that size and some that size, but flat .... There were pins, and there was a handle number, y'see and you pinned it into that bit and that bit and that bit, all the road down the eighteen yards. It was really interesting. They don't do that now, y'know.

Mrs G. 1 (1924), a boxer at a carpet mill, expressed the same sentiments. She provided a long and detailed account of the work process she undertook in the mill, of which this is only a fraction:

> A   A boxer worked for two printers and had to attend to the dyes that printers used in the wool which was used for weaving the carpets .... The printer called the number of the dye she wanted, to the boxer. Well, the boxer then took a wooden box with the dye colour and she filled it .... As soon as the boxer told the printer the box was ready, the printer started the undercarriage running .... When the printer had completed the pattern on the

> drum, she then rubbed the colour into the wool with a flat object;
> I think this was made of bone. And while she was doing this, the
> boxer had to see that she had plenty of wool bobbins to rewind
> the next drum, and see that her dye jugs were filled up. And also
> clear round her place of work ....
>
> Q   And what were you paid?
> A   I sometimes could have sixteen or eighteen shillings depending
>   on the work I did, which was very good for a person of fifteen
>   ....
> Q   And did you like the work that you were doing in the mill?
> A   Yes. But I wanted to be a printer. I didnae want to be a boxer all
>   my days, I wanted to get up there and print the patterns.

Indeed, she recalled where the premier jobs were in the mill: 'It was a very
good job to get into the weaving shop. I always thought so anyway. Maybe
other folk – but it was. It was a *very* good job to get into the weaving shop.'

The same care and pride in recounting the work process was evident in
the testimony of Mrs H. 1 (1907), a dover in a carpet-weaving factory. She
spoke especially of the skill in catching the pirns (bobbins) in her hand and
collecting them in her apron. But she also claimed to have learned every job
in the factory by watching others: 'if you were finishing up a machine and
it was running nice and smooth, you went across to talk to your partner and
she was on a different machine. I used to stand and talk to her and watch
her doing it, then I had a shot. That's how we learned – back and forward.'
Her own machine brought the greatest pride:

> Q   Were the managers walking round?
> A   Periodically they walked up and down. They used to always
>   stand at mine and I used to hate it. I used to always wonder what
>   I'd done, but after that Mr Jamieson – he had one leg – he used
>   to hobble up and I used to say: "Why does he always stand there
>   and make me nervous?" He says: "He's admiring your machine
>   because you've got the cleanest one in the factory". So there you
>   are.

Interestingly, several respondents mentioned this pride in their equipment. Mrs G. 1 (1924) worked in Youngers Bottling Store, where there was
a regime of hygiene and cleanliness. She recalled: 'And the girls that sort
of, they thought they *owned* a machine; they were in charge of a machine
but they thought they owned the machine. A Saturday morning was given
to cleaning. And these machines were brass and they were beautiful. '

The two World Wars played a significant part in opening up jobs for
women – jobs in which a skill hierarchy could enhance status. In 1915, Mrs
Q. 1 (1900) leapt at the opportunity to leave domestic service to enter work
in the local coal pits. She held a succession of jobs, her wages increasing
with each, finishing as a winder on £4. 6d per week during the inflation of
1919–20:

> A   I worked first of all on the tables .... Well, your job was at the

tables and you picked the stones out ... before they went into the
wagons with clean coal for the consumer. Then when I left the
tables, ... I got a step up further to the scraping of the hutches
that were down underneath .... I thought I wasn't making a big
enough pay, and I went to the [manager] and ... I got the job of
letting the men down the pit, up the pit, carrying their lath from
there to the blacksmith's shop to get all sharpened for the next
morning, and I put perhaps their piece boxes down the pit. Oh,
I enjoyed that job. But I finished actually up when the colliery
closed for lady workers [in 1920] ....

Q The wages that you were given when you worked in the mine
– did you feel that was a fair wage?

A Well, I thought mine's was a good wage because I found out
when I left I had the biggest paid [women's] wage in the colliery.

Many respondents acquired skilled jobs during the wars, but in every
case they had to surrender them to men at the end of hostilities.[19] Nonetheless, the experience led to many women deciding to make permanent
occupational changes – notably women who had previously been in
domestic service. After being a lady's maid (a high position in which she
had her own maid as well), Mrs R. 1 (1912) joined the Wrens as an officer
in 'a secret job', then returned in 1945 to her former employer: 'I didn't like
being in that sort of work again, not after being in the war, you know, in
the Wrens. ' As a result, she quit to be a shop assistant in an ironmongery
and china shop.

Evidence of the skill and pride in the job, and in the product, is to be
found throughout the pages of the oral-history testimony – in jobs as
varied as hotel waitressing, hairdressing, submarine-float making, hot-
water-bottle making, clerking and bookkeeping, as well as, more expect-
edly, in teaching and nursing. But the skill hierarchy had its lower end –
jobs which were not only classified as unskilled and low paid, but which
did not confer the status and pride that was evident in the extracts above.
In the testimony of some women in laundry work or in casual jobs, and of
those employed in mills with poorer conditions and exploitative managers, there is to be found shorter and less happy memories of work. In such
recollections, there is little evidence of status and skill hierarchies.

One such testimony is that of Mrs E. 1 (1901), the daughter of a plasterer,
who held a succession of low-paid, low-status jobs for all her working life.
She started at fourteen years of age as a powerloom weaver working
twelve hours from 6 a. m. to 6 p. m. , for seven shillings a week, and washed
stairs 'to get extra for the dancing and claes'. Her memory of Aitken's Mill
in Stirling is of running to beat the closing gates (and the loss of a day's
work and pay if she was too late) of her noisy machine and ever-watchful
foreman, and of a finishing room 'I never was in'. Her testimony gives a
powerful sense of alienation, exploitation and oppression. Her next job
was in the rubber works making hoses: 'I got the sack 'cause I was eating

a piece at the table. the manager caught me eating a piece an' I was sacked. And the woman told me after that, she said: "Lizzie, you got the sack for eating a piece and I go round with a table [of food] for them to pick what they want" … I went to the union. The union sent for me, but I had been to see the manager and I did the wrong thing.' She eventually found a more agreeable job in the Co-operative lemonade bottling factory, where conditions of work (notably the hours) were better. Even so, her testimony is characteristic of the minority of respondents who said comparatively little about their working lives, and in their testimony devoted greater time to, and showed greater interest in, their memories of family and leisure.

COMPANIONSHIP AND CULTURE AT WORK

But even in occupations with low status and low wages, and in which the alienation from the job was great and the sense of pride low, there were more positive attributes which can be discerned from oral testimony. Women's work provided the opportunity for personal development and immersion in peer-group popular culture. For the single woman, work constituted probably the principal opportunity for the cultivation of a sense of independence from the family home. The graduation from childhood to adulthood took place at work. Childhood friends and games were exchanged for workmates and adult activities. For married women, work could mean a release from domestic confinement, giving access to friends and companionship outwith the often claustrophobic restrictions of family and neighbourhood. And most perceptible of all is the prominent place that memories of work have for the respondents when placed beside their other memories.

In the workplace itself, the Stirling women respondents draw on a rich vein of happy recollections concerning camaraderie and companionship. Singing, hilarity and joy were to be found during the work process on a regular and even, according to some accounts, a continuous basis. Mrs G. 1 (1924) remembers the bottling factory: 'In that job you sang at your machine. I learned lots of songs from the older girls that they sang *all* the time they were working. That was a great job for [that] … They were very sad songs, some of them …. And war songs.' Mrs E. 3 (1923) remembered the same factory: 'We all used to sing …. We used to all sing together a' the old songs, unless the gaffer was in a bad mood and he said: "that'll do, keep it quiet". But often as no' we would sing. I loved it.' In the carpet factory, Mrs H. 1 (1907) recalled:

A   You used to sing the whole day, all the songs – everybody. One
     started and everybody joined in. It was grand company.
Q   Could you hear it for the noise of the machines?
A   Yes, we heard it, uha.
Q   Did the manager mind?
A   No, they didn't mind at all as long as were doing our work. I
     used to see him standing laughing, shaking his head like this:

'What a noisy crew I've got', he would say.

Q What kind of songs did you sing?

A Och, well, there was one girl from Bannockburn, she used to sing the football songs. I cannae remember what but we all joined in, and of course we always ended up with a hymn. She was one of these kinda Christian people, y'know, and a lot of other songs. Then we made up a wee one about the gaffer, and we used to see him coming we used to sing a wee song about him.

Mrs J. 2 (1905) worked in a hand-tufted carpet factory:

Q Was there a good atmosphere there?

A Oh yes, they were very nice girls and you got on with everybody, aye we got on with everybody.

Q Were you able to talk when you were working?

A Aha, and you had to sing even – a lot of good singers too.

Q Do you remember any songs?

A ... there was one girl from St Ninians, she was a lovely singer, you know. Some of them were really good singers. What was it she used to sing? Just all the old songs, you know ...

Even in domestic service, there could be gay moments. Mrs G. 4 (1918) recalled her afternoons off from a 'big house, where she and fellow maids went walking or cycling: 'And if it was raining, the underhousemaid – she used to play the mouth organ, and I used to dance away out the room. There was a happy, you know, a happy atmosphere. ' But at the pithead, Mrs Q. 1 (1900) remembered little singing; 'I think we were too busy blethering. '

Singing was only one part of the hilarity and gaiety in the working lives of many women earlier this century. Dancing and jokes – and especially pranks at the expense of male supervisors – were common expressions of female solidarity. Eleanor Gordon has noted how in Dundee such activities accompanied women's strikes, in stark contrast to the more sober and serious atmosphere attending men's strikes.[20] The role of work in women's lives had a distinctive potential for companionship which was often not achievable in other ways. Men had large numbers of work, trades union and voluntary organisations – ranging from sports clubs to the Druids – in which male companionship was often expressed. But women – certainly the Stirling respondents – had markedly fewer leisure organisations at their disposal. Very few were in unions, fewer still in sports clubs, only two were in the Co-operative Women's Guild, and only a handful mention alternative organisations. Apart from attending church or the picture-house, there were extremely few venues for either working or non-working women to indulge in organised leisure. In this vacuum, the bulk of their leisure was unorganised: impromptu dances at the pithead on a Friday night, or the gathering of women to chat and 'have a laugh' at their lunch-breaks in the factory grounds.

Perhaps the clearest indication of the role of work in respondents' lives comes from the lengthy answers given to interviewers' questions on their employment, in contrast to the short answers regarding their married lives. Testimony on work was in most cases twice the length of testimony on other aspects of post-school life. With only one exception the women said that they had enjoyed their working life, though clearly not every job in it. Former domestic servants were consistently the least pleased with their jobs, but for others memories of work prompted the most emotional responses to questioning.

For some respondents, the memories of family life were a mixture of tedium, catastrophe and exhaustion. Mrs N. 2 (1906) trained as a tailoress, fulfilling her five-year apprenticeship, but within two years gave up work to marry. Her married life turned into disaster when her only child died soon after birth, and when her husband – a church elder – ran off with another woman. Having divorced him, Mrs N. 2 remarried but could not have more children. The tailoring trade offered no positions, so she rented a small shop which she ran as a confectioners for many years in the centre of Stirling. This became her pride and joy – her place for meeting people and for making needed extra money: 'I used to love my shop. Oh yes. Used to love it. And my husband liked it too.'

Seen from the later vantage-point of domestic married life without employment, respondents put considerable stress on the significance of their years of work. Mrs O. 2 (1899) worked in a laundry and ironmongery until her early twenties when her mother died, and she then spent twenty years in the home looking after the other children and her father. Looking back, her working life appeared a very important highlight. She described in great detail the training for the different tasks in the laundry, recalling the intricacies of the machinery she used, the starching and polishing processes, and the different treatments for different textiles. She remembered her work there very fondly, despite the low wages of five shillings: 'Oh yes, it was very interesting, let me tell you .... I don't think I would have left if she'd [her employer] given me up [raised] my wages a bit.' She went into a large ironmongery: ' ... they kept all the – oh, the lovely stuff, you know: brass and copper and all that kind [of] ornaments and fancy grates. What they didn't have in that top showroom .... I had to work in the shop, you see, learn all the different parts of the shop ... you had all that to learn, and then you had to keep them all clean. Another girl and I, we did it. And then their fancy cases here were fancy knives and all these different things. Oh, some beautiful silver. Oh, I loved that shop. '

In the 1930s and 1940s, Mrs X. 2 (1920) held a succession of positions as clerk and cashier in Stirling's largest department store. After an extremely long and lucid account of her work there, she struggled to find the words to describe her feelings:

Q   And how did you feel about your work? You liked it?
A   I liked it very much. I must admit I thoroughly enjoyed all my

years. There was something, I don't know, something very nice about the – It wasn't all sort of –

CONCLUSION

The Stirling testimony suggests that historians should not marginalise the place of work in women's lives. Whilst it is customary for oral historians to note the significance of short and evasive answers to questions, it is less usual to draw conclusions from comparing the length of answers to different questions. But as Paul Thomson has noted, in contrast to matters of chronology or single events, memories are relatively good 'on the detail of a recurrent process of work or social or domestic life'. [21] In this context, comparison is valid. The Stirling material bears out the observation of Diana Gittins, quoted at the beginning of this chapter, that women's memories of work have a clear predominance over non-work memories. The women respondents were able to recall greater detail and to articulate more happy recollections from their working lives than from their domestic routine with husband and children, even though their working lives were generally of much shorter duration. In the vast majority of the testimonies, these were 'golden years' looked back on with great fondness.

Recollections of work were characterised by a notable pride and enthusiasm in describing the work process, especially among mill and factory workers. Respondents were eager to explain their occupations, giving full answers that required markedly little prompting and few 'follow-up' questions. The answers were characterised by a high level of detail regarding the work process, pay, and work colleagues. Moreover, the respondents were keen to present the skills of their work, and wherever possible to point to their upward mobility in a hierarchy of jobs. On the other hand, the social environment of work, in which camaraderie and the collective friendship of fellow women workers were evident, seemed a significant high point in the lives of most respondents. Interestingly, such camaraderie was not so frequently recalled from other portions of women's adult lives. Most respondents spoke of close personal friendship with one or two women outside of work – friendships which provided companions for going to the cinema or the dance hall. But it was in the mill, factory, workshop or department store that a collective spirit developed among women, expressed often in joviality and song. It may be that historians have difficulty in articulating the ways in which experience of employment shaped working-class women's lives. Evidence of blocked entry to men's skilled work, marriage bars and low pay are 'objective' evidence of the restricted work opportunities. But the 'subjective' reality for working-class women was that such work, however brief, was a major element in their life memories. In the pre-1939 context, in which proletarian women's access to leisure and sports was restricted, work was a crucial part of women's popular culture because the workplace provided almost the only venue in which it could develop.

Such oral testimony, we believe, does not support the general interpretation of working-class women's attitudes to work offered by Roberts, Davy, Davidoff and Westover. In the first place, some frameworks of analysis presented by these writers are flawed. For Elizabeth Roberts to dismiss women's work as a 'financial necessity' is to offer little constructive differentiation from men's work. Davidoff's and Westover's notion of women for whom 'work fits around their lives' is not evidence of any difference from men's 'compartments of home, work and leisure'; indeed, oral testimony could easily bear a contrary interpretation of the structure of women's experience of these three elements.

In addition, there are good reasons to doubt the conclusion of all four historians that domestic ideology acted so resolutely for working-class women's self-imprisonment in the home. Their conviction arises, essentially, from a view that women did not like nor want to work in low-paid, low-status positions in predominantly unskilled or semi-skilled work. The oral testimony, we believe, contradicts this. Women respondents perceive skills which the historian tends, implicitly, to downgrade because of external and historical views of occupational status. For example, the 1921 census did not even describe the jobs of forty-four per cent of women textile workers in Stirling, listing them after skilled jobs as merely 'Other workers'. Such a categorisation does not encourage the commentator to perceive skill, status and job satisfaction. Yet all but one of the textile-industry respondents quoted in this chapter came under that category, and, in spite of government, male and middle-class preconceptions, their testimony strongly displays such qualities.

Most fundamentally, the vast majority of working-class women respondents *enjoyed* their working lives, finding it a positive and rewarding experience, combining pride in work and skill with participation in the collective culture of working-class women. Roberts is too dismissive in regarding working-class women's work as 'simply a useful way of filling in time until marriage' and, for married women, as 'financial necessity'. The danger is that, at root, the historian may apply middle-class perceptions of the personal rewards of manual labour to a quite different proletarian experience.

NOTES

1   The issues raised here were first aired in J. D. Stephenson, 'Women, skill and work culture: the oral evidence from Stirling', *Scottish Labour History Review*, no. 1 (1987), 6–8. A collection of extracts relating to work has been published: J. D. Stephenson (ed.), *'Five Bob A Week': Stirling Women's Work 1900–1950* (Stirling, Jamieson and Munro, 1988). We are grateful for Dr Arthur McIvor's help with aspects of this paper.

2   L. Davidoff and B. Westover (eds.), *Our Work, Our Lives, Our Words: Women's History and Women's Work* (Basingstoke, Macmillan, 1986), x.

3   E. Roberts, *Women's Work 1840–1940* (Basingstoke, Macmillan,

1988),. 72–3. Our italics.

4   T. Davy, '"A Cissy Job for Men; a Nice Job for Girls"': shorthand typists in London, 1900–1939', in L. Davidoff and B. Westover, (eds.) op. cit. , 143.

5   E. Roberts, op. cit. 15.

6   See for example J. Lewis, *Women in England 1870-1950: Sexual Divisions and Social Change* (Brighton, Wheatsheaf, 1984), esp. 170–84.

7   F. Hunt, 'Opportunities lost and gained: mechanisation and women's work in the London bookbinding and printing trades', in A. V. John (ed.), *Unequal Opportunities: Women's Employment in England 1800–1918* (Oxford, Basil Blackwell, 1986), 88.

8   A. Phillips and B. Taylor, 'Sex and skill', *Feminist Review*, 6 (1980) quoted in J. Morris, *Women Workers and the Sweated Trades* (Gower, Aldershot, 1986), 102.

9   J. Morris, 'The characteristics of sweating: the late nineteenth century London and Leeds tailoring trade', in A. V. John (ed.), op. cit. , 95–121.

10   P. Summerfield, *Women Workers in the Second World War* (London, Croom Helm, 1984), 13.

11   E. Gordon, 'Women, work and collective action: Dundee jute workers 1870–1906', *Journal of Social History* 21 (1987), 31.

12   D. Gittins, *Fair Sex: Family size and structure 1900–39* (London, Hutchinson 1982), 125.

13   Quotations from respondents are referred to by identity codes followed in parentheses by the date of birth. The transcripts are stored in the Stirling Women's Oral History Archive, Smith Museum and Art Gallery, Stirling.

14   F. Thompson, *Lark Rise to Candleford* (Harmondsworth, Penguin 1945, reprint 1983), 332; W. Foley, *A Child in the Forest* (London, Futura, 1974), 136.

15   J. Lewis, op. cit. , 168; D. Gittins, op. cit. , 78; E. Roberts, op. cit. , 29.

16   For example, in the BBC television documentary series, 'Out of the Doll's House', first broadcast Autumn 1988.

17   E. Roberts, op. cit. , 29–32. See also F. E. Dudden, *Serving Women: Household Service in Nineteenth-century America* (Connecticut, Wesleyan University Press, 1983), 235, 238–41.

18   L. Davidoff and B. Westover, op. cit. , 16.

19   J. D. Stephenson (ed.) op. cit. , 17–20, 31.

20   E. Gordon, op. cit. , 42–3.

21   P. Thompson, *The Voice of the Past: Oral History*, 2nd ed. (Oxford and New York, Oxford University Press, 1988), 240.

SELECT BIBLIOGRAPHY

L. Davidoff and B. Westover, (eds.), *Our Work, Our Lives, Our Words: Women's History and Women's Work.* Basingstoke: Macmillan 1986

F. E. Dudden. *Serving Women: Household Service in Nineteenth- century America.* Connecticut: Wesleyan University Press, 1983.

W. Foley. *A Child in the Forest.* London: Futura, 1974.

D. Gittins. *Fair Sex: Family Size and Structure 1900–39.* London: Hutchison, 1982.

E. Gordon. 'Women, work and collective action: Dundee jute workers 1870–1906'. *Journal of Social History* 21 (1987).

A. V. John, (ed.). *Unequal Opportunities: Women's Employment in England 1800–1918.* Oxford: Basil Blackwell, 1986.

J. Lewis. *Women in England 1870–1950: Sexual Divisions and Social Changes.* Brighton: Wheatsheaf, 1984.

A. Phillips and B. Taylor. 'Sex and skill', *Feminist Review* 6 (1980).

E. Roberts. *Women's Work 1840–1940.* Basingstoke. Macmillan, 1988.

J. D. Stephenson. 'Women, skill and work culture: the oral evidence from Stirling'. *Scottish Labour History Review* no. 1 (1987).

J. D. Stephenson, (ed.) *'Five Bob a Week': Stirling Women's Work 1900–1950.* Stirling: Jamieson and Munro, 1988.

P. Summerfield. *Women Workers in the Second World War.* London: Croom Helm, 1984.

P. Thompson. *The Voice of the Past: Oral History,* 2nd ed. Oxford and New York: Oxford University Press, 1988.

2

THE WAGES OF SIN: WOMEN, WORK AND SEXUALITY IN THE NINETEENTH CENTURY

LINDA MAHOOD

INTRODUCTION

Recently studies of prostitution and philanthropy have begun to examine the role of gender in the moral regulation of the working class in the nineteenth century. Edward Bristow argues that by the 1800s a cult of sentimentality had evolved around the miserable figure of the 'prostitute'. Moral reformers responded to the 'prostitute's' plight by establishing charities called magdalene homes for the rehabilitation of 'fallen' women. The goal of these charities was the conversion of 'outcast poor into respectable and disciplined Christian poor'[1] through a strict regime of hard work and religious instruction. Olive Checkland described this 'philanthropy of piety' as the creation of a substitute for home itself, where in order to be rescued and reformed 'prostitutes' were taken into direct care.[2] Shifting the analysis, Nicole Rafter emphasises that the practice of incarcerating women as 'prostitutes' institutionalised a gender-based double standard by punishing only women for acts engaged in by both sexes.[3] Frank Mort adds that magdalene homes also institutionalised the distinction between 'pure' and 'impure' women. Once incarcerated, 'prostitutes' were subjected to a programme of physical and moral discipline which reinforced separate class and gender ideologies and widened the gap between inmates and 'respectable' women.[4] Although these studies are an improvement on those which regard philanthropy and rescue work as an apolitical pastime of Victorian gentlefolk, they do not take into account the role of wage labour within rescue homes. Both Bristow's and Barbara Brenzel's [5] studies suggest that both the particular regimes and governing ideologies of the moral regulation practised in these institutions were constantly being redefined in response to economic pressures; they do not, however, analyse this process in any systematic way.

The purpose of this chapter is to examine the management practices of the magdalene homes in Glasgow and Edinburgh in the nineteenth century, focusing on the contradictions between the directors' prejudice against women's employment in the 'public' sphere, and the institutions' dependence on its inmates' labour for its material reproduction. It is argued that this contradiction was resolved by redefining ideologies of gender in order to meet the economic realities of the institution and that this resulted in the formulation of class-specific definitions of femininity.

AN 'ARMY OF MAGDALENES': WOMEN IN THE PUBLIC SPHERE

Evidence of a public discourse on prostitution can be found in the stream of tracts and essays published throughout the nineteenth century. Public discussion intensified, however, in the 1840s around the time that the Registrar General began to publish statistical inquiries into the living conditions of Scotland's poor. These studies defined many of the traditional rural and urban working-class living arrangements as 'social problems' and aroused a wave of social consciousness in many, who awakened to what they called 'the moral state of the nation'. The Scottish establishment, which had long claimed moral superiority over its English and Continental neighbours, was seriously shaken by statistical exposés of illegitimacy, infanticide, prison convictions and intemperance and, above all by studies which reflected badly on the sexual behaviour of Scottish women.[6]

The statistics which captured the imaginations of many moral reformers related to prostitution. Between 1860 and 1890, for example, the statistics from the Glasgow Magdalene Institution indicated that over three-quarters of the inmates were in their late teens, and either orphans or from broken homes. One-quarter of these were sexually active before they reached sixteen, and fifty per cent by the age of eighteen. These statistics raised disturbing questions about the character of Scottish 'manhood' and about extra-marital sex.[7] In 1866 the asylum's directors remarked that 'the unmanliness, the unutterable baseness of some men's pleasures strikes one as he looks upon such figures'.[8]

The moral panic surrounding the subject of prostitution was generated by many social groups, and the figure of the 'prostitute' meant different things to them all. The medical profession maintained that epidemics of venereal disease were linked directly to prostitution and, recognising the debilitating effects of congenital syphilis, argued that it had a moral obligation to future generations to cure 'diseased' women.[9] Others argued that controlling prostitution and venereal disease was the joint responsibility of the physician and the police. 'The medical man must be conjoined with the policeman in this dirty and degrading work', an Edinburgh surgeon wrote; 'With speculum in hand he must go from brothel to brothel, and from door to door, examining patient by patient systematically ... like a railway porter, with a hammer in hand, examining axle by axle in a newly arrived train to see whether any may be heated or no.'[10]

The clergy, along with lay evangelists, were also prolific writers on the prostitution 'problem', which they called the 'Great Social Evil'. For many, the living habits of the rural and urban proletariat represented a threat to the future of the Empire; the escalated trade-union activity and Chartist demonstrations during the 1830s and 1840s suggested to many that

'Armageddon might be around the next bend'.[11] Some correlated prostitution with class war. William Tait, who surveyed prostitution in Edinburgh, argued that history proved that an increase in prostitution resulted in revolution, as evidenced by the large numbers of 'prostitutes' prior to the French, Spanish and American revolutions.[12] Others correlated prostitution with subversion. A Glasgow clergyman accused socialists and Chartists of seducing young female factory workers and warned industrialists against hiring them as foremen. Another clergyman, Ralph Wardlaw, attacked Owenite socialism and defined prostitution as the 'socialism of brutes'.[13] Robert Owen, who regarded prostitution as a symptom of the corrupt bourgeois social order, retaliated by accusing Wardlaw of slander and challenged him to debate the socialist doctrines.[14]

The 'prostitute' also represented a threat to the sanctity of the home. Tait stated that every family and every social class was exposed to the effects of prostitution. It brought immeasurable shame to the families of young women who 'went astray'; it corrupted the morals of young men and led to dishonesty and theft, causing shop assistants, clerks and apprentices to steal from their employers, uncles or fathers in order to finance their 'carnal pleasures'; it infected incontinent and unfaithful husbands and 'careless and dissipated wives' with diseases which were then communicated to children; it was a common cause of suicide; and finally, it was the principal reason why students of literature, science, law and medicine, who resorted to taverns and brothels to relieve the boredom of study, failed in their courses.[15] Prostitution and the 'prostitute' signified the underside of Christian social order and of industrial capitalism, both of which the bourgeoisie claimed to represent and up-hold; thus, whether the 'prostitute' was seen as victim or as polluter, she was a living violation of bourgeois notions of female sexual propriety.

In the debate about the causes of prostitution, it is significant that it was mainly working-class women who were scrutinised and stigmatised. Recruitment to the prostitution trade was therefore diagnosed in terms of environmental factors such as employment in the 'public' sphere, the frequenting of working-class entertainments, and poor education, with only a passing acknowledgement of contributing social factors such as poverty and unemployment. For example, many claimed that the poorhouse was the worst place for impressionable young girls. They predicted that without their intervention poorhouse girls would grow up to be 'prostitutes' and thieves because they remained largely uneducated and unskilled. Others argued that employment in factories, mills and warehouses led to 'prostitution' because in many cases women worked alongside men, and were exposed to 'loose conversation and example'.[16] Wardlaw, for instance, reported that 'chastity [was] almost unknown' in these establishments.[17] The statistics of the Glasgow Magdalene revealed that, unlike servants, whose 'fall' was attributed largely to seduction, the majority of former factory girls in the institution had been led astray by other mill-girls. Work in the 'public' sphere was also seen as spoiling women for work in domestic service, which was regarded as more respectable. Many families would not hire former mill-girls as household servants, 'knowing ... that the atmosphere of a factory is not the best for nourishing the moral and social qualities of females'.[18]

Moral entrepreneurs frequently used the mill-girl to typify the status of women who worked in the 'public' sphere. They worked outside the home, and many alongside men or in direct competition with them in areas which, unlike domestic service, defied the doctrine of separate spheres. To stress this, reformers did not always distinguish 'prostitutes' from mill-girls, or from any of the women who congregated unescorted by men in the streets. The following account of women at the Glasgow Fair was echoed in many descriptions of female behaviour at other venues of working-class leisure activity, such as dance-halls, theatres, public houses, and other places where 'respectable' women with 'feminine sensibilities' were not supposed to go.[19]

> The ground was teaming with street girls, some of them might be mill girls – Several mill girls were under the influence of drink ... [and] many of them were successful in their attempts to lead lads and boys away with them; two gaily dressed girls picked up young men and went off to the Green ... Saw thirteen couples lying on the Green; two couples of whom were in the very act of prostitution....

> Saw 94 prostitutes, also a large number of very young girls like mill-workers, scarcely distinguishable from prostitutes in their conduct. Saw 5 young prostitutes squatting on the grass in a very immoral manner; also one couple lying on the grass. (We speak confidently of the purpose, because a policeman on the Green assured us ... that no woman went to the Green after a certain hour, save for that purpose...[20]

Moral reformers regarded these women as 'unfeminine'. They correlated mill-girl culture – rough voices, garish dress, drinking and swearing with sexual promiscuity, although there was no evidence that this life-style led to prostitution. Furthermore, unlike the servant, whose activities were confined to the 'private' sphere, female factory labourers were seen as a potential political threat. Sharing the same working conditions as men, they were often involved in the same political movements. Historians argue that in some areas female industrial action had a significant impact on trade union development and that Scottish women were prominent among the Owenite socialists.[21] In the eyes of the bourgeoisie, female factory workers had one foot in the 'feminine' sphere of home and family and the other in the 'masculine' world of social production. Their financial independence was perceived as subverting the 'natural' role of the female sex – a role that demanded dependence and servility in relation to men.[22]

Moral reformers defined women who worked in the 'public' sphere as potential 'deviants' or 'prostitutes'. This is not to suggest that all working-class women were regarded this way, but that they engaged in behaviours that were seen as causes of prostitution. They defied bourgeois notions of 'femininity' by adopting life-styles that did not conform to the middle-class doctrine of separate spheres. Because of the realities of working-class life, especially among the poor, the 'unfeminine' woman would always be found among the poor, where overcrowding, poverty and lack of education, excluded her from the 'position and education' that confirmed the 'character' of higher class girls.[23]

Throughout the nineteenth century the expansion of the market economy and the commercialisation of traditional female tasks transformed women's household-based methods of earning a living. Traditionally, women earned money through activities such as sewing and washing which were seen as supplementary to domestic chores and thus safely outside of the 'public' sphere. Throughout the century, increasing numbers of women left their families to find wage-earning employment in the factories and mills of Scottish industry. The changing pattern of women's work challenged the division of labour dictated by the doctrine of separate spheres by undermining the foundations of the patriarchal family.[24] Controversy over the presence of working women in the 'public' arena, therefore, became an integral part of the public discourse on prostitution.

Moral reformers recognised the economic hardship faced by these women. They admitted that during depressions in the trade cycle, when unemployment was high, there was an increase in the number of 'prostitutes' on the streets. They agreed that low wages and the unstable market for semi-skilled and unskilled female labour were common causes of prostitution. But they were at a loss as to what should be done about it. Their faith in private enterprise and the Poor Law committed them to the belief that those who were prepared to earn an honest living could do so if they tried.[25] Tait demonstrated that this was not true. In order to combat female poverty, he suggested, many of the 'male' occupations such as shop assisting, tailoring, furniture polishing, engraving and coppersmithing be done by women. Similarly, he recommended implementing a price-fixing board which would guarantee seamstresses a minimum wage.[26] But Tait's suggestions were ignored by his contemporaries, who devoted their attention to rating occupations in terms of their supposed moral risk. They concluded that the chances of a woman straying from the 'path of virtue' were inextricably linked to her choice of occupation; in this respect, the most 'dangerous' occupations were to be found in mills, theatres, public houses, and agriculture. Similarly imperilled were shop assistants, seam-stresses, messengers and flower-girls.[27] Reformers admitted that the low wages paid in these trades frequently drove women from cruel and biting poverty to prostitution. However, they also claimed that 'vicious inclinations' acquired in childhood or through the influence of disreputable associates were just as likely to expose a woman to temptations as was her occupation.[28] In order to prevent women from resorting to prostitution, the majority of reformers recommended moral education and training in domestic service and other forms of work that were subject to direct patriarchal supervision or parental discipline.

Throughout the century, domestic service was regarded as an ideal form of paid employment for women because it was performed in the 'private' sphere and did not break with the feminine role. This is ironic in view of the fact that the magdalene homes reported that the majority of inmates were former servants. As one philanthropist wrote, 'Incontinence prevails extensively among the class of domestic servants... Statistics prove unequivocally that immorality in that class upon which much of the happiness of the community depends... They tell us that our maids fill the country with illegitimate children, and swarm the streets as prostitutes.'[29] By the 1870s the percentage of former servants in magdalene homes began to drop, but the percentage of former factory workers increased. This trend intensified concern about the morality of the women who worked in the 'public' sphere. Moral reformers stressed that these young women had to be taught that chastity and virginity were 'the priceless jewel in her honour – however plain her person – however humble her rank may be – which without the deepest shame and detriment, she dare not give away.'[30]

If the criteria for classifying women as 'prostitutes' appear ambiguous it is because reformers were more concerned with practical control than with systematic, academic or philosophical discussions.[31] Apparently they were confident of their ability to recognise a 'prostitute' if they saw one. The Glasgow Chief Constable stated that 'You may well know a prostitute as you would know a sweep... A man with a black face may not be a sweep, but at the same time you would say he was a sweep'.[32] Moral reformers were not satisfied with simply identifying the causes of prostitution; their primary concern was reforming the women who were recruited to the trade and, to this end, they looked to the magdalene homes as refuges where offending women could be placed under a harsh regime of moral education and training and made to conform to middle-class notions of sexual and vocational propriety.

'WHOLESOME, PATERNAL, CHRISTIAN DISCIPLINE': MAGDALENE HOMES

Scotland's first magdalene homes opened in Edinburgh (1797) and Glasgow (1815).[33] The Glasgow Magdalene Asylum was modelled on the one in Edinburgh. Both were charitable institutions which relied on voluntary subscriptions and support. They also relied on the willingness of inmates to conform to the rules of the establishment, for the asylums lacked the statutory power to detain anyone against her will.[34] According to the directors, their purpose was to rescue and reform. Those they intended to rescue were not professional 'prostitutes' with long criminal records, but young female misdemeanants, paupers and vagrants.[35] These women were usually brought to the institutions' attention (by magistrates, missionaries, the police and hospital authorities) because, driven by unemployment, extreme poverty, or illness, they had committed sexual offences or engaged in full- or part-time 'prostitution', as defined by the institution.

In Glasgow between 1860 and 1869, 61 per cent of the inmates had been servants. By 1870, the percentage of servants in magdalene homes began to fall, but those from other occupations rose. The records of the Glasgow Lock Hospital (a hospital for indigent women with venereal disease) indicate that between 1870 and 1890 33 per cent of the patients were mill-girls and 25 per cent of the patients were servants. These were followed by machinists, washerwomen and needlewomen. The hospital's surgeon remarked that although few would admit it these women were really 'prostitutes', which he defined as 'young women who had more or less given way to immoral practices'. He added that many worked at their occupations during the day and in the evenings took to the streets in order to supplement their low wages.[36]

These institutions favoured women under the age of twenty-four, who were neither pregnant nor diseased at the time of admission, and who were of reasonable intelligence and willing to submit to discipline. Inmates who received a clean bill of health from the asylum's physician were selected after a lengthy interview during which it was incumbent upon them to convince the directors of their sincere desire to reform. It was possible to fool both the committee and the physician. Inmates were frequently sent back to the hospital (for a 'course of mercury', the nineteenth-century cure for venereal disease) or to the workhouse (often a pregnancy had become obvious). Others were sent on their way shortly after admission as it became clear that they would be 'highly dangerous' to the institution. Still others, – such as one Margaret Richie, who was wanted by the police – were arrested when their whereabouts became known to the legal authorities. Inmates who passed the probationary period were fully admitted to the institutions where they were expected to stay for two years. Those who completed the programme were given a certification of character and guaranteed the protection of the institution for as long as they behaved well and received favourable reports from their employers.

Life in a magdalene home was organised around the premise that inmates could be reformed only if order were put into their lives and a strict regime of 'mild, wholesome, paternal, and Christian discipline' were enforced. Accordingly the day was organised around work and prayer, and strict discipline governed all routines.[37] After admission, inmates were expected to take a 'hot or cold bath' and were given a uniform. Their own clothes were cleaned, ticketed and laid aside and would only be returned in case of dismissal. The daily routine, which varied little throughout the century, was designed to mirror that of an efficiently run home, and to emulate the 'respectable' family life in the households of the directors. The only exception was that inmates were prohibited contact with anyone outside the institution. The management believed that inmates were more likely to internalise the reformatories' teachings about how women like themselves ought to behave if they were isolated from contradictory examples. This applied particularly to inmates with family and friends whom the institution regarded as troublesome.

On a typical day in the Glasgow asylum in 1820, inmates arose at dawn; washers began work at 5. 30 a. m. , laundry workers at 6.00 and sewers at 7. 00. The sewers took turns doing domestic chores around the asylum. Before breakfast, the 'sisters' gathered with the matron for 'family worship'. Breakfast (porridge) was between 8.00 and 9.00, after which the inmates resumed their revenue-generating employment in the laundry or sewing room. Dinner was between 1.00 and 2.00 and supper between 7.00 and 8.00. After supper there was 'family worship' again. It was not unusual for inmates to work for an hour or two after supper. One hour was set aside each day for the education of illiterate inmates and each girl was given her own Bible as soon as she was able to read. The entire inmate population was examined regularly in reading and reciting portions of Scripture. Throughout the day the staff were expected to take every opportunity to instruct inmates in the principles and duties of religion. Bedtime was at 10. 30, making the average working day at least ten hours long. With only minor exceptions the regime was the same in Edinburgh.

The programme was strict and the rules numerous. The directors expected a high standard of conduct from the inmates who were in turn expected to observe a 'becoming silence' at all times. No 'snuff ... no letters, or parcels, or messages' were allowed in the house and felonies such as swearing, fighting and lying (which were always a problem) were punished by expulsion, solitary confinement or hard physical labour. At the Edinburgh Asylum, Mary Buchan was put in solitary confinement twice – for insolence and for the bad quality of her work. Margaret Reid was rebuked for striking Robina Miller on the side of the head; whereas Jean Marshall was given a week's confinement and a week washing the stairs for a similar offence. Between 1833 and 1835 discipline was so bad that the directors resorted to shaving inmates' heads in order to keep the inmates from escaping.

> [b]y the adoption of the practice alluded to, an advantage has been gained, as no woman likes to leave the Asylum without her hair; and, before it has grown a proper length, she has become habituated to her situation, and by instruction and example, made to see the sinful course she had been pursuing. This effect has failed in only two out of fifty cases![38]

Although women came voluntarily and the institution could not detain them against their will, once admitted it was rather difficult to leave. It was against the asylums' policies to release anyone before she demonstrated that she was capable of a 'change of life' whereupon she was either reunited with her family (if the directors approved of their character) or placed in domestic service. Country service was always preferable because many of the inmates were too well known to be returned to their former communities. Inmates who desired to leave before being formally discharged were required to give a month's notice and were frequently put in solitary confinement to think it over. After that time, those who could not be prevailed upon to stay were reprimanded, scolded, relieved of their uniforms and dismissed.

A similar procedure was followed in cases where inmates rebelled against or resisted the institution's attempt to control their behaviour. Inmates who were expelled for misbehaving were reprimanded in front of the other women, and a report upon their expulsion was sent to the police. Nelly Sutherland and Bell Evans were dismissed from the Edinburgh Asylum in this way for deliberately setting fire to their bedroom. Inmates who were so anxious to leave that they ran away were charged with the theft of their uniforms, denied any money they had earned, and prohibited from re-admission. When Margaret Peat ran off she was brought back to the Edinburgh Asylum under guard and sentence by the magistrates to two months in the Bridewell. Ann Robertson was given six months for the same offence. Circumstances were better for Ann Wallace, however, who ran away from the Edinburgh Asylum in 1811 with 'the Society's clothes. Mrs. Coutts [the matron] met her on the street 2 days afterward and brought her back to the Asylum ... took her clothes ... and turned her away; and she having promised to go to the harvest; they gave her 1 [shilling] to buy a Hook'.[39] Although the merits of each case were carefully weighed against the circumstances, the rules were strictly followed.

Two main strategies for moral regulation were developed in the institutions: moral education and industrial training. It was believed that both could be accomplished through a regime of hard work and Bible reading. One historian states that religious indoctrination in magdalene asylums had one overriding aim: to replace deceit and pride with guilt. The directors found nothing more disturbing than an inmate's unwillingness to confess her sin.[40] The thinking behind the policy of giving each inmate her own Bible as soon as she had learned to read was that the scriptures would reveal the extent of her sin, defilement and guilt; and she would thus learn to accept herself as a 'sinner'. Scripture reading and prayer were combined with periods of solitary confinement. According to Michael Ignatieff, the significance of solitary confinement was that it offered the perfect reconciliation of humanity and terror. It epitomised a punishment so rational that offenders punished themselves in the 'soundless, silent anguish of their own minds'.[41] Furthermore, by individualising punishment, the directors glossed over the class inequalities, poverty and hypocrisy which were responsible for the inmates' troubles.[42] Finally, through Bible stories, inmates were taught a morality centred on self-sacrifice and duty. Through the Christian chain of command, which parallelled the Victorian social class hierarchy and which sanctioned female inferiority, self-abnegation and duty, each inmate learned her appropriate gender-role and social class position.

In addition to religious education, inmates were provided with a secular education ranging, as the literacy level of the general population improved, from basic reading and writing early in the century to special classes in geography, arithmetic and music; also included were weekly lectures on 'homely and interesting' subjects, as well as Gospel Temperance meetings. Education classes were intended to be a pleasant break from the other activities of the day, and it was believed that it was important for inmates to develop their minds. What is striking about the evening curriculum and special events is their overall 'gentility' and similarity to the activities with which middle-class women might occupy their evenings. The emphasis on gentility reflects how closely penitentiaries associated middle-class manners with reform. It was not intended that inmates become learned, or 'ladies', but rather, that they should come to appreciate the values associated with being a lady,[43] in order that they might make better *servants.*

Education was supplemented with training for domestic service so that inmates would be able to support themselves after they left the institution. Asylums intended to return inmates to their families wherever possible. In cases where inmates were orphans or the family was unsuitable, inmates were returned to the 'private' sphere as competent and submissive servants. As servants, inmates could act out their femininity in paid employment, which conveniently enabled bourgeois women to protect their own femininity.[44] This letter from a former Glasgow inmate in 1881 illustrates this nicely.

> I have a good situation, and I am doing the very best to give satisfaction... The one baby is eighteen months old, and the other five months old, and very delicate, but my mistress says the young baby has grown this last week. I am coming to see you on Thursday evening first to get a lesson in shirt-ironing. I got all the washing done up nicely. I did the collars and cuffs, but I was afraid of the shirts, so they were sent out ... Mrs S. said to me last night, I hope you will not be going away and leaving me, for she knows very little about housekeeping and less about children, so I am going to be the baby's mother...[45]

The directors were prejudiced against women in 'public' paid employment and preferred to place inmates in situations where they would be dependent upon others for food and board, and where they hoped the girls would be closely supervised by 'respectable' members of the middle class. Rafter argues that the very concept of an institution dedicated to the rescue and reform of women over eighteen was rooted in the perception of women as child-like creatures. [46] If the directors felt any concern about sending inmates into service, the same situation that got so many of them into trouble in the first place, they soothed their consciences with the belief that the moral education inmates received would neutralise and fortify them against 'evil influences and temptations'.[47]

As the century progressed, an increasing number of inmates, especially those from Glasgow, had previous work experience in mills and factories and refused to be placed in service. The directors regarded these inmates with a certain degree of frustration and disillusionment.[48]

> [W]ith this class, who are too often the offspring as well as the associates of the low, the drunken, the dissolute, who have not ever had the elements of religious or moral training, and who have previously been employed as field-workers, mill-workers, char-women, hawkers etc. the directors have some difficulty, as they are manifestly unsuited for domestic service...[49]

In the early days, girls such as Betty Finlay, who declared that she 'could not bring her mind to that kind of employ [service]', were sent to David Dale's cotton-mill at Lanark. This is ironic because, although the directors applauded Dale's system of patriarchal paternalism, under the influence of the Owenite socialists in the 1830s, reformers attacked the community at New Lanark and charged socialism with causing prostitution.

By 1835 a change in ideologies of moral regulation and gender can be observed. The Edinburgh directors discovered that 'discontent and riotous behaviour' could be controlled by moving certain women from sewing to washing. They discovered that those women who were used to 'roving' would not conform to sedentary work, and they concluded that this energy could be 'harnessed' in the laundry room. By mid-century more emphasis was placed on industrial training in laundries, which had proven to be the most financially profitable activity anyway. Through training in the laundry the directors promised to turn out a highly skilled and well-disciplined industrial labour force.

To summarise, the system of moral regulation developed in these institutions depended on moral education, religious training and strict discipline. In addition, however, the directors had to develop strategies other than corporal punishment for dealing with inmates who resisted their programme. Their solution was to try to manage 'discontent and riotous behaviour' – in other words resistance – by shifting 'troublesome' inmates from sedentary work to active labour. They argued that certain inmates, generally those with previous employment in the 'public' sphere, were 'manifestly unsuited for domestic service'. So they developed two streams for moral regulation. The first was designed for inmates who had never been unsexed, so to speak, by employment in the 'public' sphere. These would be returned to the 'private' sphere as competent and submissive domestic servants. The second stream transformed inmates, mainly those with prior employment in the 'public' sphere, or those who refused to become deferential, into well-disciplined industrial labourers.

THE 'SANCTIMONIOUS SWEATSHOP'

The ideologies of moral regulation were frequently altered in response to economic pressures within the institution and in the community at large.

Behind the directors' idealised image of the morally reformed female proletariat lay the material realities of reproducing the institution: paying the bills and possibly making a profit. This resulted in a contradiction between the need, endemic to charities, to maintain the institution on a day-to-day basis, and the desire, unique to magdalene homes, to bring about the moral reformation of its inmates. Similarly, the directors recognised by the middle of the century that there was a demand from the community for female labour in industry and that more women preferred this work. The directors astutely resolved their dilemma by constantly adapting their ideology of moral regulation, a process which can be observed in a series of experiments in Edinburgh and Glasgow throughout the century. It should be emphasised that these were charitable institutions; at no time in their histories did subscriptions pay for more than a fraction of the administration cost. The directors, therefore, were faced with the difficulty of creating the right balance of 'work and religion'.

Although the directors recognised that prostitution had many causes, they attributed it mainly to the inmates' previous unwillingness to work. In order to re-proletarianise the inmates, the institution operated in what sociologists call the 'long-shadow of work', basing their regime on training in deference and subordination – qualities the inmates would need as suitable servants or labourers. The organisational structure of magdalene homes was based on a paternalist model, which recast elements of the factory system in the image of the patriarchal family, thereby reproducing the patriarchal and class-bound order of society.[50] The 'fatherly' male directors reigned supreme as the chief disciplinary officers. The 'motherly' matrons, usually middle-aged spinsters or widows, acted as the subordinates of the male directors and as role-models for the inmates. The other members of staff, also unmarried women, were expected to set an example of cleanliness and tidiness in their own person and to see that this was followed by the inmates. They were also expected to maintain a professional distance from the inmates and to report any signs of 'levity, or any thing on the part of inmates at variance with good order'.[51]

Upon admission the inmates were separated according to their past employment records and education, as well as moral character. Those who had been 'seduced' were segregated from the more 'depraved', who had actually been 'on the street'. Women on 'probation' were strictly forbidden from communicating with the other women, Even during family worship they sat 'behind a screen'. Once fully admitted to the institution, inmates were further segregated on the basis of the status of the employment they performed and contact between the kitchen maids, sewers and laundresses was discouraged. The higher-status workers such as sewers were segregated from the kitchen help; the washers, manglers, and glazers were segregated from 'the other classes above stairs'; and the laundresses from 'the other classes above or below stairs'.[52]

Early in the histories of these magdalene homes the directors discovered that getting a good day's work out of the inmates would be a continual battle. Many had never held a steady job and others were totally unskilled and illiterate. These problems were compounded by general bad health, malnourishment, and a range of complaints and physical disabilities common to the population in general. Getting work out of even the 'able-bodied' was a challenge. In order to induce the inmates to 'industry' the Edinburgh directors decided to give each inmate a daily quota of work; the surplus gains, roughly one third, would then be given to them for clothes. Those who failed to meet the quota only received one-quarter of the profit. Allowing inmates to keep part of their wages would teach them the value of 'honest' labour, plus the diligence and thrift they would need in the work force.[53] In contrast, the Glasgow Asylum did not pay its inmates for the quantity of work produced, but gave one shilling to inmates who behaved well for six months after leaving the institution.

The opportunity to earn a little money for clothes, however, inspired few inmates. They were frequently reprimanded for the insufficient amount of work they produced. This resulted in stricter rules in Edinburgh. In 1800 a few looms had been purchased so that inmates might be taught a trade. In order to force inmates into taking an interest they stressed that 'any women who left the loom without permission would be dismissed'. Furthermore, idle inmates were always publicly reprimanded and rule violators were punished with solitary confinement. For example, when Margaret Reid refused to do the laundry she was given '3 days solitary confinement to think it over'. In addition to corporal punishment, the directors recognised the value of positive reinforcement and gave material rewards for good work and moral behaviour. Special dinners and 'dishes of tea' were regarded as rewards for 'diligence' and a few positions, such as messenger and door-porter were reserved for girls of merit. These tasks were to be viewed as a means of 'exciting a spirit of emulation amongst the rest, that they also may be put in places of trust'. Finally, 'as a means of promoting emulation', inspirational tracts and books were awarded to the best scholars.[54]

When an institution was in financial trouble it changed its views about the moral significance of profit-sharing. In 1833, for example, the Edinburgh Asylum, was £650 in debt and the directors were faced with a choice between reducing the inmates' stipend from one-quarter to one-sixth or abolishing it all together. After learning that the Glasgow Magdalene Asylum did not pay their inmates directly, the Edinburgh directors abolished the girls' allowance and decided to give them some clothes when they left instead. In the more affluent 1850s, the directors felt free to reinstate their profit-sharing system, but this time the highest-paid inmates only received one-twelfth of the profits. The washers and kitchen maids only earned a sum equal to the average earnings of the best sewers; whereas the glazers could earn the best sewers' average plus one-quarter. The directors had high hopes for their experiment but, as it happened, the free-enterprise system had a number of unforeseen consequences. First, it did not increase the productivity as expected and led to a decrease in the quality of the work as women rushed to get as much done as possible. Second, the girls became dissatisfied with tedious work which did not pay well. Third, the inmates refused to help one another. And fourth, it promoted 'individuality and made it difficult to arrange work tasks collectively'. After two years the experiment was abandoned and replaced with a series of 'reward tickets' which had no direct cash value.

In 1877, the Edinburgh Asylum boasted that the 'long hours of work had been shortened' in order to give time for 'intellectual and moral training'. On closer examination, however, it turns out that the matron had found another money-making scheme. She converted the 'odds and ends of time … to good account' by getting inmates to knit stockings. In total they earned four guineas for the one hundred and fifty pairs of stockings made 'in time which might otherwise have been wasted, while their hands have been trained in work, which is essential to domestic economy and comfort'.

By the middle of the century the managers discovered that laundry work was the most profitable and easily learned of the trades tried in the institution. It was, however, a problem in Edinburgh, where the institution was located in the centre of the city. The clothes were frequently damaged by the soot from the Gas-Light Company and had to be rewashed, which 'required double quantity of soap'. Patrons complained of stains being left in the clothes, and the matron was afraid to 'mention gas as the cause of it, as families might be disposed to withdraw their employment'. On 14 August 1821 a whole greenfield of clothes was destroyed by the gas and the institution sued the Gas-Light Company for damages; two girls worked around the clock scrubbing out stains with 'salts of lemons'. Consequently, the laundry in Edinburgh never really got off the ground until 1864 when the institution moved to the country.

In contrast, Glasgow's laundry, which employed forty women in 1867 was a booming success. By 1870 the directors boasted that their institution was 'not only a refuge to unfortunates, but what is of still more conse-quence, it is a training school for them in good conduct and in some homely branch of usefulness and of what many prove remunerative occupation'.[55]

The economic success of laundries among rescue homes did more than help to cut the cost of an inmates' confinement. More importantly, laundry work served a symbolic function: through laundry work, women daily performed a cleansing ritual.[56] They enacted 'penance for their past sins and purged themselves of their moral contagion'.[57] It is not surprising, then, that in 1877 the directors of the Glasgow institution imbued laundry work with great moral significance. They regarded it as … 'not only more healthful and more remunerative, but, in its moral tendencies, far superior to needlework…[which] is monotonous and less profitable'.

Glasgow experienced a trade depression between 1877 and 1883[58] and the difficulties women faced finding employment, together with the clamp-down on street soliciting resulting from the amended Police Act, drove many to the institution to escape poverty and police harassment. The depression also decreased the amount of laundry work available by increasing competition between commercial laundries and charities; the Magdalene Institution was not the only charity that did laundry work. Nevertheless, throughout the 1870s and 1880s laundry work became an increasingly important part of the annual revenue of the institution. The directors boasted that it paid for two-thirds of the cost of maintaining the home, and also played an indispensable part in the training of girls for 'future usefulness'. Prior to 1886 work had been done by hand, but with the advent of steam technology it became clear that modernisation was necessary if they were going to compete with commercial enterprises. In order to finance this, the directors actively solicited funds. They claimed that at least two thousand pounds were needed to modernise the machinery and extend the plant. 'It would be no kindness', they explained,

> to the inmates to give them the shelter of the Home for a given period, and to keep them in semi-idleness, the condition of idleness having been the bane of many of them in the past. On the contrary, an endeavour is made to impress them with the dignity of labour, and to teach them self-respect and independence, thus raising them to a higher moral platform, to breathe a purer and nobler atmosphere.[59]

The loyal patrons responded and the money was raised within a year. The plant acquired a steam engine and a boiler along with washing and calendering machines. The directors were beginning to regard the laundry more and more as a competitive business and began to advertise in annual reports and charity pamphlets. In order to pass this entrepreneurial spirit on to the inmates and to entice them into taking a more active interest in the 'domestic and industrial' work, they introduced a system of of profit-sharing in 1887. Premiums varying from one to seven shillings were allocated to girls according to merit, conduct, industry, and the class of promotion obtained. Thus, every inmate would be made to feel that the 'prosperity of the Homes, [was] her prosperity in which she ha[d] a direct personal interest'. By 1909 the directors observed that laundresses had become highly skilled workers. 'Such great strides had been made in the laundry trade', since the 'time when it was thought that any female could wash and dress clothes. It has become a skilled industry that can only be successfully pursued after a period of prolonged and careful training; and to bring such women as the inmates ... up to this high standard is not an easy task'.[60]

Finally, it should be noted that this remark was made in the same year that the residence requirement for inmates was under review by less sympathetic board members. Throughout the asylums' histories the two-year residence requirement had been a regular source of controversy. There were many who argued that they could reach more girls if residency was reduced to four months. But the directors were attempting to create an industrial labour force and many argued that keeping inmates for shorter periods would be too expensive because by the time an inmate was physically and technically capable of earning her keep, she was likely to leave the institution. Financial motives, and the need to make profit out of the inmates' labour, therefore, lay behind the two-year residence requirement, which is another example of the shaping of moral reform ideology by economic incentives. In sum, although the directors never ceased to espouse the claim that these were voluntary organisations, subtle incentives such as the premium scheme and the promise of material goods, which were reinforced by the activities of the Edinburgh and Glasgow police and magistrates, served to keep inmates in the homes until the directors were satisfied that they were morally reformed, and until they produced a significant income for the institution. Economic necessity, therefore, reinforced ideology in the 'making of a sanctimonious sweatshop'.[61]

CONCLUSION

This study of the goals and objectives of the magdalene homes in Edinburgh and Glasgow tells us as much about the nineteenth-century view of women's roles in the home, at work and in society as it does about the institutional practices themselves. It has also provided an unique opportunity to examine the relationship between moral regulation and the construction of gender and class ideologies. The directors of these institutions never ceased to extol the virtues of domesticity for women and preferred to return inmates to their families and friends where they would continue to have a dependent status, or to place them in domestic service where they would be supervised in 'respectable' middle-class households. Their efforts to create the ideal working-class woman, however, collided with social reality in ways they had not anticipated. These institutions were subjected to social, political, economic and internal pressures that prohibited them from becoming a 'rehabilitative utopia'.[62] By mid-century the increase in the demand for female labour in industry, together with the inmates' preference for this work forced the directors to shift their emphasis from training in domesticity to industrial labour.

Similarly, behind the institutions' programme of moral regulation lay the contradiction between the material reproduction of the institution itself and the moral regulation of working-class women. The strategy the directors developed to resolve this contradiction was to attach a moral significance to work. The challenge, then, was not simply a matter of re-socialising women for service or factory work, but of realising a moral mission. The directors assigned a moral meaning to certain forms of female labour; thus they not only created women fit for work, but work fit for women. As the century progressed, and as more women resisted employment in the 'private' sphere as domestic servants, the directors were able to resolve their bias against placing women in the 'public' sphere. But, before they could make the fact that women worked in the 'public' sphere palatable to themselves and to their middle-class patrons, they had to convince themselves that these women had been properly socialised. Although the first goal of the magdalene home was training in domesticity, the increased emphasis on industrial training was rationalised as its second goal, but one equally important for the acquisition of appropriate working-class gender roles.

In conclusion, this chapter has enabled us to examine the process whereby sexualities are defined and controlled along gender and social class lines. Behind the nineteenth-century definition of the 'prostitute' was a contemporary vision of the ideal-type of working-class woman; in the process of defining the 'prostitute', reformers also defined her antithesis, the ideal working-class daughter, wife and worker. This definition was not a direct copy of the middle-class feminine ideal, but was designed distinctly for the working class. The ideal working-class woman was pious, subservient and thrifty.[63] But more importantly, according to the directors of the magdalene homes 'respectability' for working-class women could include a role in both the 'public' and 'private' spheres, at least until marriage. This was not the case for 'respectable' middle-class women, who were 'unsexed' by paid employment. Finally, it should be emphasised that the symbol of the 'prostitute' was not merely the product of the charities designed to save her; she had a far wider cultural significance. Although working- and middle-class women were separated by a vast economic and social gulf, the middle-class women who entered the medical profession or became social reformers were as threatening to the social order as the mill-girls and 'prostitutes' were. [64] The symbol of the 'magdalene', therefore, was also used as a threat to all women who dared to defy established class and gender roles.

ACKNOWLEDGEMENTS

I would like to thank Vic Satzewich for assisting me with collecting the Edinburgh material and commenting on various drafts of this paper, and the editors for their helpful advice.

NOTES

1 E. Bristow, *Vice and Vigilance* (London, Gill & Macmillan, 1977), 63–64, 67.

2 O. Checkland, *Philanthropy in Victorian Scotland* (Edinburgh, John Donald Publishers, 1980), 3.

3 N. Rafter, 'Chastizing the Unchaste: Social Control Functions of A Women's Reformatory', in *Social Control and the State*, ed. S. Cohen and A. Skull (Oxford: Martin Robertson, 1983), 291.

4 F. Mort, *Dangerous Sexualities* (London, Routledge & Kegan Paul, 1987), 81.

5 B. Brenzel, 'Domestication as Reform: A Study of the Socialization of Wayward Girls, 1856–1905', *Harvard Educational Review*, 50 (May 1980), 197–213.

6 A. Thomson, *On the Licentiousness of Scotland and the Remedial*

Measures Which Ought to be Adopted (London, J. Nisbet Co. , 1861), 3.

7   Checkland, op. cit. , 1980, 232.
8   Glasgow Magdalene Asylum, *Annual Report*, 1866.
9   *Glasgow Courier*, 11 February 1805.
10 J. Miller, *Prostitution Considered in Relation to its Causes and Cure* (Edinburgh, 1859), 30.
11 T. C. Smout, *A Century of the Scottish People 1830-1950* (London, Fontana Press, 1986), 40.
12 W. Tait, *Magdalenism* (Edinburgh, P. Richard, 1840), 203.
13 W. Logan, *An Exposure, from Personal Observation of Female Prostitution* (Glasgow, 1843), 13; R. Wardlaw, *Lectures on Female Prostitution* (Glasgow, 1842), 9.
14 *The New Moral World*, 15 October 1842, 127.
15 Tait, op. cit. , 1840, 171–98.
16 Logan, op. cit. , 1843, 13.
17 Wardlaw, op. cit. , 1842, 105.
18 J. Myles, *Chapters in the Life of a Dundee Factory Boy: An Autobiography* (Edinburgh, 1850), 49.
19 M. Sumner, 'Prostitution and Images of Women' unpublished M. Sc. (Economics) thesis (University of Wales, 1980), 154.
20 Glasgow Magdalene Institution, *Report on Glasgow Fair*, 1863, 7–9.
21 Sumner, op. cit. , 1980 182; E. King, *The Scottish Women's Suffrage Movement* (Glasgow, Glasgow Museums and Art Galleries, 1978); E. Gordon, *Women and the Labour Movement in Scotland, 1850–1914*. (Oxford University Press, 1990 forthcoming); J. D. Young, *Women and Popular Struggles* (Edinburgh, Mainstream Publishing, 1985), 68.
22 Sumner, op. cit. , 1980, 179; also see H. Ware, 'Prostitution and the State', unpublished Ph. D. diss. (University of London, 1969).
23 Sumner, 1980, op cit., 154.
24 E. Hellerstein, L. Hume, and K. M. Offen, *Victorian Women* (London, Harvester, 1981) 273.
25 Ware, op. cit. , 1969, 117.
26 Tait, op. cit. , 1840, 210.
27 W. Logan, *The Great Social Evil* (London, 1871), 53.
28 W. Acton, *Prostitution* 2nd ed. (London, John Churchill & Sons, 1869), 80; Wardlaw, op. cit. , 1842, 117; Miller, op. cit. , 1859, 7.
29 A. C. C. List, *The Two Phases of the Social Evil* (Edinburgh, 1859), 18.
30 Miller, op. cit. , 1859, 15.
31 Sumner, op. cit. , 1980, 113.
32 Select Committee on the Contagious Diseases Acts (1866–69), P. P. 1881 (351), viii, 193, 382; hereafter cited as *Select Committee.*
33 The data on the Edinburgh Magdalene Asylum in this section is found in the Sub-Committee Minute Books, (1797–1880); the Ladies' Committee Minute Books, (1780–1900); the Monthly Report on Women's Conduct, (1800–1807); and the Annual Reports, (1800–1890). The information on the Glasgow Magdalene Institution is found in the Annual Reports (1820–1909). In 1840 the Glasgow Magdalene Asylum merged with the House of Refuge for Females and was then reincorporated as the Magdalene Institution in 1860.
34 F. Finnegan, *Poverty and Prostitution* (London, Cambridge University Press, 1979), 169.
35 See Rafter, op. cit. , 1983, 290.

36 *Select Committee* 4 April 1882, 123; A. Patterson, 'Statistics of the Glasgow Lock Hospital Since its Foundations in 1805: With Remarks on the Contagious Diseases Acts, and on Syphilis', *The Glasgow Medical Journal*, 6 December 1882, 410.

37 J. Walkowitz, *Prostitution and Victorian Society* (London: Cambridge University Press, 1980).

38 Edinburgh Magdalene Asylum, *Annual Report*, 1835.

39 EMA, Subcommittee Minute Book, 30 October 1811.

40 See F. K. Prochaska, *Women and Philanthropy in Nineteenth Century England* (Oxford University Press, 1980), 156.

41 M. Ignatieff, *A Just Measure of Pain* (London, MacMillan Press, 1978), 213.

42 Finnegan, op. cit. , 1979, 211.

43 See Rafter, op. cit. , 1983, 296, 307.

44 See Sumner, op. cit. , 1980, 166.

45 Glasgow Magdalene Institution, *Annual Report*, 1881.

46 See Rafter, op. cit. , 1983, 299.

47 Glasgow Magdalene Asylum, *Interim Report*, 1859.

48 See Brenzel, op. cit. , 1980, 205.

49 Edinburgh Magdalene Asylum, *Annual Report*, 1880.

50 See Walkowitz, op. cit. , 1980, 221.

51 Edinburgh Magdalene Asylum, *Sub-Committee Minute Book*, 12 May 1835.

52 Ibid.

53 See Bristow, op. cit. , 1977, 65.

54 Edinburgh Magdalene Asylum, *Sub-Committee Minute Book*, 4 August 1801; 6 September 1814; 30 June 1823.

55 Glasgow Magdalene Institution, *Annual Report*, 1870.

56 See Bristow, op. cit. , 1977, 71.

57 See Walkowitz, op. cit. , 1980, 221.

58 See Cage, 'The Nature and Extent of Poor Relief', in *The Working Class in Glasgow, 1740–1914*, ed. R. A. Cage (London: Croom Helm, 1987), 76–97; Glasgow Magdalene Institution, *Annual Report*, 1879, 1886.

59 Glasgow Magdalene Institution *Annual Report*, 1886.

60 Ibid. , 1909.

61 See Bristow, op. cit. , 1977, 71.

62 See Brenzel, op. cit. , 1980, 109.

63 See L. Nead, 'The Magdalene in Modern Times: The Mythology of the Fallen Woman in Pre-Raphaelite Painting', in *Looking At Images of Femininity in the Visual Arts and Media*, ed. R. Betterton (London: Pandora Press, 1987), 80.

64 See Hellerstein, op. cit. , 1981, 289.

SELECT BIBLIOGRAPHY

Acton, W. *Prostitution*. Second Edition. London: John Churchill & Sons, 1869.

Brenzel, B. 'Domestication as Reform: A Study of the Socialization of Wayward Girls, 1856–1905. *Harvard Educational Review* 50 (May 1980); 196–213.

Bristow, E. *Vice and Vigilance*. London: Gill & Macmillan, 1977.

Checkland, O. *Philanthropy in Victorian Scotland*. Edinburgh: John Donald Publishers, 1980.

Finnegan, F. *Poverty and Prostitution*. London: Cambridge University

Press, 1979.

Logan, W. *An Exposure, from Personal Observation of Female Prostitution.* Glasgow, 1843.

Miller, J. *Prostitution Considered in Relation to its Causes and Cure.* Edinburgh, 1859.

Patterson, A. 'Statistics of the Glasgow Lock Hospital Since its Foundations in 1805: With Remarks on the Contagious Diseases Acts, and on Syphilis'. *The Glasgow Medical Journal* 6 (December 1882): 401–418.

Rafter, N. 'Chastizing the Unchaste: Social Control Functions of a Woman's Reformatory'. In *Social Control and the State,* ed. S. Cohen and A. Skull. Oxford: Martin Robertson, 1983.

Tait, W. *Magdalenism.* Edinburgh: P. Richard, 1840.

Walkowitz, J. *Prostitution and Victorian Society.* London: Cambridge University Press, 1980.

Wardlaw, R. *Lectures on Female Prostitution.* Glasgow, 1842.

3

WOMEN IN THE PRINTING AND PAPER TRADES IN EDWARDIAN SCOTLAND

SIÂN REYNOLDS

'Oh I loved my work. I'd have worked weekends if they'd have let me!' [Former woman compositor in Edinburgh, interviewed in 1986]

'The heavy work in printing is done by men. In the main, women's skills are needed at the completion of the printing process... Take this leaflet for instance: it has two folds and these folds were made by a machine operated by a woman. Quite a simple operation! Others require more skill however, like putting covers on magazines and books, ... and making holes in printed work for binding. Putting numbers on tickets and coupons. Book sewing and wire stitching ... checking, sorting, counting, packing and so on'. (*Jobs for Girls in Printing*, leaflet produced by the British Federation of Master Printers in 1973)

The first quotation comes from one of the last survivors (she has since died) of an unusual group of women: skilled compositors who worked in the Scottish printing trade in the early years of this century. The second quotation, blandly relegating all girl trainees to jobs of which most are neither demanding nor rewarding, indicates how unlikely it was that a woman would be directed towards skilled work in printing in Britain even as late as the 1970s. It is still the case that fewer women than men are recruited to advanced technical jobs in printing and binding, despite the new technology and supposed equality of opportunity of the late twentieth century.[1]

In Edwardian Scotland, however, a number of women were employed in the thriving printing and paper trades, not all of them in unskilled jobs. As well as women bookbinders, who would equally have been found in London firms, there were also for about fifty years, from the 1870s to the 1920s, a number of women compositors, mostly in Edinburgh. Far from marking the opening-up of this kind of industrial employment to women, their presence, both as binders and compositors, was the cause of bitter conflicts between employers and male trade unions, since women were invariably paid less than men. The conflicts came to a head in the years 1900 to 1914, and left a legacy of segregation and exclusion. This chapter looks first at the kind of jobs available to Scottish women and girls in this sector and then at the problems encountered by women who entered the printing and paper trades. It is neither a story of the unchanging 'oppression' of women, nor one of gradual improvement in their position. Rather, it illustrates the complexity of relations between the sexes in an industrial context.

JOBS FOR THE GIRLS?

Jobs in the paper and printing trades were only available in significant numbers in the towns. Some idea of what was on offer for a girl leaving school comes from a survey, carried out by a charity organisation, giving information about 781 working-class families living in the Old Town of Edinburgh. One family, picked more or less at random, could be described as follows: both parents were alive; the father, a tailor, was not often in work; the mother, at home, was 'weary-looking but hardworking'. Of the seven surviving children, two were still at school. The five oldest daughters went out to work and three of them were employed in the printing or paper trades: the 23-year-old is described as a 'stationer', the 20-year-old as working, 'in letterpress', presumably as a compositor, and the 17-year-old as a paper box maker. The other two worked in a rubber factory.

This family is unusual only in having a large number of daughters of working age. Printing and paper trades figure quite prominently in the survey, which covered the families of children attending North Canongate school in a poor part of town but one with 'an admixture of ... the thoroughly respectable working class'.[2] Of the fathers, 40 – the largest single occupational group – were employed in these trades, mostly as skilled journeymen. A total of 30 sons were also in the trades: 16 of them as 'printers', 5 as bookbinders, 2 as typecasters and 7 in paper trades. Perhaps more surprising than any of these figures is the very large number of daughters in the same occupations. No fewer than 45 working daughters are described as 'compositors' or 'printers'; a further 17 were 'bookbinders' and 17 more 'bookfolders'; 23 were envelope-makers or held similar jobs, 20 were paper bag or box makers and 6 were employed in miscellaneous jobs such as laying-on and ticket-printing. The total number of daughters employed in printing and paper trades was 128, and thus far larger than the total of sons.[3] (Table 1).

As will be evident from other chapters in this volume, working-class women and girls in Scotland had a limited choice of work in the 1900s. Domestic service, farm work, clothing and textiles accounted for 60 per cent of women's employment in the 1911 census. It made a great deal of difference where one lived. In Edinburgh by far the biggest employer of women and girls was still domestic service, but as a centre of the paper and printing industry the city offered jobs in this sector to both men and women, especially after the extraordinary expansion in the demand for

TABLE 1. Canongate survey, Edinburgh 1906, printing and paper trades

	Fathers	Mothers	Daughters	Sons
Printers'	33	-	45	16
'Bookbinders'	7	2	17	5
Bookfolders	–	7	17	–
Envelope makers	–	1	23	–
Paper bag/box makers	–	5	20	6
Misc. printing	–	–	6	1
Typecasting	–	–	–	2
TOTALS	40	15	128	30

Source: CECOS Report, 1906, analysis of case studies. Again nomenclature is a problem. 'Printers' includes all who thus described themselves, plus 'compositors', 'letterpress' etc. It may include semi-skilled printing workers. Girls or women who are described as 'bookbinders' were probably stitchers, but may have been folders.

books and periodicals of every kind in the later nineteenth century.[4] The same was at least partly true of Glasgow, which had several large printing firms, and to some extent of other Scottish towns such as Perth and Aberdeen.

As the Canongate survey indicates, while most men in the trade were likely to be skilled journeymen, women were scattered over a number of jobs, most of which were not rated as skilled by the norms of the time. To take the paper trades first: in paper-making, for instance, a few women worked at the unpleasant and ill-paid task of sorting rags; in stationery, which employed a good many women, they worked as envelope-makers, relief-stampers, show-card mounters, black-borderers, and paper bag or box makers. Most of these jobs could be learned quickly and usually consisted of folding, creasing and gumming by hand paper or card which had been cut to size on machines operated by men. The exception to prove the rule was paper-staining, a more exacting trade, which took two years to learn and recruited girls 'from the better sort of working-class family', some of them 'coming to the factory on cycles'.[5] One way or another, there was virtual segregation in the stationery trades: men worked machines and handled complex processes; women and teenage girls did routine, repetitive tasks. Consequently, there was no competition from men for women's jobs, the lowest paid and the least desirable.

A similar division of labour marked bookbinding and printing although, as we shall see, the segregation was beginning to break down by the beginning of the Edwardian era. One example, midway between stationery and printing, was machine-ruling. The production of ledgers and the fast-growing need for school jotters and notebooks had prompted the introduction of various kinds of ruling machines. At first, women were employed simply to feed the machines, but by 1904 in Scotland, (by contrast with England, except for Birmingham) they were 'sometimes promoted to the supervision of simple ruling machines... One firm is said to have only two men ... where once there were forty'. Whereas the men had been paid 28s, the 'girls', as they were called, were paid 17s a week – a high wage for a woman.[6]

Bookbinding had by the 1900s been a segregated trade for some considerable time. Both in Scotland and in England, for reasons apparently inspired by the domestic division of labour, women had established a historical claim to certain parts of the work; essentially, these were folding the sheets and stitching them into sections. As Felicity Hunt has pointed out, these seemed to be 'gender appropriate tasks'.[7] 'Men are never employed in folding', it was said in 1904, nor did they ever attempt to replace women at stitching, even when this began to be done with machines: 'sewing machines are domestic implements in men's eyes'. After it had been sewn, the book was srappered (that is, covered with end-papers) and that was the last a woman saw of it. 'At this stage, the book passes into the hands of men, to be touched no more by women, except perhaps in a few subsidiary processes'.

The 'hands of men', of time-served journeymen that is, took charge of a number of tasks: the book was pressed and nipped, the edges of the pages guillotined; the spine was glued to muslin, rounded, grooved and backed; boards and cloth were cut and pasted on; the cover design and lettering were stamped on in the blocking room; and, finally, the book was 'pasted down' and 'built up' in a large press. If gold leaf was to be laid on, as was common at the turn of the century, this was sometimes handed to women to do, but otherwise all these processes – by 1900 involving the use of quite powerful machines – were men's work, as was every kind of leather work. To quote a Glasgow observer, 'as a rule the men do the heavier and more complicated work, while women do that which is reparatory or supplementary'. Although it was arguable that stitching, if not folding, was at least as skilled as many of the later processes, 'use and wont' had declared it to be merely 'preparatory'.[8]

On the whole, however, and despite segregation, bookbinding offered good opportunities for women. The expansion of book production brought high employment to the trade.[9] In working-class families in Glasgow and Edinburgh, bookbinding was thought of as a thoroughly respectable trade for a girl to enter. In Glasgow, according to one report, 'the girls engaged in folding and the allied process are as a rule of higher intelligence than mill girls and machine feeders, and drawn from different social strata', although it goes on to say that some are 'frail and underfed, from very poor homes'.[10] Stitchers and folders are reported elsewhere in the same study as 'looking down on' machine-feeding girls. As women's work went, bookbinding was skilled, normally requiring a two- to four-year apprentice-

TABLE 2. 'Printers' and 'bookbinders' in England/Wales and Scotland, 1901

	Printers		Bookbinders	
	Men	Women	Men	Women
England & Wales	89,306	9,463	11,608	18,933
Scotland	9,643	2,852	1,422	3,522

Source: Census, cited J. R. Macdonald, *Women in the Printing Trades*, 1904 employed persons only.

TABLE 3. Totals in selected printing and paper trades, Scotland, 1911

	Glasgow		Edinburgh		Scotland	
	Men	Women	Men	Women	Men	Women
Printers	3,059	1,036	3,502	1,802	11,031	4,083
Bookbinders	620	2,121	688	1,219	1,658	4,023
Envelope-makers	193	704	156	458	572	1,786
Bag/box makers	165	1,304	26	408	348	2904

Source: Census, Scotland, 1911. NB. The total population of Glasgow (784, 496) was more than twice that of Edinburgh (320,318), so the numbers in printing represented a larger share of the workforce in the latter. These figures include employers and employed, and no distinction was made by the census between skilled and semi-skilled 'printers' etc.)

ship, and it was accordingly somewhat better paid than the stationery trades. In the 1900s, folding and sewing girls in Scotland started at 4s or 5s rising to 10s by age 16 to 18, with the possibility of earning between 12s 6d and a maximum of 15s for experienced workers.[11] A letter to the *Edinburgh Evening Despatch* in 1913 said that 'the wages are better than those obtained by shop girls and conditions incomparably better than those prevailing in domestic service today'.[12] Genteel and reasonably well paid, bookbinding was an attractive calling, despite what might seem to have been the repetitive nature of the work. Both in England and in Scotland, women outnumbered men in the trade overall, but the disproportion was higher in Scotland, where there were more than three women to every man (see Tables 2 and 3).

Finally, we come to printing proper. Here, women would normally have been few in number. They were to be found in the low-paid role of machine-feeders and layers-on in the press room, where the skilled and heavy work of machine-operating was all done by men. But, for most of the nineteenth century, they would not normally have been seen in the composing-room. The 'art and mystery' of composing was practised in an all-male community, traditionally proud of its skill, its literacy and its elaborate vocabulary and ritual whose gender exclusiveness has been well described by Cynthia Cockburn.[13] But, in the late nineteenth century, it began to occur to employers as well as to promoters of women's employment that there was no reason why women should not learn the compositor's trade. Composing was still done by hand, and women's supposed 'dexterity' was regarded as making them particularly suitable recruits. Basic typesetting essentially consisted of picking individual metal characters from a type case and fitting them into a clamp (the composing 'stick') until one had a solid line. Lines of type were first transferred to 'galleys' (metal trays) and, then locked into 'formes' to 'make up' pages. In the process called 'imposition, the pages were ordered in correct sequence for printing. Of the three main branches of letterpress printing from which male compositors could choose – newspapers, bookwork and jobbing – it was bookwork which was regarded as most suitable for women, and to which they began to be recruited both north and south of the Scottish border.[14]

In England, the employment of women as compositors never really became accepted. Despite the fact that some experimental printing-houses employed women in the period 1860 to 1880 (notably the Victoria Press and the Women's Printing Society) women were effectively kept out of the trade in the English capital, mainly because of the determined and successful opposition of the men's trade union, the London Society of Compositors. Women were, however, to be found working for firms in the Home Counties now beginning to challenge London printers, but even here they were not numerous. It was estimated in 1899 that the total number of women compositors outside Scotland did not exceed three hundred. So the large-scale employment of women in Edinburgh printing houses in the 1900s – about eight hundred by 1909 – created rather an exceptional situation.[15]

How had this come about? During a strike by Edinburgh printers in 1872–3, several large firms, including Constable's and Blackwood's, advertised for 'girls of good education' to train as compositors. Contrary to later mythology, the girls who replied cannot seriously be regarded as having broken the strike; the records show that this was essentially achieved by hiring non-unionised men from outside. But the employers certainly took advantage of the strike to introduce girl apprentices. At first, the returning men did not object much to their entry – indeed they agreed to teach them the trade and began to put their own daughters into it. Following the Edinburgh lead, print employers in Aberdeen, Perth, and elsewhere began to take on girl beginners. But girls were never employed in any large numbers in Glasgow, both because there were fewer large book-printing firms and because the local trade union branch was stronger. Since trade was brisk in the late 1870s, no men's jobs were immediately threatened. Gradually, however, as trade fluctuations became more common, the Edinburgh men realised how great a threat was posed by women, who were being paid at half the rate for men: a maximum of 16s as opposed to the 32s paid to a 'stab hand' (that is, a journeyman on time rates). The men's union, the Edinburgh Typographical Society (ETS) – the local branch of the Scottish Typographical Association (STA) – was still in a state of some weakness after the strike, and was unable to prevail against the employment of women; nonetheless, it raised its voice increasingly against women workers as the nineteenth century drew to an end.

Were women compositors really doing the same work as men? Yes and no. At least until the 1900s most of the women, who worked mainly in the larger book-printing firms like Morrison & Gibb and R. & R. Clark, were doing what was known as 'straight setting', that is, setting line after line of unbroken copy, and were paid at piece-work rates. 'We girls just did handsetting', as one survivor assured me. With few exceptions, they were not trained to handle later processes such as upmaking and imposition. One skilled man could make up the type set by several women, rather as spinners once supplied the handloom weaver with thread. The key to this job segregation was training. Women did not do a full apprenticeship, but learned the lay of the typecase and practised setting lines of type quite without supervision ('we just looked at the card') until they were proficient. This wasted no material, whereas learning the later processes could not be done without the risk of possibly expensive mistakes and was, as far as the employer was concerned, altogether unnecessary. This was the real reason why it could be claimed with some truth that women 'did not do the whole job', rather than the argument, much heard at the time, that women could not lift the heavy type-cases and formes: this was hardly a significant task since, no matter who did it, lifting was neither skilled nor time-consuming.

All in all, it must be conceded that women compositors were not doing the entire job as, under ideal circumstances, the time-served journeyman learned it. However there were many male compositors who were no longer doing the whole job either. Edinburgh was notorious for employing 'linesmen', who had completed apprenticeships but had never been taken on as 'establishment' hands: they worked at piece rates – mostly on straight typesetting – and had less security of tenure. They were paid more than women, but less than the 32s of the stab hand. So women were doing much the same work as *some* men. Arguments raged about whether women did the typesetting work as well as, better, or worse than men, and the evidence is so flawed by special pleading as to be unhelpful. What can be said with certainty is that they fitted very well into what was already a fragmented work process (typesetting being separated from other tasks). Although they were certainly doing skilled work – more highly skilled than virtually any other women's industrial employment – and although the sums they earned looked like high pay to most women, they were indeed being employed as cheap labour.[16]

What does this brief survey of the openings for women in stationery and printing as a whole tell us? First, simply that in the 1900s these trades offered enough alternative industrial employment, at least in the big cities, to be a significant component of the women's labour market, as is illustrated by the choices of the girls and young women in the Canongate survey. Secondly, that these choices might have been influenced, in part, by the trade's 'gentility' quotient: the stationer's, the binder's or the printing office was a respectable workplace (albeit with its own internal hierarchy of respectability). Thirdly, that men and women were usually in single sex groups. Even if they worked in the same room, the men would be in charge of machines and the women occupied with manual tasks at a bench. Women compositors might seem to be an exception to this but, in practice, most firms employing women had a separate composing-room for them, generally referred to as the 'Girls' Caseroom'. The apparent rationale of the segregation might be the machinery used, or the materials and activities involved (paper rather than leather, stitching rather than pressing). But the essential distinction was that women did the least demanding or skilled jobs within any given category: even the women compositors could be so described. The corollary of segregation was that while by the 1900s most of the men belonged to a trade union – generally a craft union such as the STA – the women were not unionised, and were indeed debarred from the craft union on the grounds that they were not being paid the rate for the job.

Fourthly, on the question of pay, not only were women's rates always lower than men's, but they were also subject to some sort of iron law of their own: the differentials between a woman envelope-maker, bookfolder, book-stitcher and compositor were not very great. The average weekly wage for a woman aged 20 in envelope-making was 10s; in bookfolding and stitching, it could be 12s 6d to 15s; the Edinburgh women compositors were said to average 13s to 16s and, as we have seen, some machine rulers were earning the very high rates of 17s. But, in practice, very few women took home anything over 15s. The male printer's apprentice would also be earning abut 15s at age 20, but on completing his seven years at 21, his wage normally jumped to the 32s of the journeyman.

The reason for the difference was that women's wages were only partly related to skill, being determined rather by the general level of wages for women's work in the economy. These in turn reflected not so much the work done, or the aptitude of the individual, as the belief held firmly by employers in all industrial sectors, by working men, and indeed by women themselves, that while a man needed a wage sufficient to keep a family, a woman was only contributing to a household, usually her parents' rather than her husband's, and did not 'need' the money.[17] It was in fact the widespread practice of Scottish women to leave full-time employment on marriage, with some exceptions, notably among the jute workers of Dundee. Two of the four surviving women compositors interviewed said they would have liked to continue working after marriage, but their husbands 'would not allow them to'.

The low average pay of women meant that even those in what might be thought of as skilled trades earned considerably less than the male rate. So long as women had remained in quite different jobs from those of men, no great concern was expressed about their low wage levels. But once there was possibility of their replacing skilled men, conflict between employers and unions was inevitable.

There is no space here to detail the arguments advanced by employers in favour of, and by trade unions against, the practice of hiring women. The basic economic conflict was sometimes frankly stated; sometimes it was adorned with cultural arguments which added up to a profile of 'the woman' as an occasionally useful but basically unreliable and essentially temporary visitor to the industrial world, whose true vocation lay outside it. Thus employers liked to argue that certain jobs were particularly 'suited' to women: when the Monotype composing machine (the detonator for a major conflict) was introduced into the Edinburgh printing trade, one employer remarked 'Seeing women at the keyboard or monotype as it is practised in my own office, sitting in a comfortable parlour, I feel strongly that it is eminently suitable work.'[18] The feint line ruling in 'children's exercise books', another claimed, 'is simple enough work to be given to girls'. However since employers also had to justify paying women less, they had to be careful to balance any praise of their dexterity, for instance, by complaining of their drawbacks. They 'needed more accommodation'; they 'make more mistakes'; 'they are always going off for sickness of some kind, or their mother is ill ...That is the greatest trouble, their mother is ill constantly'.[19]

From the trade unions, along with straightforward complaints that women were being used to undercut wages (occasionally accompanied by admissions that their work itself was competent), arguments about health and motherhood were more likely. 'They are constitutionally not so strong'; 'it is not a trade for them from the health point of view'. They might be affected by 'phthisis' (tuberculosis), 'the scourge of the printing trade' and, leaving 'with the germs of the disease in their system', later contribute to the 'degeneracy of the race'. 'After all is said and done', one union negotiator said in 1913, 'is bookbinding a proper trade for a woman?[20]

Both masters and men were agreed on one point: that '99 out 100 of these girls, when they go to the trade expect that they will be married' before a full apprenticeship could be served, so that it made no sense to 'train them properly'. This argument served both groups of men: employers, because they could legitimately pay women less; workers, because they could claim women were less skilled than men and therefore less satisfactory. But such arguments simply led to a stalemate. Meanwhile, women compositors continued in work at Edinburgh, while women bookbinders and machine rulers in several centres were increasingly being asked to handle some of the processes the men regarded as their own preserve. Resentment was soon to result in open conflict.

SHUTTING THE DOOR (1910): THE BAN ON WOMEN COMPOSITORS

The compositors' dispute was the first to emerge.[21] The Edinburgh men's longstanding anxiety about women compositors came to a head in 1909–10 for several reasons. First, many more girl apprentices were recruited in the 1900s, so that by 1909 there were 850 of them, as opposed to about a thousand men. Secondly, after years of weakness and difficulty, the Edinburgh branch of the STA was re-unified, and had the backing of the newly-formed local Printing and Kindred Trades Federation (PKTF). Thirdly, the coming of new technology in the shape of Monotype composing machines to Edinburgh's book printers was a new and serious threat – since the first Monotype operators were all women. The Monotype consisted of a keyboard, like that of a typewriter, attached to a roll of perforated ribbon. It could be completely separated from the casting of the hot metal and Edinburgh employers considered it ideally suited to women, for it was clean work, 'like typewriting'. Unlike their counterparts elsewhere, the Edinburgh men refused to learn monotyping when it first appeared. Consequently, big contracts such as the printing of the *Encyclopaedia Britannica* were soon being machine-composed by women. For the first time ever, women now had a skill that men did not, since the men's traditional seven-year apprenticeship was largely irrelevant to the Monotype. But they were still being paid half the men's wage.

By 1909, the Edinburgh men, under pressure from both the rest of the STA and the PKTF, had seen the danger. Backed by the other unions, they presented the master printers with a memorial requesting (a) that no new girl learners be hired for six years and (b) that all new Monotype keyboards be given to men. Significantly, the masters scarcely demurred to the first, but stalled for several months on the second. During the summer, the workers of two of the largest firms threatened to strike; these firms capitulated and accepted the men's demands, and after further strike threats and the holding of well-attended meetings in September 1910, the remaining firms followed suit. The result was effectively to stop women from becoming compositors again. No woman then in work lost her job but thereafter (the six-year limit passing almost unnoticed during the Great War) no girls were recruited as apprentices. The women working Monotypes were allowed to keep their machines, but were eventually outnumbered by male operators. Of the 800-plus women working in 1910, about three-quarters had left the trade through marriage or retirement by the late 1920s; about 200 remained at work, some of them as late as the 1950s. But they were the last women compositors in Scotland, and almost all of them must now be dead.

This dispute was remarkable for the intervention of the women compositors themselves – and on both sides of the argument. About half the women took the side of the men, that is they agreed to the ban on girl apprentices and agreed to come out on strike with their male colleagues, if it should come to that. It was indeed their participation that drove the larger firms to settle sooner. At first sight it might seem odd that women should collaborate in their own exclusion. But the episode demonstrates the peculiar pressure on working-class women at the workplace itself. They were working literally alongside their own fathers, brothers and future husbands, with whom they had no personal quarrel. Indeed for all the men's aggregate hostility, workplace relations were usually friendly. Nor was any woman threatened with losing her own job. Moreover, the ban was nominally for six years; how could they know it would be permanent? Asked to choose between their sex and their class, many women responded to the very powerful call of class solidarity. As one survivor put it, 'it was only natural' to support the men, who thought 'women were taking their jobs away from them. '

To oppose the men of one's own class required both courage and a commitment to something more abstract than one's own interest (since that was not threatened): the right of women to enter the trade in future. The other half of the women, led by Amelia McLean, who did take this line, had to face the opprobrium of being called class traitors and accused of hob-nobbing with the middle class. In fact they, too, specifically expressed sympathy with the men's case. The petition they presented to the masters, the 'We Women' memorial, reads in part: 'While recognising that the men have had a real grievance in that some firms have employed an unfair proportion of young girls at apprentice wages, or nearly so, we women regard it as a great injustice that one of the main skilled industries in Edinburgh should be closed against them.'[22]

It could be argued that theirs was the harder path to choose. Unlike the men, the women compositors had no tradition of solidarity as a gendered group. Nor was any man asked to choose between his class and his sex. As we know, these women lost the battle, the result being described as a victory for 'the working class', but as Cynthia Cockburn has rightly remarked, the price was paid by women and 'perhaps we might say ... by the working-class properly perceived'.[23]

This is illustrated with particular clarity by the later history of the women's section of the Edinburgh Typographical Society. After 1910, partly in order to control the women in the trade, a branch of the men's craft union was opened for the remaining women. Now at last, when it was too late, men and women compositors were organised in the same craft union, and relations between them were cordial as never before. But it must be the only example in British trade union history where satisfaction was expressed – by the men's executive committee – that the numbers of one of their branches were actually *falling*, as women retired from the trade.[24]

DRAWING THE LINE: THE BOOKBINDERS' DEMARCATION DISPUTE (1912–13)

The Scottish bookbinders' dispute, two years later, took a different turn. he bookbinders had wholeheartedly supported the stand made by the Edinburgh male compositors, and the 1910 dispute was much mentioned during negotiations leading to their own strike. For them, the issue – a longstanding and familiar one – was what they termed the 'encroachment' of lower-paid women, and a few men upon jobs regarded as the work of journeymen bookbinders: 'our craft which used to be our own ... [is being] filched from us by underpaid labour ... sometimes done by girls'. Their memorial to the master binders in September 1912 asked that 'female and non-apprenticed male workers' be excluded from the bookbinding and a paper-ruling trade, 'except as to one or two auxiliary processes such as folding and sewing and the feeding of machines'. Because this was fought as a demarcation dispute rather than a demand that no more women be employed, the processes which journeymen insisted belonged to them were spelled out in great detail:

> *Leatherwork*: all leather and vellum cases, including siding and piecing; all edgework, cutting and paring leather; making of all end-papers; endpapering; headbanding, fixing in, pasting up. *Stationery forwarding*: all end papers quarter bound, turned in, hand indexing, cutting and paring leather. *Machinery*: all blocking, casemaking, casing in, 'glueing up to Crawley,'[glueing the pages onto the spine] lining, pinching, board cutting, bevelling, cutting and cloth cutting machines. *Clothwork*: rounding, backing, pasting up, lining, pressing, 'glueing up to Crawley'. *Paper ruling*: all machines in paper ruling.[25]

The situation that had prompted the dispute, although familiar, was not clear-cut. What happened was that in certain firms women were moved from task to task depending on the volume of work to be done. As the above very comprehensive list indicates, there were plenty of processes they might be asked to handle, if a bottleneck occurred. In practice, employers did not ask women to do what they regarded as 'really' men's work, using heavier machines or greater skill. The tasks most often mentioned in the talks (apart from machine ruling which was a special case) were glueing (this is the 'laying of the foundation of a book and shouldn't be given to girls', a union man stated), endpapering in leather and cloth work, headbanding and guillotining. No one knew exactly how many women were involved: the men said about two hundred, the masters about seven hundred (their argument in part was that they were short-handed).

As the nature of the disputed tasks suggests, both masters and men were agreed on the basic gender division of labour: in the words of the chairman, an employer, 'women are doing work best done by women and men are doing work best done by men, and the question is whether work in the middle is better done by men than by women'. But the men were surprisingly frank in their admission that women were actually quite competent at some of the disputed tasks.

I know that many of those girls that are referred to are capable of doing work which would stagger the older binders, capable of doing much better than some of the men, because they have had the opportunity. *We want to do away with that opportunity. We want to keep the craft to ourselves* ...Surely that is not anarchism?[26](My italics)

Such an admission carried all the more weight because of its candour, the speaker, Mr Dempster, the Glasgow representative of the National Union of Bookbinders and Paper Rulers, was a resolute opponent of setting up a women's union and would frankly have liked to see women out of the trade.

The employers argued their side on practical rather than principled grounds. They had no present intention of using women to do what was clearly men's work, but they did not wish to have their hands tied by a demarcation ruling that might create bottlenecks in the work process. And secondly, they argued, they would not be able to find male replacements for the women workers in the disputed areas: 'not one male bookbinder is out of work'.

After three conferences had failed to bring a solution, the men came out on strike in November 1913. Unlike in the case of the printing dispute, little evidence has come to light about the attitude of the women bookbinders themselves, and the little that exists is conflicting. The employers stated that the women were all at work: 'they certainly recognise that the men are out against them... there is not one single instance of the girls striking out of sympathy with the men later in the strike, however, a newspaper reported that several women had been sacked for refusing to handle the work of strikers. These two statements are not incompatible, of course. Women could have continued working at their normal tasks without necessarily strike-breaking. But unlike the Edinburgh dispute, this strike does not seem to have caused any loud outcry by women's organisations: 'if the suffragettes were any good they would take this up instead of breaking windows', one employer testily wrote to another.[27] Were the Scottish women bookbinders neither sufficiently in solidarity with the men to take their side, not sufficiently angry about demarcation to protest? This may have been the paradoxical result of the position in which they found themselves: safe in the knowledge that the men were not disputing their right to the folding and stitching jobs that were theirs by 'use and wont'.

Had the women bookbinders threatened to strike, the employers might have been under greater pressure. As it was, however, the men returned to work after three weeks, with an agreement that gave them only minimal satisfaction. No demarcation pact was included. Instead, a permanent conciliating committee was to be set up to examine all such disputes. But the male machine rulers obtained a partial victory in the shape of a 'first claim' clause on any machine vacated by a man. The outbreak of war in 1914 interrupted any further serious moves on this front. It was during the war that the National Union of Bookbinders eventually reversed its long-standing policy and allowed women's branches to be created. The first two were in fact in London and Edinburgh. Unlike the Edinburgh women compositors, whose union branch was, in effect, programmed to wither and die, women bookbinders did at least gain a permanent foothold in the union, and have remained part of the bookbinding workforce to this day.[28]

The Scottish employers, meanwhile, had kept their flexibility of action and, unlike their English equivalents, successfully resisted any agreement on demarcation between men and women. They were thus in a position envied by their colleagues south of the border. In 1920, an Edinburgh master binder wrote that 'there is a great deal of jealousy in Manchester at the conditions enjoyed in ... Scotland'. But this masks the fact that *in practice*, women continued to do very much the same as before. In 1919, the secretary of the Scottish Master Printer's Association explained to an English colleague that the Scottish bookbinders had come back to work in 1913 'without achieving their object of establishing demarcation [*sic*] between men and women's work, and to day there is no Agreement on the subject in Scotland. ' But, he continued,'the practice follows generally the *use and wont* of former days'[29] – in other words, the trade remained by and large segregated, with women continuing to do folding and sewing and relatively little else – a familiar-enough story in the context of women's employment in twentieth-century Britain down to the present day.

CONCLUSION

The final result of these conflicts was to fix the situation for most of the twentieth century as it stood in 1914. Despite their different outcomes, the printing and bookbinding disputes were both resolved in ways ultimately acceptable to both masters and men, at talks where no women were present. They effectively put an end to the partial intrusion by women into sectors of the trade other than those listed in the pamphlet quoted at the beginning of this chapter.

The whole question of women's employment in this sector can be viewed in different ways, depending on what one sees as its appropriate context. From the perspective of the Scottish economy, for instance, it could be seen as an episode in the history of printing and publishing, one such a flourishing industry north of the border. For book-printers in particular, competition from the south of England was a powerful incentive to cost-cutting through the employment of women. Meanwhile, male craftworkers in the industry, formerly among the highest-paid aristocrats of labour, had by the 1900s lost their leading position to the engineers and metal-workers of Scotland's developing heavy industries. The nineteenth-century Scottish craft unions appear to have been less successful than their English counterparts at debarring women from their trades, and this was reflected in the proportionately greater number of women employed by Scottish firms in disputed occupations such as machine-ruling and typesetting, or in those areas of bookbinding claimed by men.

From the perspective of labour history, consequently, the episode can be interpreted as part of the wider historical attempt by employers in Scotland and elsewhere, at this stage in industrial capitalism, to fragment the work process and introduce new technology, thus making it easier to employ less-skilled labour. Until comparatively recently, at least, labour history accounts tended to present women workers as vulnerable, manipulated, apathetic to trade union organisation, viewing their employment as essentially short-term and willing to accept low pay. In short, they were seen as an ideal weapon in the hands of employers, in the same way that, at times, rural migrants, young people and immigrant workers have also been characterised.

That the women we have been discussing were willing to accept low pay and that they were not organised into unions is of course true. If, finally, one wants to bring the perspective of feminist history to bear on their case and ask why things were as they were, one has to be attentive to structural factors and, above all, wary of assuming that 'women' were somehow doomed to be vulnerable to exploitation and oppression by 'men'. What we have here, rather, is a historically specific case with identifiable features. The three features that might be singled out as most significant are the age structure of the workforce, attitudes to equal pay, and trade union membership.

The age structure of the women's workforce was not the same as that of the men's; consequently, to refer to 'women' in opposition to 'men' is perhaps as misleading as the regular use of 'girls' to refer to women of any age, as documents of the time often do. We know that most women left this kind of employment on marriage: the result was that the workforce remained predominantly young, made up to a large extent of teenage girls. There were some older women – single, widowed and, in a few cases, married – but never enough to provide the critical mass of experience and know-how taken for granted among the men, among whom all age-groups were represented. Significantly, married women were reported by employers, who did not much like them, to be lacking in docility.[30]

To the senior trade unionists who generally handled negotiations with the employers, the 'women' might have seemed more like their own daughters than like a group of adults on an equal footing. This may help to explain the impression one gets of a greater gulf existing between the men and women workers than between the men and the employers. Among many examples of *bonhomie* and male fraternity to be found in minutes of bilateral talks, a striking one comes from the end of the bookbinders' strike. The writer, an employer, remarks on:

> the informality that reigned over the proceedings. When the pipe or rather pipes of peace are going full blast and the smoke wreaths are rising serenely towards the ceiling, when the fumes of Glasgow mixture and Edinburgh shag are mingling together in delightful

juxtaposition, producing an atmosphere that only dogs and smokers can exist in – it is difficult to maintain the dignified air, the strict attention to one's p's and q's so usually apparent at a large conference.[31]

We have here a picture of men of mature years, who although sitting on opposite sides of the table, had a shared lifetime in the trade behind them (masters had often started out as journeymen). Their immediate task was to dispose of the appropriate employment for – as they saw it – a lot of girls young enough to be their daughters. They agreed that while these 'girls' might be able to 'stagger the older binders' on occasion, they were 'really' best suited to their sewing machines for the few short years they would remain in the trade. The women bookbinders were at a disadvantage not so much because they were women, but because they were young women without the benefit of any collective tradition; they had no place in the smoke-filled room.

This helps to explain the attitude of most of the women in the printing trades to equal pay. Equal pay for women was not seriously suggested by any of the parties to the disputes discussed above. Employers thought it out of the question, and while trade unionists sometimes held it up as a possibility, they did so on the strong assumption that if men and women were paid equally, employers would prefer to employ men. Both groups assumed that women were not 'really' doing the same work as men. The women themselves, while not necessarily accepting this low valuation of their work, were desperately afraid of losing their jobs if equal pay were introduced. The 'We Women' manifesto of the Edinburgh compositors, for instance, contained a clause (dropped from the published version) which read as follows:

> We recognise that the demand on the part of the men that women should immediately be paid the same wage as women means the elimination of women, since at present women have neither the same apprenticeship as men nor the same opportunities for all-round experience in the composing room.[32]

Those women who are on record as discussing wage rates tended to argue that they should be paid a 'fair' wage for the job: not as much as a man, but more than they were then getting. The use of the word 'fair' is revealing: it accepts the logic of the fragmented work process, rather than 'trade union logic', according to which what mattered was not so much the skill required for a certain job as the skill of the person doing it.

It was hard to use trade union logic when one was not a member of a trade union. The particular trade unions involved in this case were craft unions with historical traditions. The male apprentice bookbinder or compositor learned about them from the moment he entered the door of the workshop and found it was a 'chapel'. The great majority of men in the trade were, by the 1900s, members of their craft union and benefitted from the cumulative experience of their elders, acquiring cultural baggage to accompany their craft training. Women, on the other hand, while they might be initiated into the skills of the trade, had not been invited to acquire the collective mentality. They long remained barred from the craft unions where they might have learnt it, though they were beginning to be encouraged at this period to join the newer general unions for the less skilled. Even so, the earliest attempts to unionise women got off to a slow start, partly because established trade unionists did not always appreciate the considerable practical problems women faced in joining in union activity; partly because trade union thinking was an acquired habit (can one imagine a male printer saying 'I'd have worked weekends if they'd have let me'?); and partly because unions did not seem to be addressing the dilemma of the woman worker. So-called 'apathy' has to be read against this background. When, as in the case of the Edinburgh Typographical Society after 1910, there was genuine co-operation from the men in introducing women workers to the procedures and aims of the union movement, membership and commitment among the women soon reached acceptable levels.

But the women's section of the ETS was a rare case, doomed as we have seen, by the 1910 agreement to eventual death; craft unions thereafter for many years remained closed to women, and segregation remained the rule in the printing trade. The trade unions must accept part of the responsibility for this outcome. They were selective in their protests at women's low pay and failed to tackle the problem as a whole, reacting only when it affected men's pay or employment. And they were extremely slow in admitting women to union membership of any kind. On the other hand, the collective action needed to resolve the anomalies in the different employment of the sexes could hardly emerge from a working class or a labour movement divided both consciously and unconsciously by gender, and in a society where marriage and employment were compatible for one half of the population but mutually exclusive alternatives for the other.

At this distance, it is perhaps hard to appreciate what had been lost, and how welcome an opportunity the printing trades offered, compared to the drudgery that passed for women's work at the turn of the century. After Queen Victoria's death in 1901, the envelope-makers and black borderers all had to work overtime: an observer described meeting one such girl coming home late on a 'bleak and wet' Saturday afternoon, who said cheerfully: 'It is "larks" working late... I love the factory and should hate to be out of it'.[33] And as one former compositor, very elderly, said to me, 'I'd go back tomorrow, but they don't take women now!'

ACKNOWLEDGEMENT

For permission to quote from papers held in the National Library of Scotland, I am grateful to the keeper of Manuscripts, to the Society of Master Printers of Scotland and to SOGAT 82.

NOTES

1   See Cynthia Cockburn's excellent study of compositors in London, *Brothers: Male Dominance and Technological Change* (London, Pluto, 1983), for a description of the contemporary printing trade and an analysis of gender relations within it.

2   The City of Edinburgh Charity Organisation Society, *Report on the Physical Condition of Fourteen Hundred Schoolchildren in the city together with some account of their homes and surroundings* (London, P. & S. King & Co, 1906), hereafter referred to as *CECOS Report*, 2. Research for the survey was carried out in 1905. The school, unnamed in the report, is identified as North Canongate by Robert Q. Gray, *The Labour Aristocracy in Victorian Edinburgh* (Oxford University Press, 1976).

3   Personal analysis of the *CECOS Report* case studies. No great statistical claims can be made for this data, given the incomplete information on which it is based – for instance, children living away from home were not counted. But it may be taken as indicative.

4   On Edinburgh as a printing centre, see Lorne McCall, 'Of Making Books There Is No End: aspects of Edinburgh's printing industry', *Scottish Book collector*, no 6 (June-July 1988): 8–12, on the early history; and Siân Reynolds, *Britannica's Typesetters, Women Compositors in Edwardian Edinburgh* (Edinburgh, Edinburgh University Press, 1989), chapter 1, for the period under discussion here. See also Gray, *The Labour Aristocracy*, esp. chapter 1.

5   The information in this paragraph is based on chapter 1 of J. R. Macdonald, (ed.), *Women in the Printing Trades, a sociological study*, (London, P. S. King & Co., 1904). Chapter 1 was in fact written by Clementina Black. This survey contains a wealth of information, some of it on Scotland. On paper-staining see ibid., 177.

6   Ibid., General Glasgow Report, Appendix III, 177, (probably written by Margaret Irwin).

7   Felicity Hunt, 'The London trade in the printing and binding of books: an experience in exclusion, dilution and de-skilling for women workers', *Women's Studies International Forum*, VI, 5 (1983), 518. See also her 'Opportunities lost and gained: mechanisation and women's work in the London bookbinding and printing trades' in *Unequal Opportunities, Women's Employment in England 1800–1918* ed. Angela V. John (Oxford, Blackwell, 1986), 71–94.

8   The account of bookbinding is based on chapter 1 of Macdonald, *Women in the Printing Trades*, and on the section on bookbinding in the Glasgow Appendix, ibid. 174 ff, from which the quotations in these two paragraphs are taken.

9   See Gray, *The Labour Aristocracy*, 62: The effect of introducing machines, and the large-scale employment of women bookfolders 'was not however to displace skilled men, but to make more efficient and specialised use of them'. Cf. ibid., for a report that in 1895, a 'great amount of surprise 'was expressed by a delegate meeting of the bookbinders' union both at the 'extent of female labour' in Edinburgh, and the 'classes of work allocated' to women.

10 Macdonald, *Women in the Printing Trades*, Glasgow Appendix, 174–5; cf. Gray, *Labour Aristocracy*, 63, where bookbinders (male) are described as 'a comfortable-looking class of workmen ... everything about them seemed to indicate steadiness in the workshop and comfort at home'.

11 Note that these are Scottish wage rates, lower than in London. Cf. rates quoted in Felicity Hunt's two articles, cited above, note 7.

12 *Edinburgh Evening Despatch*, 26 November 1913.

13 Cockburn, *Brothers*, 19: 'It would have been an odd family that was willing to see a daughter enter so male-oriented a trade'. But in the early days of printing, it was not uncommon for a master printer's widow to take over running the business on her husband's death; and some wives and daughters of printers did work in the family shop in the eighteenth and occasionally nineteenth century. The most famous example of a printer's widow in Scotland was Agnes Campbell Anderson, who had a monopoly on Bible printing in Scotland between 1676 and 1712 and for whom no one seems to have a good word to say; cf. McCall, 'Of Making Books There Is No End', cited above, note 4.

14 Newspaper work required compositors to work at night, from which women were barred by the Factory Acts; jobbing was usually carried on in small family firms; bookwork, on the other hand, called for a larger workforce, and more 'straight dig'.

15 On London and the Home Counties, see Felicity Hunt's two articles cited above, note 7. On numbers in the London area, see Barbara Bradby and Anne Black, 'Women compositors and the Factory Acts', *Economic Journal*, 1899, 261–6.

16 See Reynolds, *Britannica's Typesetters*, for a full history of the women compositors; see also Sarah Gillespie, *A Hundred Years of Progress 1853–1952: the record of the Scottish Typographical Association* (Glasgow, STA, 1953), chapters 9 and 16.

17 Formulated, by no means untypically, by a writer to the *Edinburgh Evening News* (29 November 1913), anent the bookbinders' strike: a man 'has a home to maintain', while a woman's earnings 'are generally in addition to those of a father'. On the family wage see John, *Unequal Opportunities*, 25 and references, and on Scotland, Eleanor Gordon, *Women and the Labour Movement in Scotland* (Oxford University Press, 1990, forthcoming).

18 Master Printers' Papers, Minute Book, 1910, National Library of Scotland (Acc 8291).

19 Fair Wages Committee (P. P. 1908, vol. XXXIV, para. 4573 ff.), Mr Fraser's evidence. Fraser was managing director of the Edinburgh printing firm, Neill & Co.

20 See Fair Wages Committee (ibid. , paras 2869–2973, evidence of Messrs Templeton and Simpson for the STA, for remarks about health; 1913 quotation from *Annals of the Scottish Printing Trade*, National Library of Scotland, (Acc 8166 B, book 8, 1913) Hereafter known as *Annals SPT*, this is a collection of documents made by the secretary of the Scottish Alliance of Masters in the Printing and Kindred Trades, J. Maclehose.

21 Cynthia Cockburn gives a clear and readable account of the incident, based chiefly on the *Scottish Typographical Journal* in chapter 6 of *Brothers* op. cit. ; for a more detailed narrative see Reynolds, *Britannica's Typesetters*, chapter 5. I have therefore kept this account to a minimum.

22 The Manifesto, or rather memorial 'We Women' is reproduced in Cockburn, *Brothers*, 156. (See also below, note 27).

23 *Brothers*, 159.

24 Mary Alston's report to the Women's Section of the ETS, 1920, Edinburgh Typographical Society papers, Women's Section

Minute book, National Library of Scotland (Acc 4068).

25 Second memorial, October 1913, *Annals SPT*, book 8, 1913.

26 Ibid. , record of third conference between employers and union representatives, book 4, p. 59 of printed booklet. Mr Dempster's words were widely reported in the press. The entire progress of the strike can be traced in the *Annals SPT*, series B, (bookbinding), books 4–8.

27 Ibid., for quotations and press cuttings. The writer 'Justitia' to the *Edinburgh Evening Despatch and News* (26 November 1913) asked, 'what are the women in the bookbinding trade and what are the organisers of the National Federation of Women Workers and other kindred bodies doing? Are they dumb that they raise no protests...?'. Cf. *The Vote*, 21 November 1913, article signed EGM, unfortunately short and ill-informed. *The Vote*, the organ of the Women's Freedom League, had played an active part in supporting the Edinburgh women compositors in 1910.

28 For the full story of the women's bookbinding unions and their amalgamation with the men's, see Barbara Drake, *Women in Trade Unions* (first published 1920, now re-issued by Virago, 1984), chapter 7, and C. J. Bundock, *The Story of the National Union of Printing, Bookbinding and Paper Workers* (Oxford University Press, 1959), 105 ff. and index. (This also contains a useful pull-out summarising the bewildering number of name-changes in the bookbinders' union).

29 Italics added. *Annals SPT*, series B, book 14, 2 December 1919 and 5 July 1920.

30 See in particular Macdonald, *Women in the Printing Trades*, chapter 9 which juxtaposes the information that it is the custom 'in these trades that married women should not work in them', and that married women had an annoying tendency to press for *higher* wages. (The investigators had been asked if there was evidence that married women lowered wages). See also the Glasgow Appendix, ibid.

31 *Masters' Strike Bulletin*, December 1913, *Annals SPT*, series B, book 8.

32 Papers of the Edinburgh Master Printers' Association, National Library of Scotland, Manuscripts, Acc 8291, Box 4, section III; the memorial as received by the masters on 9 June 1910 contains this section as clause 5, but it has been crossed out and does not appear in the version made public. The men's demand was indeed made for strategic reasons.

33 Macdonald, *Women in the Printing Trades*, 87.

SELECT BIBLIOGRAPHY

C. J. Bundock. *The Story of the National Union of Printing, Bookbinding and Paper Workers*. Oxford University Press, 1959.

Cynthia Cockburn. *Brothers: Male Dominance and Technological Change*. London: Pluto, 1983.

Sarah Gillespie. *A Hundred years of Progress 1853–1952: the Record of the Scottish Typographical Association*. Glasgow: Maclehose, 1953.

Eleanor Gordon. *Women and the Labour Movement in Scotland*. Oxford University Press, 1990. Forthcoming.

Robert Q. Gray. *The Labour Aristocracy in Victorian Edinburgh.* Oxford University Press, 1976.

Felicity Hunt. "The London trade in the printing and binding of books: an experience in exclusion, dilution and de-skilling for women workers', *Women's Studies International Forum* VI, 5 (1983).

Felicity Hunt, "Opportunities lost and gained: mechanisation and women's work in the London bookbinding and printing trades', in Angela V. John (ed.), *Unequal Opportunities: Women's Employment in England 1800–1918.* Oxford:Blackwell, 1986.

J. R. Macdonald, *Women in the Printing Trades, a sociological study.* London: P. S. King & Co. , 1904.

Siân Reynolds. *Britannica's Typesetters, Women Compositors in Edwardian Edinburrgh.* Edinburgh University Press, 1989.

4

EARLY GLASGOW WOMEN MEDICAL GRADUATES
WENDY ALEXANDER

Most of the literature on the entry of women into medicine is biographical, focusing on the famous original pioneers. This chapter attempts a rather different exercise, looking at some of the first groups of women doctors to qualify from the University of Glasgow. The objective is to assess the 'typical' experience of early Scottish women doctors. The methodology is to examine and compare the social origins, education and subsequent career patterns of two groups of graduates, sixty-two in total, from 1890–1900 and 1908–10. These were very early years in the history of women doctors and to understand the Glasgow experience it is vital to trace briefly the history of the women's medical movement.

THE EARLY STRUGGLE FOR ENTRY

From the middle of the nineteenth century women across Europe struggled for acceptance into the medical profession. The first women to succeed at the end of the nineteenth century were predominantly middle class. Their struggle directly challenged prevailing notions of femininity and of appropriate social spheres for women. To most contemporaries, the prospect of higher education for women, let alone the study and practice of medicine, was regarded as uneconomic, physically debilitating and positively dangerous.

The Victorian medical profession was one of the foremost proponents of separate spheres of activity for men and women. The all-male medical profession was virtually unanimous in its claim that the middle-class woman who dared to venture beyond her domestic sphere would seriously jeopardise her health and fertility.

The second line of defence advanced against women doctors by the medical profession was that female innocence – the source of the innate moral superiority of women – would be fatally undermined by the study of subjects such as anatomy. Thus, all contemporary conventions of fitness and decency militated against the pioneers. However, arguably a more important factor in the almost unified opposition of the medical profession was the potential economic threat women doctors posed to their male colleagues, 'crowding out' an already overcrowded profession.[1] Thus, most male practitioners were willing to tolerate or even encourage the female nursing movement, whilst vehemently opposing all developments in female medical education.

The entry of women into medicine in the UK coincided with the increasing professionalisation of medicine. From 1858 onward the Medical Register distinguished those with a professional qualification from the quacks. The first women to be admitted to the Medical Register was Elizabeth Blackwell (1821–1910), a native of the United Kingdom who graduated from a US medical school and after a long struggle won recognition in the UK. The second woman licensed to practise in Britain was Elizabeth Garrett (1836–1917), who succeeded partly through private study and partly through a loophole which the licensing bodies then quickly moved to close. For twelve years these two were the only women qualified to practise in Britain.

The next scene of struggle to gain women entry into medicine in Britain was Edinburgh. The case of Sophia Jex Blake (1840–1912) and her four colleagues is well documented elsewhere.[2] Following a failed attempt to obtain a professional qualification in 1874, Sophia became the moving force behind the establishment of the London School of Medicine for Women, the first teaching establishment for women doctors in the UK. The women students had to sit the exams of one of the recognised licensing bodies to be eligible to practice. The Kings' and Queens' College of Physi-cians in Ireland was first to accept women candidates, in 1877; the University of London followed in 1878; and finally, in 1886, the first Scottish licensing body, the Scottish Conjoint Colleges (the Royal College of Physicians in Edinburgh, the Royal College of Surgeons in Edinburgh and the Faculty of Physicians and Surgeons of Glasgow) opened their doors to women. Those qualifying obtained a Licentiate qualification, less prestigious than a university degree but sufficient to practise. Candidates for the Licentiate studied at Scotland's non-university medical schools, but these proved re-luctant to accept women. Ever anxious to promote the cause of Scottish women doctors, Sophia Jex Blake (who had opened her own dispensary in Edinburgh in 1878) responded to this state of affairs by establishing the Edinburgh School of Medicine for Women. However, the School was to be fairly short-lived. Sophia's single-minded approach generated opposition. Disagreements within the School led to the establishment of cheaper classes in the name of the Medical College for Women in Edinburgh. In 1898, after the University of Edinburgh finally opened its doors to women medical graduates, the Edinburgh School of Medicine for Women closed, having successfully pioneered medical teaching for women in Scotland.

Meanwhile, the Scottish universities, still smarting after the Jex Blake affair, which had attracted so much adverse publicity in the 1870s, contin-ued to resist women entrants despite the more progressive attitudes being adopted in England. Scottish women had taken the first steps as early as the mid-1860s to advance the cause of higher education for women in Scotland; by 1882 Queen Margaret College (QMC), a women's college associated with Glasgow University, had opened its doors to arts students. From 1884 to 1892, QMC's teaching developed until a full course of study equivalent to an M. A. degree was available.

The decision to open a women's medical school in Glasgow as part of QMC was taken in 1889 in response to a request from QMC students to the College Council. Legislation that year had made it clear that women would finally be admitted to sit Scottish university medical examinations. Thus it was decided to establish the new medical course at QMC exactly on university lines so that students could eventually be examined for the University of Glasgow's medical degree.

When the Medical School opened in 1890, Queen Margaret College became unique in Scotland as a women's college that offered university-level teaching in both arts and medicine. In Britain, QMC became the fourth centre for women's medical study after London, Dublin and Edinburgh. Unlike the Edinburgh schools, QMC was to prepare its students for a medical degree rather than for the less demanding Licentiate.

At QMC Medical School the sessions, class fees and regulations were identical to those of the University. The attitude of the University professors to women students was also changing. No longer did University lecturers excuse the shortcomings of a lecture on the grounds that it 'was prepared for the weaker intellects of QMC'. Unlike other Scottish Universities, which all opted for accepting women into mixed classes (except in one or two medical subjects such as anatomy), Glasgow chose separate tuition, a decision much regretted by later students but which reflected the very high standard of organisation and tuition that had been established at QMC.

The remaining archival material concerning QMC in these years suggests it was the centre of a highly organised corporate life. The College itself was never residential on the English pattern but Queen Margaret Hall was opened to accommodate some female students. Two important student societies were the QM Suffrage Society (which was addressed by Christabel Pankhurst on the need for more militant suffrage activity) and the QM Settlement Association, through which medical students undertook pioneering work on infant care, including the distribution of free milk to pregnant mothers.

By 1892, when women were first matriculated as students at the University of Glasgow, there was a history of almost fifteen years of medical instruction for women in London and Dublin, five years in Edinburgh and two years in Glasgow. However, the University of London was the only institution other than Glasgow offering a medical degree to aspiring women doctors in the country. In total there were scarcely more than one hundred women qualified to practise in Britain.

In the pre-war years the number of women graduating in medicine at Glasgow fluctuated from 4 per cent to 20 per cent of the total number of graduates averaging at around 10 per cent. Although quotas later operated against women entrants there is no evidence of their operation in this period. Students were admitted or not according to the results of a preliminary examination. The number of female students at Glasgow was constant rather than growing as more provincial medical schools opened in England and as other Scottish universities developed a tradition of women's medical teaching. However, from 1908–9 there was a steady increase in the number of women medical students, a trend that continued throughout the First World War and beyond.

SOCIAL AND GEOGRAPHIC ORIGINS

The very high level of education (by contemporary standards) required of prospective entrants and the high cost of a medical education meant that Glasgow's women medical students were drawn overwhelmingly from the middle class. Over half came from professional backgrounds and another third from the commercial classes. The aristocracy was conspicuous by its absence.

But most interesting are those women who came from less elevated backgrounds – from the margins of the middle class and even from the more prosperous working classes. These women were more prominent in the later period when alternative sources of financial assistance had begun to emerge. The sample of women considered by this study included the daughters of: craftsmen – a blacksmith, a lithographer and block maker; small shopkeepers – a butcher, draper and flesher; and of a commercial traveller and a collector of inland revenue. No woman came from an unskilled or semi-skilled background. However, it remains an unresolved puzzle how in the 1890s the daughters of a butcher and flesher and even of a master mariner managed to finance the substantial costs associated with a medical education. The fact that they somehow managed is a tribute to the perseverance of the women and of their families.

The cost of a medical degree far exceeded the cost of other degrees. The absolute minimum sum for a five-year medical education in Glasgow for a student living away from home was around £400. One of the attractions of a Glasgow medical education was its relatively low cost. Nevertheless, £400 was still a very high figure in relation to the incomes of many of these women's fathers. Many women were excluded from pursuing a medical career through lack of funds; others, along with their families, endured considerable hardship in order to do so. Most contemporaries, even those associated with the University, were unaware of the scale of the problem and mistakenly assumed that the opening of bursaries to women would solve any financial problems. In fact, only twelve bursaries were open to the three hundred women medical students and a majority of these were also open to male applicants. Furthermore, the fact that women usually did not have the benefit of professorial teaching disadvantaged them in competition.[3]

The availability from the early 1900s onward of grants to all Scottish students facing financial hardship from a fund established by the Scottish-born American multi-millionaire, Andrew Carnegie, did assist many struggling students. However, the costs associated with a medical education remained far too high for daughters of the working classes to contemplate entry and the main impact of Carnegie grants was to ease the financial burden on less prosperous middle-class families. Nevertheless, in a still fairly restrictive Victorian age, young women from a surprisingly wide social spectrum came to Glasgow at the age of seventeen to study medicine.

EDUCATION

The impact of separate teaching on the Glasgow women's medical education was vigorously debated at the time and by later commentators. Although the persistence of separate teaching declined through time, in 1909 women still had separate classes in all the clinical subjects. The women bombarded the University Court to no avail with petitions for mixed instruction. Several public complaints voiced by QMC students were made through the *Glasgow Herald* in the 1890s. They concerned the limited opportunities for midwifery training. Women students were restricted to the Glasgow Maternity Hospital which in turn only admitted women to its West End Branch. This annex was so underdeveloped that it was overseen by a visiting nurse and had no permanent physician attached to it.

The extent to which women were disadvantaged by separate teaching, especially in the clinical field, was taken up in an article in the *Glasgow Herald* in the 1890s.

> It is acknowledged by most people of average intelligence that women final candidates are at some disadvantage. The men, in nearly every subject, are examined by their teachers, and this is especially desirable in the clinicals. When a girl has been brought up to recognise certain methods and statements as truth it is hard, at the critical point of her final examination, to discover that medicine and surgery are far from exact sciences, and that teacher and examiner are two different men, who differ in opinion as only men can do. Such is the state of affairs with the women students, the pathetic part being that to find a remedy is practically impossible unless the Western Infirmary opens certain wards to the Queen Margaret Medicals.[4]

The persistence of separate teaching prevented women from achieving equality of opportunities with their male counterparts at any time during the pre-war period. This goes a long way toward explaining why the women's average marks trailed those of their male colleagues, although the differential declined as common teaching increased. Yet even at these early stages a few women were able to overcome all the disadvantages and excel in their academic performance. Women from the Glasgow sample were commended in subjects as challenging as clinical medicine and surgery.

POSTGRADUATE QUALIFICATIONS

The increasing professionalisation of medicine in the nineteenth century continued in the twentieth century. An ordinary medical degree was no longer sufficient to guarantee entry into many parts of the profession. Increasingly, hospital consultancy positions could only be obtained with a higher qualification.

For women, the need for second degrees posed particular problems. The higher postgraduate qualifications were awarded by the Royal Colleges which did not even accept women candidates for their senior examinations until 1911. The highest qualification, the Fellowship, was dependent on nomination by other Fellows of the College and many male Fellows were reluctant to nominate women, although two women from the sample considered here did succeed in obtaining these highly prestigious awards. The main postgraduate qualification, the Doctor of Medicine (M. D.) degree, was obtained by over a third of the sample. The fact that all but one of these M. D. s was awarded by Glasgow University suggests that young women doctors experienced difficulties in gaining acceptance at other institutions. Certainly in the early years the tradition of women's medical study was more advanced at Glasgow than at other Scottish universities. Some of the women postgraduate students were highly distinguished; several were commended; another took the prize for the most distinguished thesis; two others were awarded postgraduate research fellowships. Other postgraduate qualifications included Diplomas in Public Health and in Tropical Medicine and, most commonly, Licentiates in Midwifery. The academic performance of an individual student at the undergraduate level did not appear to be a particularly strong determinant of her capacity for postgraduate studies nor, significantly, did marriage appear to have been a bar to further study.

MARRIAGE

There was a fear among contemporaries that educated women would neither want to marry nor be regarded as suitable partners. Professional women in particular were castigated for selfishly shunning the prospect of rearing of a family in favour of the glories of a career – a particularly worrying prospect at this time of increasing imperial preoccupation. Patriotic citizens enquired anxiously, 'who will bear the future sons of the Empire if women go to University'?[5] But was there any foundation to this popular belief that professional women did not marry? The evidence from this sample appears to confound the conventional wisdom.

Over half of this sample of Glasgow medical women married – that is, a proportion only 10–15 per cent smaller than the national average. This differential would probably be even smaller if the comparison were made directly with middle-class women, who tended to have a lower propensity to marriage. Qualifying in medicine raised the social status of a significant number of these women who also overwhelmingly married into the established professions. Unfortunately, it was not possible to trace the childbearing patterns of this sample.

CAREER PATTERNS

Women doctors throughout Britain made rapid progress in the early years of the twentieth century. The resolution, passed in 1878, excluding women from membership of the British Medical Association was rescinded in 1892.[6] In 1881 there were only four women doctors practising in Scotland, but by 1901 the total had risen to sixty.[7] The British total was approximately 100 in 1891, 200 in 1901 and almost 500 in 1911.[8] In 1911, the Association of Registered Medical Women was formed, to promote fellowship among medical women and to protect their interests, especially the need for equal pay.[9]

The major obstacles these new women doctors faced in the pre-war period were access to: hospital residencies; hospital appointments; and postgraduate teaching facilities. The First World War, which created both a rising demand for doctors and a shortage of young male applicants, significantly altered the position of women in medicine: from the pursuit of a minority, medicine was transformed into a fairly popular profession for women.

By the turn of the century the importance of residency posts – short-stay, live-in hospital appointments taken up soon after graduation – was growing. Although still not compulsory, they were now crucial for advancement in hospital medicine. As no records of rejected applications now exist it is difficult to establish precisely the difficulties experienced by women in securing such appointments. However, contemporary press cuttings do highlight the experience of some of these early Glasgow graduates and illustrate the wider problems experienced by women doctors everywhere.

Throughout this period the most prestigious hospitals were the voluntary general hospitals, financed by paying patients and supplemented through subscriptions and bequests. Only one of Glasgow's three large voluntary general hospitals, the Royal Infirmary, accepted women residents. Glasgow's foremost teaching hospital, the Western Infirmary, did not admit women to clinical instruction until 1920 and did not appoint women residents until forced to do so during World War II.[10] Undoubtedly, the opposition to women residents in the prestigious voluntary general hospitals severely curtailed their advance into Glasgow hospital medicine. Women were accepted to residencies in only two of a total of over ten specialist hospitals in Glasgow. The two accepting women residents, the Samaritan and Maternity Hospitals, both dealt exclusively with gynaecology, indicating the early emergence of the ghettoisation of women into 'female' sectors of medical practice.

Despite the difficulties of access to the hospital sector, 27 of the 62 Glasgow graduates (44 per cent) took up some sort of residency post in Glasgow, eleven (18 per cent) went directly into foreign mission work and

12 (19 per cent) took up residency posts in other parts of the country, leaving only 12 (19 per cent) who took up no residency posts. Unfortunately, these figures do not reveal how many of the women who did not take up any residency posts had made unsuccessful applications, nor do they reveal the range of posts open to women. It is not possible to compare male and female success rates in obtaining residencies, as no detailed studies have been undertaken of male access patterns. Nevertheless, the total number of posts available and the wide range of potential specialities as compared to the narrow range of posts actually taken up by Glasgow women indicate that women's access, especially in the more prestigious sectors, was much more restricted than for their male counterparts.

The limited number of hospital posts open to women is revealed by an examination of the residency posts accepted by Glasgow graduates in London. Six Glasgow women accepted fourteen residency posts in London, but all of these posts were limited to four hospitals, two of which were run by women: the New Hospital for Women, founded by Elizabeth Garrett Anderson, and the Clapham Maternity Hospital. For the Glasgow women who took up residency posts elsewhere in England, the spread of institutions is inevitably more varied but the limited range of posts open to them is remarkably consistent.[11] Women were forced to take residencies in the less prestigious sectors – asylums, poor law infirmaries and dispensaries. The only two women who did succeed in obtaining residencies in the prestigious voluntary general hospitals faced a tremendous storm over their appointments. Both these appointments at Macclesfield Infirmary, as we will see, were marked by controversy and considerable press interest.

The pattern emerging from this study indicates that women found great difficulty in obtaining residency positions (the lowest rungs on the hospital ladder) in the voluntary general hospitals, especially the teaching hospitals. These appointments were the most favoured route to advancement in hospital medicine. Even those women working in the voluntary specialist sector were often highly concentrated in the fields of obstetrics, gynaecology and paediatrics. The acceptance of less prestigious Poor Law and dispensary positions by many highly qualified women graduates reflected the limited opportunities available to them, the need for secure employment and the desire for wider medical experience in the period immediately following their graduation.

PUBLIC REACTION TO WOMEN MEDICAL GRADUATES

In April 1901 the governors of Macclesfield Infirmary made a new departure in unanimously appointing a woman, Miss Marion J. Ross who had taken high honours at Glasgow, as Junior House Surgeon. However, on 18 November 1901, the *Glasgow Evening Citizen* reported that Dr Ross had left to take up general practice locally and another female Glasgow graduate, Dr Clark, had been appointed to her post. This prompted the honorary medical staff, i. e. the visiting general practitioners, to resign in protest against the appointment of another woman. Initially the press was sympathetic:

> The resignation of the medical staff has not been taken very seriously by the directors, who have too much common sense to be dismayed by this somewhat petty proceeding. It is also rather late in the day for any such display of disapproval over the appointment of a woman, to have much effect on the medical woman's movement. The staff all along protested at a woman holding the post, and the election of a second has proved too much for them.[12]

The *Macclesfield Courier* recorded the progress of the dispute. On two occasions the Governors refused to dismiss Dr Clark despite the resolute opposition of the medical staff. Even the Governor who put forward the motion for her dismissal acknowledged that 'the medical men have not said all they might have said in justification of their action' but, the task of the Governors, he maintained, was not to fight the wider battles for women doctors, but to act in the best interests of the Infirmary. Dr Clark did have strong support among some Governors who suggested that her predecessor, Dr Ross, now working locally in general practice, should replace the medical staff who had resigned as the Infirmary's honorary physician; others advocated a compromise whereby Dr Clark would be retained to work amongst the women and children. However, despite continued support for her case Dr Clark, feeling under increasing pressure and fearful of the implications for patient care, felt she had no option but to offer her resignation.[13]

Dr Clark's resignation relieved the Governors who promptly capitulated to the honorary medical staff's demand that they should have a virtual veto over the appointment of future staff by handing the medical staff the right to draw up the short list of candidates in the future. Nationally, the stance of the honorary medical staff at Macclesfield was supported by *The Lancet*, the medical journal which had traditionally been at the forefront of opposition to all women's medical training.

Having resigned her position at the Infirmary, Dr Clark entered general practice in Macclesfield for five years before marrying and moving to Hong Kong. During the First World War she came back briefly and worked as Assistant Tubercular Officer in Glasgow, before returning to Hong Kong as Acting Medical Officer of Health for the duration of the War. She later took a Doctor of Medicine degree, published articles on Cerebro-Spinal Fever and spent ten years in public health work. It is difficult to assess the precise impact of the initial opposition Dr Clark met in Macclesfield on the future development of her career. However, despite her distinguished career she never again worked in hospitals. This suggests that the early opposition she met at Macclesfield was effective indeed.

The second incident involving a Glasgow graduate concerned Dr Eva McCall, who applied for the post of Medical Officer for Birkenhead Poor Law Infirmary; she was initially rejected on grounds of sex. But, when no men applied to the re-advertisement, the Guardians relented and she was appointed.[14] Why no male doctors applied on re-advertisement is not clear, but may reflect the relatively low status and remuneration, in this case £120 p. a. , attached to Poor Law appointments.

What makes this particular case revealing is the calibre of the woman doctor involved. Dr McCall had a very distinguished academic record and had already held three residencies in prestigious London hospitals. Within a year of her appointment at Birkenhead she had obtained a Doctor of Medicine degree and published two articles in the *British Medical Journal*. She remained in public health for the rest of her life, rising to the position of Assistant Medical Officer of Health for London County Council. If Dr McCall had been a man she would undoubtedly have been offered the opportunity to pursue a career in hospital medicine in London; it would have been highly unlikely for her to apply for a Poor Law position. Furthermore, local Poor Law Guardians would have been delighted to have such an impressive applicant. The rejection of Dr McCall's initial application on the basis of her sex again points to the level of prejudice confronting early women doctors.

The third incident to involve a Glasgow graduate and which attracted press coverage was the case of Dr Jane Gilmore Cox in 1901.[15] Dr Cox had been Junior Assistant Medical Officer at Bracebridge Asylum in Lincolnshire. Her immediate predecessor had also been a woman, the first to be appointed at the Asylum, and the experiment had proved a great success. Dr Cox was not so fortunate. The circumstances surrounding her resignation aroused controversy and led to a dispute over whether a third woman should be appointed. The Alderman supporting the reappointment of another woman explained some of the background to the resignation:

> He had heard that Dr. Cox attended to her patients most minutely, and if she erred at all, it was because she attended too much to them. She received a less hearty welcome because she did not attend any of the croquet parties or tennis parties and did not go out to the race meetings. If, on the first advertisement, they did not get the proper lady to apply, he should say 'Advertise again until you do'. He supported the resolution to appoint a lady doctor who would get on well with Dr Torney (the Medical Superintendent), and whom they should require Dr Torney also to get on well with.

The Medical Superintendent of course denied these allegations that Dr Cox had been edged out because of her disdain for the medical staff's social round and the motion went against advertising for a woman doctor, although women were free to apply.

These cases illustrate the prejudice that obstructed the early careers of Glasgow medical women. In each case the woman was a highly competent graduate with residency experience. In every case she met opposition either from a male-dominated governing body or from an all-male medical staff. Yet, this opposition did not dissuade these women from persisting

with their chosen profession, although it did influence patterns of specialisation.

Dr Flora Murray, writing in the *New Statesman* in 1913 on career
prospects in hospital medicine said, 'Staff appointments are professional
prizes. They are made by the Council or governing body, generally
consisting entirely of men, upon the advice of a medical staff composed of
men'.[16] No amount of academic excellence or diligence in performing one's
duties could overcome such obstacles. However, these deficiencies were
somewhat ameliorated by the nation-wide network of hospitals run by
women for women. By 1927 there were 183 women-run hospitals across
Britain; however, only three of these were in Scotland, a circumstance that
forced most Glasgow women to work in male-dominated hospitals and
frequently endure obstacles to advancement.[17]

All the evidence, both quantitative and qualitative, relating to the
Glasgow sample reinforces the claims of contemporaries about the general
prejudice – whether formalised or subconscious – amongst male governing bodies against women graduates. However, any study of the collective
experience of early women doctors must attempt to assess the extent to
which they were able to use their professional training. This means
building up a picture of their entire career patterns. Only then is it possible
to assess how far their patterns of speciality was a product of choice or of
compulsion.

A common argument advanced in opposition to women entering
medicine is that they never practise medicine after graduating and so the
investment in their education is wasted. In fact only two women (3. 2 per
cent) from this sample appear never to have worked and even this is not
certain as one returned to her parents' home in India and may have worked
temporarily in general practice. Perhaps more surprising is the fact that
only five women (8. 1 per cent), seem to have stopped work on marriage.
Three of these five had excellent academic records, suggesting that a good
undergraduate performance was no guide to subsequent commitment to
the profession. Overall, these results suggest the Glasgow women's remarkable commitment to a full professional life even after marriage. It is
even possible that some of the five women who appear to have given up
practising on marriage may in fact have taken up general practice – a
possibility difficult to verify from existing records. Many women, then as
now, may have found that the flexibility of hours in general practice better
suited their domestic responsibilities. However, since the existing records
do not allow us to confirm this, it cannot be assumed.

Fifteen (24 per cent) of the women did interrupt their careers for a period
of years or stopped work in middle age. Some of them may have been
active in general practice and in at least six cases their past record of work
would suggest this was a possibility; but again, this cannot be verified. The
reasons for giving up work included having to move abroad with one's
husband, poor health, childbearing and, in one case, the elevation of her

husband to a knighthood. Another factor may have been temporary periods of unemployment. In 1926, the London School of Medicine for Women found that 6 per cent of its graduates from 1923–25, were unemployed because they could not obtain paid work.[18] Therefore excluding the two who never worked, the five who gave up on marriage and the fifteen who took breaks from employment, the remaining forty women (65) per cent of the sample) worked throughout their lives. Adding together all those who worked throughout their lives and those who worked for most of their lives, 89 per cent of the sample are accounted for. The results exceed even those for a contemporary American study indicating that over 80 per cent of American women doctors continued in practice.[19] The figure of 89 per cent actively practising is comparable to the rates for their male contemporaries, a substantial number of whom did not devote their entire lives to a medical career, temporarily venturing into other fields such as business, politics or estate management.

This evidence comprehensively refutes the notion that women made markedly less use of their education than did their male colleagues. Similarly it contradicts the popular belief that marriage was incompatible with a career. The two women who never worked were not married, and the five who may have dropped out after marriage represent only 15 per cent of the married women in the sample. Furthermore, two of the four women in the sample who achieved outstanding success were married.

The validity of these findings on the number of Glasgow women using their professional training are reinforced by the figures from Manchester University for all women medical graduates before 1938. Ninety per cent of Manchester graduates also made use of their training and, as in Glasgow, two-thirds did so on a continuous full-time basis.[20] Similarly, only one-fifth of the Manchester graduates gave up practice on marriage. The remarkable correlation between the Glasgow and Manchester patterns of work is further evidence of women doctors' commitment to utilising their training to the full, whatever the obstacles.

AREAS OF SPECIALITY

Although specialisation was on the increase at the turn of the century, the medical profession was still much more fluid than it is today. Most women worked in several medical fields throughout their careers. However, it is usually possible to identify one main specialism for any particular member of the Glasgow sample.

Excluding the 18 per cent entering the mission field, the most popular specialism amongst the early graduates was general practice (24 per cent) followed by public health (19 per cent). In the later period public health overtook general practice as the most popular specialism, attracting almost twice the numbers of graduates in any other specialism. The distribution of women in other specialisms altered little. Thus, the main change between the two periods was the large shift towards the expanding public health sector as more government funding became available, especially for maternal and infant care. Legislation such as the Notification of Births (Extension) Act and the Maternal and Child Welfare Act, had made compulsory much of the existing voluntary work of local authorities with mothers and infants. In 1918 Dr Janet Campbell became head of the Maternal and Child Welfare Department at the new Ministry of Health and immediately appointed six women doctors as her inspectors.[21] By 1922 there were approximately 2000 infant welfare centres in Britain, staffed largely by women doctors.

Without detailed figures on the occupations of male practitioners in this period, comparisons must be general and tentative. However, the pattern of specialisms amongst women probably differs substantially from the male pattern in two respects: the smaller number of women in general practice and voluntary general hospitals; and the higher number of women in public health. The obstacles for women wishing to enter voluntary general hospitals have already been noted, but their lower concentration in general practice was also tied to problems of access. Many male practitioners in established practices were reluctant to take on a woman partner often for less-than-convincing reasons. Sometimes this reluctance was explained on grounds of delicacy – that is, it was deemed unsuitable for a woman to treat male patients. Allegedly, women doctors could not be restricted to women patients as emergencies would always arise. Public caution also affected the growth of women's practices as women doctors were sometimes expected to have wider experience in other medical fields before they could build up a flourishing practice. In an age when a general practitioner's income relied on the number and wealth of his/her patients, some women found that general practice did not offer them sufficient security of income. This was because most women G. P. s relied overwhelmingly on women patients – either because they refused to treat men or because men were reluctant to come. Women were invariably poorer patients as they neither possessed independent incomes nor were likely to qualify for health insurance under the National Insurance (Health) Act.

Comparing these figures for early-twentieth-century women doctors with recent surveys on the distribution of women doctors, the similarities are more striking than the contrasts. In some cases the range of specialities had actually narrowed over the century. By 1979 the number of women doctors working in hospital medicine had not increased. A comparison of the proportion of women from this sample employed in hospital medicine, including those working in Poor Law hospitals, with the modern-day proportion reveals that a higher 9 per cent were engaged in hospital work then than today. Furthermore, although a wider variety of medical opportunities are available to women today and women have better access to senior posts than they did fifty years ago, progress has been very slow given the rising percentage of women in medical schools, where they now account for almost half the undergraduates in Scotland. These recent patterns suggest that when women did make progress into hospitals in the 1920s and 1930s this was not part of an inevitable 'onward and upward' movement, but a more hesitant pattern characterised by both advances and retreats.

Mary Walsh has examined the specialisms of early American women doctors. She has explained the concentration of women in certain specialities in the following way:

> For a society that has reservations about female competency, the result is often a decision by women to opt for the least threatening patients, women and children, the poor, the mentally ill. Another option is to move into public health with its captive clientele – the indications are that many pioneers became involved in public health after their exclusion from other fields due to sex discrimination.[22]

Walsh's analysis concentrates on the negative factors pushing women towards public health, stressing that it was one of the few areas of relatively easy access where women could exercise authority with comparative ease. It is, however, possible to view this concentration in a more positive way. Many women entered medicine in order to have the opportunity to treat other women. Personal experience of ill health or the knowledge that many women wanted to be treated by their own sex motivated many young women to enter medicine. Similarly, other women were motivated by a humanitarian instinct to treat the most vulnerable in society. This impulse drove many overseas into the mission field, whilst many others stayed at home in Poor Law posts. The disappointing feature here is that so few women had their skills recognised through advancement in their chosen field.

The examination of career patterns by specialisms does not tell the whole story. It reveals nothing about the relative seniority of the positions women held in their various specialisms. How can the 'average' experience of early Glasgow women doctors be assessed? Did the majority of women from Glasgow manage to obtain a variety of positions, and at what level?

In the area of public health, despite the high concentration of women in junior posts, none of this sample became a senior Medical Officer of Health for a city or district. It was not until the thirties that a woman was appointed as a City Medical Officer in York.[23]

Poor Law appointments followed much the same pattern as public health. Many women were employed in infirmaries or asylums, but none of them received the more coveted posts of parochial Medical Officers, who oversaw the provision of outdoor relief. (The only exception was to be found on the island of Colonsay, where the authorities had no option because the woman was the only doctor on the island!)

Flora Murray, writing in the *New Statesman* in 1913, argued that 'when applying for posts in Poor Law infirmaries and asylums women candidates are heavily handicapped. However capable and experienced they might be they never obtain the higher posts of Senior Assistant or Superintendent.[24] Very soon after Dr Murray wrote this article, women started gaining appointments as Superintendents, but these women were rare exceptions and no woman from this sample was appointed to such a post. In the two cases where Glasgow graduates were in charge of Poor Law institutions, the hospitals and asylums were so small that the appointment of a Superintendent was unwarranted.

In hospital medicine the now characteristic concentration of women in gynaecology and paediatrics was already evident. It is remarkable how little has changed with respect to women obtaining senior appointments or entering certain hospital specialities. Even today only 6 per cent of Britain's consultant general surgeons are women.[25] None are employed in Scotland's major hospitals and consultant female physicians are still a rare breed.

The dilemma for any observer is to balance the achievements of a few highly talented women, who defied all the odds and reached the pinnacle of the profession, against the obstacles encountered by the majority. Invariably, a woman had to be better than a male applicant and even then she was not guaranteed the job. For example, two of the four women from this sample who were appointed to large voluntary hospitals held fairly junior positions – one as an assistant to the bacteriologist, the other as assistant to the pathologist at the royal Infirmary. Both post-holders were highly talented women. One had taken the highest points at graduation, been commended for her M.D., and later undertook full-time research work at the Lister Institute in London. The other had taken the Bellahouston Gold Medal for the best M.D. thesis and had already been awarded a Beit Memorial Research Fellowship. It is unlikely that men with similar qualifications would have considered such junior positions as these women accepted. Furthermore, the fact that these were the only two women appointed to work in the Royal Infirmary in a non-residency capacity highlights the abnormally high standard that was demanded of women doctors.

Just over a quarter of the sample published medical articles and books. The graduates of 1900 alone included two authors on childbirth, one on birth control, another on immunity and a fifth on venereal disease. One early missionary wrote extensively on health and women in East Africa; another, on childbirth in India. In total, the members of the sample published almost seventy books and articles among them – by any standards, a substantial contribution to current medical scholarship.

Yet not everyone was held back by the formidable obstacles. Four outstanding women in the sample defied all the prevailing trends against women's advancement and achieved remarkable success. All four became consultants and two became professors. Three – Dr A. Louise McIlroy, Dr Agnes Savill and Dr Gertrude Campbell – came from the early period and one, Dr Margaret Rorke, from the later period. Dr Campbell achieved her success abroad, starting out as a missionary and rising to be Principal and

Professor of Obstetrics and Gynaecology of the Lady Hardinge College in Delhi. Dr Margaret Rorke became the Chief Consultant in Venereal Diseases at the Royal Free Hospital in London in 1935, a Member of the Royal College of Obstetricians and Gynaecologists, and President of the Medical Society for the Study of Venereal Disease. Dr Rorke was also a member of the working party that prepared the influential 1930s social study, 'Working Class Wives'.

Dr Agnes Savill was one of the two women in the sample to become a Fellow of the Royal College of Physicians. Her early experience had included work in a Liverpool workhouse, an unusual experience for someone destined for the heights of the profession. From early in her career she specialised in dermatology, working as a physician in a variety of London skin hospitals, and the women-run 'South London Hospital for Women'. In 1940 she became a Consultant Physician at the London Skin Hospital, Fitzroy Square. Her other area of work was radiology and she wrote several academic articles on this subject. In 1935 she became Vice President of the Electro-Therapy section of the Royal Society of Medicine. She was a prolific writer, her publications including over twenty articles in the medical press and a dermatology manual. For thirty-two years she edited revisions of her deceased husband's medical textbook.

Dr Anne Louise McIlroy was the most distinguished Glasgow graduate; in 1929 she was created Dame of the British Empire for her services to medicine. Her numerous postgraduate qualifications were complemented by honorary degrees. Her whole career was one of 'trail-blazing' for future generations of women doctors. Before the First World War, she became the first woman to be appointed a 'senior assistant' to a professor in Glasgow University's Medical Faculty. (No woman was to be appointed to a medical professorship at Glasgow until the later 1970s) Dr. McIlroy was the first woman to be elected President of the prestigious Metropolitan Branch of the BMA, and she later joined its General Council. In 1920, at the age of forty-five, when she was already a Consultant in obstetrics and gynaecology at the Royal Free Hospital, she became Professor at the London School of Medicine for Women. She was to hold this position for almost twenty years and for the last five she was also a surgeon at the Marie Curie Hospital for Women, for the treatment of cancer.

The success of these four women indicates that despite the obstacles, women of exceptional talent could make it to the head of their profession. Yet a note of caution is necessary. The fact that three out of the four women achieved this success in women-dominated institutions and in specialisms primarily concerned with women's health raises questions about the opportunities open to even these most able women. Dr Campbell became a professor at an Indian ladies college where there were still taboos against men teaching gynaecology to women. Both Drs Rorke and McIlroy became consultants at the Royal Free, the only London teaching hospital to accept women and an institution firmly tied to the tradition of women in medicine through its association with the London School of Medicine for Women. Only Dr Savill received her consultancy in a male dominated general London hospital. This failure even among the most talented to penetrate the hierarchies of mixed general hospitals must serve to confirm earlier evidence regarding the debilitating and institutionalised prejudice against women entering influential areas of the profession.

All the evidence suggests that the ability to succeed in professional terms was dependent on appropriate postgraduate qualifications and, more importantly, on wide-ranging residency experience, particularly in general hospitals. Perhaps if undergraduate qualifications – the first barrier to entry which women had already conquered – had been a more crucial factor, women would have been better placed. As it was, more invisible barriers obstructing access to residencies and to hospital appointments were more vital determinants of progress. Nevertheless, substantial progress had been made by the thirties. Future retrenchment and even retreat later in the century would confirm the relative speed and success of advances in these years. One of the factors in hastening women's advancement in this early period was the impact of the First World War.

WAR WORK

The coming of the First World War offered women from all walks of life the opportunity to move into many areas of work from which they had previously been excluded. In medicine, the contribution of women doctors, especially that of Scottish women through the Scottish Women's Hospitals (SWH), convinced many sceptics that women medical practitioners were as competent as men.[26] The SWH was founded in October 1914 by Dr Elsie Inglis, an Edinburgh graduate, in response to the refusal of the War Office to employ any female medical volunteers. Women were thus forced by the War Office to continue the tradition of separatism that had grown up, of necessity, in much of their hospital work over the previous thirty years.

The nucleus of the SWH was the women's suffrage associations. It has already been pointed out that there were a number of active womens' suffrage organisations at Queen Margaret College in the early years of the century and there is evidence that a number of early Glasgow women doctors remained active in the movement after qualifying, although the anecdotal nature of the remaining evidence makes it impossible to determine the numbers involved. Nevertheless, the fact that the SWH grew out of the Scottish suffrage movement suggests that the overlap in personnel and activity was considerable.

Ignored by the War Office, the SWH wrote directly to the Allies offering their services, and subsequently served in six nations. All members of the Fourteen SWH units, from stretcher-bearers to commanding officers, were women. At least seven women from this sample were attached to SWH units working in the field.

Two SWH commanding officers were drawn from this sample. Dr Keer, a Glasgow graduate of 1910, was placed in charge of a Unit based in Corsica to nurse Serbian exiles. The other Glasgow graduate to command a Unit was Dr Louise McIlroy. In light of her subsequent achievements – her professorship and elevation to a peerage – the choice of Dr McIlroy as a commanding officer may seem an obvious one. But in 1914 most of her experience was concentrated in the fields of obstetrics and gynaecology – not particularly relevant to the needs of a military hospital. Her Unit left Scotland in May 1915 for six months' work at Troyes in France, a few weeks in Serbia and finally three years in Salonica, all under the French War Office. In 1917 Dr McIlroy oversaw the establishment of the only orthopaedic centre in the Eastern Army. She also established a nursing school for Serbian women, as most of the nation's training centres had been destroyed. After the Armistice, the Unit moved to Belgrade to establish the Elsie Inglis Memorial Hospital.[27] Three other Glasgow graduates from this sample also served in her Unit. For her four years of continuous service, Dr McIlroy received a Croix de Guerre avec Palme and many other decorations.

The proven record of work of the SWH and its English counterpart, the Women's Hospital Corps, forced the Ministry of Defence to relax its ban on women, who were subsequently invited in 1916 to become non-commissioned civilian auxiliaries to the Royal Army Medical Corps.[28] Three women from the sample accepted such appointments to serve overseas.

The War offered women opportunities to run large general hospitals in a manner that had been impossible in peacetime. None of those serving overseas remained surgeons after the war. This again raises questions about female access to the highly prestigious specialisms of which surgery is the most notable.

The benefits accruing from women's war service were collective as well as individual. As Eva McLaren concluded,

'in 1914 positions on the staffs of general hospitals were only open to women in very few instances, and the opportunities afforded to them, especially in general surgery, were extremely limited. That medical women could successfully staff War Hospitals of three to six hundred beds, dealing with all sorts of casualties and with the various diseases affecting the armies, was a proposition that still lacked proof.'[29]

In the initial stages of the War, a few women by their actions abroad had proven that women could in fact run large mixed general hospitals. Their example (together with the acute shortage of doctors) encouraged professional recognition of women doctors on the domestic front. Medical schools, no longer filled to capacity, began to admit more women. Although there was much retrenchment again after the War – an example being the exclusion of women from London teaching hospitals – it was no longer possible for opponents of women doctors to claim with any legitimacy that they had been excluded on grounds of competency.

MISSIONARY WORK

The mission field also gave women access to medical opportunities that were denied at home, particularly in the early years. Indeed, it was the publicising of the humanitarian case for women physicians in India in the 1870s and 1880s – to treat Indian women whose religious customs prevented them from being examined by men – which at a crucial juncture undermined professional and public opposition to women's medical training in Britain.[30]

The history of Scottish women medical missionaries in India began with Dr Matilda MacPhail, who went out in 1887 with the Free Church of Scotland Mission. In 1891 she opened a twelve-bed hospital at Rajapurum, Madras. The hospital grew and in 1914 the Christina Rainy Hospital in Tondiarpet, Madras, opened supported entirely by fees from local private practice.[31] Dr McPhail continued as Superintendent of the hospital until the mid-1920s; during this period four women from this sample worked under her.

Slightly over 20 per cent of the Glasgow women became missionaries, a proportion far higher than the male average but in line with the importance of missionary work in the early movement for women's medical training. The proportion of missionary graduates was fairly constant throughout the pre-war period. The main destination of Glasgow medical women missionaries was India, which accounted for ten of the original thirteen. The other three worked in China, Egypt and British Central Africa, respectively. These figures demonstrate the impact of the work done in pleading the case of Indian women in Britain.

As one might expect, marriage rates among missionaries were much lower than for the sample as a whole, with only four in ten marrying. All those who married wed missionaries and at least four of them continued to work after their marriage. Thus, in missionary work, as in other branches of medicine, marriage does not seem to have been a bar to continued service. Finally, the fact that all these women entered the mission field immediately after graduation – only three even waiting to do residencies – dispels the oft-quoted myth that women doctors only entered the mission field to escape domestic unemployment. Increasing domestic opportunities in medicine does not seem to have diminished the desire to embark on missionary work. Indeed, the missionary impulse amongst Scottish women seems to have increased in this period. The reasons for this are not altogether clear: perhaps the availability of Carnegie grants helped more aspiring missionaries cover the cost of their education; perhaps missionary societies were more willing to fund women students; or perhaps the growing awareness of Scottish women doctors already working in the field encouraged more prospective women medical missionaries to pursue this career.

At least twelve other women from this sample worked or at least lived abroad in non-missionary capacities. This total excludes those involved in war work; thus, a remarkable 42 per cent of the sample spent considerable periods of their lives abroad. The evidence of their overseas employment is sparse. The existing records confirm that many turned to general practice, particularly if they had been drawn overseas by their husband's career, as prior to World War I it was almost impossible for women to get government or colonial appointments overseas.

After the war colonial appointments became slightly more accessible to women, for the war and the consequent shortage of medical personnel had opened up new opportunities for female physicians. One Glasgow graduate became Medical Officer of Health for Hong Kong; another, Medical Officer at the African Hospital in Lagos. A third joined the Child Welfare Association in Jamaica and a fourth became a District Surgeon in South Africa.

CONCLUSION

Any conclusions about these women's careers must acknowledge that the story of their working lives is one of contradictions. Examples can be found of continued advancement and retrenchment alike. The vast majority of women did make good use of their training, despite the obstacles they faced. Most women did find residency posts, although they tended to be concentrated in the low-status sectors of medicine. The continuing bar on women doctors in most large general hospitals prevented all but a few from obtaining the prestigious hospital residencies that offered the prospect of future employment in the hospital sector. The women-run hospitals managed to compensate for some of these deficiencies in the mainstream hospital experience, but there were few such institutions in Scotland.

Public hostility to women graduates was not uncommon but it was the medical profession and male boards of management that offered the greatest resistance, as they felt most directly threatened by women doctors. The perseverance of the overwhelming majority of women graduates in their professional careers even after marriage was remarkable.

More pessimistically, many of these women were apparently forced to settle for low-status positions, in low-status sectors, treating low-status patients. Perhaps personal reservations about seeking positions of authority in a hostile climate may also have operated in a vicious circle with common prejudice. For many women, who found that the voluntary general hospitals were closed to them, public health offered a growing and relatively secure field of alternative employment.

The war service of many women certainly heightened public acceptance of women physicians even if many hospitals still held out against them. However, some outstanding women also received official recognition from their fellow physicians in the form of honorary positions. Rising opportunities at home do not seem to have deterred a constant flow of women throughout the pre-war period from heading for the mission field. Almost all of them departed very soon after their graduation and subsequently gave a lifetime's service. Thus it seems implausible to posit the simple explanation that they were driven abroad by lack of opportunities at home.

Perhaps the most significant finding of this study is the total number of women, in excess of 88 per cent, who practised after graduation either for a lifetime or for a long period. These results entirely refute the claim that women were less committed to practising medicine than their male contemporaries and indicate the extent to which these women valued the vocational nature of their training. Similarly, the high marriage rates, approaching national norms, suggest that marriage and domestic commitments could, and frequently did, co-exist with an active professional life.

Nevertheless, opposition to women in medicine persisted on the grounds that the profession entailed many responsibilities that contravened prevailing and remarkably durable notions of female delicacy. The separate-spheres ideal that upheld the virtues of gentility, fragility and leisure for middle-class women survived into the twentieth century and continued to underlie popular opposition to women doctors. However, the separate-spheres ideal had itself undergone considerable modification by the early years of the century as its emphasis shifted from stressing female purity to the virtues of motherhood. The early twentieth century was a period of rapid progress for middle-class women as they moved out into society; their intellectual horizons broadened as increasing currency was given to notions such as sexual equality and female suffrage. Women doctors were not immune from these wider societal trends, especially those as dramatic as the impact of war on popular perceptions of women and on the opportunities for women in various environments.

However, male doctors continued to fear the threat women doctors posed to their economic position, particularly with regard to treating other women. These fears, in combination with the popular ones on grounds of delicacy, all well-rehearsed on overwhelmingly male governing bodies, accounted for the exclusion of many women from the prestigious centres of the profession such as the voluntary general hospitals, and certain high-status and allegedly 'indelicate' specialities such as surgery. However, opposition to the employment of women doctors in the lower-status sectors of the profession diminished as new opportunities opened up, notably in public health, thereby allaying the fears of male contemporaries about the impact of female colleagues on their economic security. Perhaps such low-status sectors as public health were so isolated from the prestigious voluntary sector that female penetration of them posed relatively little danger to the overall status of the profession. Indeed, by guaranteeing many women jobs, these low-status sectors served a useful function in reducing the competition in the prestigious sectors.

The entry of women into medicine coincided with the continuing process of professionalisation. The rising undergraduate academic requirements for medicine (which formed part of this process) do not appear to have inhibited women's entry or performance. The increasing importance of postgraduate qualifications as specialisation advanced left many women in a Catch-22. Their inability to obtain residency posts as a result of both formal and informal barriers prevented them from getting the wider experience that was necessary for many postgraduate qualifications, which, in turn, were increasingly demanded for permanent hospital posts. Certainly, the areas of speciality adopted by these women do reveal the widespread prejudice amongst male medical staffs, boards of governors and the general public. However, this was not the only factor in operation. Some women deliberately chose to work in sectors like public health with its captive clientele or opted to work exclusively with women and children to avoid the problems of having to tackle reluctant male patients or face enforced competition with male colleagues.[32] Some women were undoubtedly reluctant to accept positions of authority over male colleagues because of the problems it might pose. Yet others may have been less ambitious, or restricted by domestic responsibilities and childbearing. But, given the inadequacy of the evidence on this point it cannot accurately be emphasised as an explanatory variable for womens' general position in medicine.

The relatively greater successes of the women in the earlier period suggests that the ongoing battle against prejudice was not one of sustained intensity. It seems possible that the earlier graduates performed better than the later ones because they faced less sustained opposition in the prestigious sectors, where their numbers were still so insignificant that they were viewed more as 'individual exceptions' than as a part of a real threat to male domination. If fears of a 'flood' of women did peak later, this would account for the lesser progress by the later group. The details of the timing and intensity of any such backlash and its relationship to the decline of women-only institutions lies outside the scope of this enquiry, but certainly merits future investigation. Irrespective of any possible backlash, the positions of authority finally attained by some of the early medical women far exceeded the achievements of women in other professions.

Thus, in conclusion, the most remarkable findings of this study are the number of women who made use of their education, and the advances made in the very early period, relative not only to womens' advances in other professions, but also to the current position of women in medicine. The success of the very early women, relative to their total numbers, appears only to have been matched in the last twenty years by similar levels of diversity of speciality amongst medical women. The findings of this study, which has traced the progress of early women graduates, highlights the need for further work – on the contrasting male/female experience, on Anglo-Scottish comparisons, on further developments in the inter-war period and on the impact of the decline of female-only institutions – to develop a more complete picture of the position of women within the medical profession in Scotland and the UK as a whole.

NOTES

1   J. Woodward and D. Richards, *Health Care and Popular Medicine in Nineteenth Century England* (London, Croom Helm, 1977), 118.

2   Margaret Todd and E. Lutzker, *Women Gain a Place in Medicine* (New York, McGraw Hill, 1969) *The Life of Sophia Jex Blake* (London, Macmillan, 1918).

3   *Glasgow Herald* (23 May 1901), QMC Press Cuttings, Glasgow University Archives, p. 78/23407a/.

4   *Glasgow Herald* (June 1899), QMC Press Cuttings, Glasgow University Archives p. 11/23407/.

5   Willystine Goodsell, *The Education of Women* (New York, Macmillan, 1923), 31.

6   I. Thorne, *Sketch of the Foundation and Development of the London School of Medicine for Women* (London, the Women's Printing Society, 1915), 37.

7   David Hamilton, *The Healers*, (Edinburgh, Canongate, 1981), 221.

8   Lutzker, op. cit. , 153.

9   Thorne, op. cit. , 57.

10   Olive Checkland (ed.), *Health Care as Social History: The Glasgow Case* (Aberdeen University Press, 1982), 137.

11   *Medical Directories.*

12   *The Glasgow Evening Citizen* (18 November 1901), QMC Press Cuttings, Glasgow University Archives, p. 172/23407a.

13   *The Macclesfield Courier* (11 January 1902), QMC Press Cuttings, Glasgow University Archives, p. 184/23046a.

14   *Glasgow Evening News* (15 July 1901), QMC Press Cuttings, Glasgow University Archives, p. 124/23407a.

15   *Lincolnshire Echo* (17 October 1901), QMC Press Cuttings, Glasgow University Archives, p. 145/23407a/.

16   Dr Flora Murray, 'The Position of Women in Medicine and Surgery', *New Statesman*, Special Supplement (Nov. 1913), xvi–xvii.

17   E. Moberly Bell, *Storming the Citadel: the Rise of the Woman Doctor* (London, Constable, 1953), 148. See also Dr. Margaret W. M. Campbell's unpublished manuscript: *Three Scottish Women's Hospitals from their Foundation to 1948* (Glasgow 1981), held in the Mitchell Library.

18   Bell, ibid. , 171.

19   S. Virginia Drachman, 'The Limits of Progress: the Professional Lives of Women Doctors, 1881–1926', *The Bulletin of the History of Medicine* (March 1986), 69.

20   Mabel Tylecote, *The Education of Women at Manchester University* (Manchester University Press, 1941), 121.

21   Bell, op. cit. , 182.

22   M. R. Walsh, *Doctors Wanted: No Women Need Apply* (New Haven, Yale University Press, 1977), 259, 261.

23   Bell, op. cit. , 184.

24   Murray, op. cit. , xvi–xvii.

25   'Royal College of Surgeons', *The Times* (5 April 1989), 10

26   See Eva McLaren, *The Scottish Women's Hospitals* (Glasgow, James MacLehose, 1919) and Lady Frances Balfour *Dr. Elsie Inglis*

(London, Hodder and Stoughton, 1918).
27 McLaren, ibid. , 329.
28 Bell, 166.
29 McLaren, op. cit. , 373.
30 Margaret I. Balfour and Ruth Young, *The Work of Medical Women in India* (London, Oxford University Press, 1923), 182.
31 Balfour, ibid. , 32.
32 Walsh, op cit. , 342

SELECT BIBLIOGRAPHY

Balfour, Lady Frances. *Dr. Elsie Inglis*. London, Hodder and Stoughton, 1918.

Balfour, Margaret, I and Ruth Young. *The Work of Medical Women in India*. London, Oxford University Press, 1923.

Bell, E. Moberly. *Storming the Citadel: The Rise of the Woman Doctor*. London, Constable, 1953.

British Medical Council. *The Book of Glasgow*. Glasgow, Alex Macdougall, 1922.

Chaff, Sandra L. , ed. *A Bibliography of the Literature on Women Physicians*. New Jersey, Scarecrow, 1977.

Checkland, Olive and Margaret Lamb, eds. *Health Care as a Social History: The Glasgow Case*. Aberdeen, Aberdeen University Press, 1982.

Chigston, T. L. 'The Medical Schools of Scotland', *Scottish Review* 23 (Jan. 1894).

Coutts, James. *A History of the University of Glasgow*. Glasgow, James MacLehose, 1909.

Drachman, Virginia S. 'The Limits of Progress: The Professional Lives of Women doctors 1881–1926, *Bulletin of the History of Medicine* (March, 1986).

Hamilton, David. *The Healers: A History of Medicine in Scotland*. Edinburgh, Canongate, 1981.

Jex Blake, Sophia (1). *Medical Women: A Ten year's Retrospect*. Edinburgh, The National Association for Promoting the Medical Education of Women, 1888.

Jex Blake, Sophia (2). *Medical Education of Women: A Comprehensive Survey of Present Facilities*. Edinburgh, The National Association for Promoting the Medical Education of Women, 1888.

Lovejoy, Esther Pohl. *Women Doctors of the World*. New York, 1957.

Lutzker, Edythe. *Women Gain a Place in Medicine* New York, McGraw Hill, 1969.

McLaren, Eva. *The Scottish Women's Hospitals*. Glasgow, MacLehose, 1919.

Medical Directory, 1899–1950. London.

Medical Register, 1899–1950. London, General Medical Council.

The Medical Who's Who, 7th ed. London, 1925.

Murray, Dr. Flora. 'The Position of Women in Medicine and Surgery', *New Statesman* Vol. II (1913–14): 1 November 1913 Special Supplement.

Patrick, John. *A Short History of Glasgow Royal Infirmary*. Glasgow, Glasgow Royal Infirmary, 1940.

Thorne, Isabel. *Sketch of the Foundation and Development of the London School of Medicine for Women*. London, The Women's Printing Society, 1915.

Todd, Margaret. *The Life of Sophia Jex Blake*. London, Macmillan, 1918.
Walsh, Mary Roth. *Doctors Wanted: No Women Need Apply: Sexual Barriers in the Medical Profession 1935–1975*. New Haven, Yale University Press, 1977.

5

'YE NEVER GOT A SPELL TO THINK ABOOT IT.'
YOUNG WOMEN AND EMPLOYMENT
IN THE INTER-WAR PERIOD:
A CASE STUDY OF A TEXTILE VILLAGE*

JAMES J. SMYTH

INTRODUCTION

This chapter is concerned with young women workers in a textile village in Fife during the inter-war years. Historical background is provided on the linen industry in the area and on the employment of women and children in the nineteenth century. The chapter focuses, however, on the experiences of women who entered the labour market in the 1920s and 1930s and draws largely on oral testimonies. Particular attention is paid to the extremely limited range of jobs available to these women, to the initial impact of starting work in the Mill and to the question of authority and control exerted over young women at work and at home.

The experience of young women workers has attracted little attention from historians. While women in paid employment have been a subject of study and debate since the beginning of the factory system, most work has focused on married women, as if the fact of young women going out to earn was unproblematical.[1] Although the early working lives of young men have received detailed attention, there have been no studies of young women similar to those undertaken by Ferguson and Cunnison on 'Glasgow boys'.[2] Perhaps this absence can be explained by the differing social expectations of women and men's employment career. While most men would work for nearly all their adult life, women, in general, would only expect to be in paid employment for a relatively short period, until they married and had children. Paid employment in this instance refers to regular, full-time, paid work done outside the home. Married women continued to work both in the home without pay and outside the home in paid jobs which tended to be casual and/or part-time.

The sudden decline of women aged twenty-five or older in paid employment 'owed everything to the impact of matrimony upon the female labour market'.[3] But did this period of leaving school and 'earning' a living

*The research on which this chapter is based was carried out as part of the ESRC's Social Change and Economic Life Initiative. I am grateful for the support of the University of Edinburgh team. I would particularly like to thank Jan Adams for her invaluable work in transcribing the taped interviews.

have no meaning or value for women themselves? Was it simply a case of marking time until they got married? Given that the majority of young women would go out to work and were prepared to leave home in order to do so[4] it is surely of interest what this common experience meant to women.

It has been pointed out recently that the figure of the factory- or mill-girl was not typical of women workers in the nineteenth century.[5] Yet, while it is clear that there is a need for more industry- and locality-based research on the particular nature of women's 'work' experience, the sheer scale of the textile industries as sources of employment for women makes them impossible to ignore. Young workers were in particular demand at textile factories, which very often were the major employers in specific localities. Going from school to the mill may not have been a universal experience for women in Scotland but it certainly was a common one. Given the significance of the linen industry in Fife over the centuries and its location in numerous centres throughout the county, it would appear to be an ideal case-study in the history of women's work. Linen was the main manufacture of Scotland in the eighteenth century[6] and remained the largest single industry in Fife throughout the nineteenth century.[7] Although Fife is most commonly associated with the coal-mining industry, it was only in the twentieth century that coal replaced linen as the largest employer.[8] While the former has received considerable attention from historians, the latter has, by comparison, been neglected.[9] Given that in the 1950s over one-fifth of all employed males in Fife worked in the coal industry it is hardly surprising that it should have received the attention it has, but the neglect of linen is surely more than partly due to it being a predominantly 'female' industry. Despite its continuing decline, the linen industry in Fife remained a significant source of employment throughout the first half of the twentieth century and beyond: in Kirkcaldy Burgh, for instance, linen remained the largest employer of both men and women until after the First World War[10] and in 1951 it was once again employing more people than coal.[11]

The village of Prinlaws only came into existence in about 1798 when the construction of a flax-spining mill, dressing shop and bleachfield was started.[12] The need to attract workers necessitated building houses and so an archetypal 'factory village' was created. This industrial complex went through a series of changes of ownership until it was purchased in 1828 by John Fergus, who continued to build up and develop the site; by 1836 Prinlaws employed some 320 people and by 1858 some 1500, making it the largest linen concern in Fife.[13] The Prinlaws Mills remained in production until 1957 when the firm suddenly ceased trading. Prinlaws was situated right beside the Town of Leslie; although there was never any natural barrier between them it was only with the closure of the Mills that Prinlaws became part of the Burgh of Leslie. Until then, Prinlaws 'might even [have been] described as a small kingdom'.[14]

The control that the firm exerted over the workers and inhabitants of the village makes Prinlaws a very distinctive case. The 'company village' was not an unusual phenomenon in the early 1800s – in fact, it was rather the norm for factory production – but what is unusual is that such a situation should have lasted into the second half of the twentieth century. The power of the firm lay in the double control it enjoyed, providing both jobs and housing, with one being dependent upon the other; even at the point of closure the firm still owned all the 200-odd houses it had build over the years. This is not to say the authority structure of Prinlaws remained unaltered from 1800 to 1957 – over a century and a half fundamental changes did occur – but it is important that the extent of 'paternalist' authority held by the company be fully recognised.[15]

HISTORICAL BACKGROUND: WOMEN AND CHILDREN IN THE LINEN INDUSTRY

The manufacture of linen, as of other cloths, was traditionally undertaken in the home as night-time seasonal work and was extremely labour-intensive. Although the whole family could be involved there was a clear division of labour whereby it was always women who spun the yarn and men who wove the cloth. Amongst women the knowledge of spinning would appear to have been almost universal, as most women worked at least part-time at the spinning wheel in order to supplement the family income. The linen industry expanded enormously during the eighteenth century – to such an extent, in fact, that it became the largest source of employment in Scotland apart from agriculture – and did so not through mechanical, factory production but by increasing the total numbers employed and increasing individual productivity.[16]

Maxine Berg has pointed out how, in the cotton industry, improved technology allowed the 'direct producers' to take advantage of increased productivity while the new 'machines' were still located in a domestic environment.[17] This window of opportunity was not to last long but it can also be evidenced in linen which was slower to develop into factory production than cotton. In Leslie Parish (where Prinlaws is situated), by the end of the eighteenth century but before the introduction of mills, technological changes not only increased employment opportunities for men and women, but increased their earnings. Over a generation, the time spent by women at the wheel had increased as had the amount of thread they produced; from a previous weekly output of one-and-a-half spindles of yarn, women were now producing two-and-a-half spindles. The crucial innovation was the two-handed spinning wheel, 'unknown in the parish' before 1770 but used exclusively by the 1790s.[18] There was no immediate or complete revolution in the production processes of the linen industry, since flax was a particularly difficult fibre to work with. By 1800 there were around twenty-five water-powered linen mills in Scotland, all located in the east.[19] Mechanical improvements continued to be made, however; by 1815 machine-spun yarn had supplanted hand-spun except in the very fine ranges and steam-power had been introduced into the mills.[20] By 1839 there were five flax mills in Leslie Parish – powered mainly by water but with one steam-engine in operation – which together employed 456 people. Of this total workforce 337 (or 74 per cent) were female, 260 (57 per cent) were under the age of 21 and 101 (22 per cent) were under the age of 16. No children under the age of 12 were employed (or were admitted to by the employers).[21] Given that the total population of the Parish for 1841 was 3625, the importance of the spinning mills in the local economy is quite clear. Between 1821 and 1841 the population of Leslie Parish grew by almost two-thirds; this increase resulted from the development of the linen industry – in particular, the building of spinning mills and bleachfields.[22]

According to the New Statistical Account, which refers to the position in 1836, there were 6 flax mills in the Parish employing some 200 people. Although approximate, the latter figure gives us a clear indication of the growth of employment in the industry (even with the closure of one mill) in just three years. The Account also states that there were 260 handloom weavers and a further 140 workers employed in three bleachfields.[23] If we add these to the number given as working in the flax mills in 1839 we get a grand total of 856 people employed in the flax industry, that is, 23.6 per cent of the total population for the Parish in 1841.

Once established, John Fergus bought over neighbouring mills and rebuilt his own. With the growth of Prinlaws the demand for labour could not be satisfied from within the village itself. We know that in the 1920s and 1930s young women from neighbouring villages (especially from mining areas) came to work in the mills, often having to walk some distance in the process; presumably, this had been occurring for some time.[24] However, the 'core' workforce consisted of those who lived in the company-owned houses in Prinlaws. In 1891 (the latest date for which we can extract details from the Census) there were some 1023 people living in Prinlaws; this group accounted for 26 per cent of the total population of Leslie Parish (3886 persons).[25] There were 548 persons listed as economically active in Prinlaws in 1891, of whom 430 (78.5 per cent) worked in linen. There were no handloom weavers left in Leslie Parish by 1891[26] so all those employed in linen would have been industrial workers and almost certainly employed in the mills and bleachfields of John Fergus & Co. This workforce was predominantly female: of the 548 economically active persons, 305 (55.7 per cent) were women; of the 430 employed in linen, 270 (62.8 per cent) were women. There were very few opportunities for work outside the mill or bleachfield; 65.8 per cent of economically active men were employed in linen while for women this proportion reached 88.5 per cent.

Tables 1 and 2 provide detail on the employment of young people in the linen industry for the Leslie area in 1839 and 1891. Table 1 is extracted from 'Factory Returns' which aggregate the five mills in Leslie in 1939 and, as such, includes more than the Fergus Mills.[27] Table 2 is extracted from the 1891 census schedules and deals only with the population of Prinlaws. As

TABLE 1. Age and Sex of young persons employed in flax mills, Leslie Parish, 1839

| | Males | | Females | |
Age	No. employed	% employed	No. employed	% employed
10	-	-	-	-
11	-	-	-	-
12	-	-	2	0.6
13	14	11.8	13	3.9
14	18	15.1	14	4.2
15	15	12.6	25	7.4
16	4	3.4	19	5.6
17	2	1.7	7	2.1
18	14	11.8	61	18.1
19	-	-	24	7.1
20	-	-	28	8.3
Total Under 21	67	56.3	193	57.3
21+	52	43.7	144	42.7
TOTAL	119	100.0	337	100.0

Source: PP 1839 (41) XLII, *Returns Relating to Fctories*
(This table refers to the males and females employed in the flax mills of Leslie Parish in 1839. It details the numbers employed at each age and what proportion of they represent of the total male and female workforce.)

such, it represents only a proportion of the total workforce in the Fergus Mills but does include workers in the bleachfield. The two tables are not, therefore, strictly comparable but would appear to be as close a comparison as we are likely to get.[28]

Perhaps the most interesting and surprising contrast between the two dates is the lack of very young children employed in 1839. The Factory Act of 1833 restricted the employment of children under 9 years of age in all textile factories apart from silk mills. In 1835 the number of hours worked by children under 12 was restricted to 48 per week; in 1836 this restriction was applied to all children under 13. Given this limitation of hours, which made it necessary to employ some children for 8 hours in mills geared to 12-hour shifts, there was a pressure on employers to employ children of 13 and above. However, it was recognised at the time that many children were being fraudulently certified as being older than they really were.[29] That the latter was the reason for the absence of children under 11 is likely, especially given the evidence of employers to the Factory Commission of 1833 in which there was virtual unanimity over the need to get children into the Mill at a very early age if they were to become good spinners.[30]

TABLE 2. Age and sex of young persons employed in linen. Prinlaws, 1891

Age	Males		Females	
	No. employed	% employed	No. employed	% employed
10	2	1.3	2	0.7
11	–	–	5	1.9
12	5	3.1	5	1.9
13	9	5.7	4	1.5
14	23	14.5	9	3.3
15	9	5.7	16	5.9
16	4	2.5	11	4.1
17	10	6.3	20	7.4
18	6	3.8	17	6.3
19	2	1.3	10	3.7
20	3	1.9	10	3.7
Total Under 21	73	45.9	109	40.4
21+	86	54.0	161	59.6
TOTAL	159		270	

Source: Census Manuscript Schedules 1891, Country of Fife.
(This table details the numbers of males and females employed in linen at each age and what proportion they represent of the total male and female workforce.

In 1874 the full-time employment of children under 14 was prohibited, with the exception of those who had a certificate proving that a certain educational standard had been reached. In 1891 an Act was passed prohibiting the employment of children under 11, though this did not come into effect until 1893.[31] In 1901 the age limit was raised to 12 and in 1918 exemption from school was disallowed, though this legislation operated only from 1921 onward.[32] For most of the nineteenth century, therefore, following the legislation of the 1830s, there was little change in the age at which children could enter the Mill and the world of paid employment. It was only in the mid-1890s that the number of young people employed began to fall again; this can be seen as the beginning of a new period of child protection which culminated in 1921 with statutory full-time education up to the age of 14.

The notion of childhood as a sheltered or protected period in the life-cycle of the individual became extended over the course of a century until children aged 13 or under could no longer be employed either full-time or half-time in *any* industry. How thoroughly enforced the legislation was is an open question – children certainly continued to take a variety of part-time jobs such as delivering milk or newspapers – but formal entry into the world of paid employment was now postponed until the age of 14.

In the transition from childhood to adulthood one can identify a number of key ages: at 14 one left school and started work; at 19 one was entitled to receive an adult wage; at 21 one came of age in society as a whole and had (if one were a man) the right to vote. However, both men and women remained 'children' in a sense as long as they continued to live in their parents' house. It was only through marriage and setting up their own home that young people became full members of the adult world. Deciding on any particular age as the dividing-line between childhood and adulthood, therefore, is problematic but one can regard 'young workers' as those under 20.

The core group of workers for the mills at Prinlaws was composed of young women. Tables 1 and 2 both show a higher number of very young (i.e. those 14 and under) boys than girls. However, the number of boys over 14 years declined rapidly while the relative number of girls increased dramatically. This was because for most boys there was no future in the Mill; they were employed as cheap labour and knew they would be paid off at 19 when they could expect a 'man's wage'. Boys did not train in spinning, since this – as in Dundee[33] – was a wholly female trade. The handful of young men still employed in Prinlaws in 1891 (Table 2) at ages 19 and 20 would likely continue in the mills permanently as tradesmen, labourers or foremen. In contrast, most girls would expect to continue working in the mills as spinners and piecers. Women would leave the mills when they got married but if they did not marry they could spend the rest of their lives working in the Mill. They could not expect to become forewomen, however.[34]

A direct comparison of Tables 1 and 2 appears to show that towards the end of the nineteenth century men constituted a larger proportion of the labour force than before and that this labour force was getting relatively older. However, Table 2 only includes those workers from within Prinlaws itself; all of the oral evidence suggests that the workers from outside the village were exclusively female and young. In 1891 women workers comprised 81.5 per cent of the total workforce in flax and linen in the County of Fife and women under 20 accounted for 36.6 percent.[35] This compares to the situation in Leslie Parish in 1839, when women as a whole and women under 20 made up 73.9 per cent and 36.2 per cent of the total workforce respectively. If anything, therefore, the role of women in the industry had increased during the latter half of the nineteenth century and the proportion of young women employed remained much the same. Unfortunately we do not have the same detailed information as regards age for the inter-war years but it is clear that, while the proportion of men employed increased, the linen industry remained a female-dominated industry. In 1921 in the County of Fife women still accounted for over 73 per cent of the total workforce in the manufacture of flax and hemp.[36] The oral evidence also serves to show that, certainly as far as Prinlaws was concerned, the main concern of the mill-owners was to secure a plentiful supply of young women workers.

While the people interviewed for this study contrasted (generally unfavourably) their position as young workers in the twenties and thirties with that of subsequent generations, they made a more positive contrast with their parents' generation, particularly with regard to their own escape from the half-time system. They were also aware that this had been imposed upon the mill-owners by Government legislation.[37]

> (Mrs B) …You used to work half a day in the Mill and half a day at the school.
> *That was between twelve and fourteen, is it?*
> (Mrs B) … a lot o them went at twelve years old and did half time. They were a half a day at the school and half a day to work – some o' ma aunts did it.
> *All of you would have started work at fourteen?*
> (Mrs B) Fourteen. Oh aye.
> (Mrs C) That was the law. That was passed.
> (Mrs B) That was the law, that was the law at that time and of course ye had to wait till you were fourteen.

ENTERING THE MILL

Even if their entry into the labour market was delayed these young people were faced with the same opportunities (or lack of them) as their parents had been. Growing up in the inter-war period there was little likelihood of anything but going to work at fourteen, and for girls the choice of jobs was much more circumscribed than it was for boys. The Prinlaws labour market was a very distinctive one but, at a time of persistent mass unemployment the Mills did at least provide local jobs.

> (Mr A) I think when you left school in the thirties, like say I left school in '36, you would get a job of some kind. I don't think y' had any doubt that you would get a job, no matter what it wis.[38]
> (Mr G) There were nae shortage o' jobs. If you worked in – if yer faither or yer folks worked in Prinlaws there were a job for you tae. Irrespective.
> (Mrs G) Oh aye, that wis one thing, yes, if there wisnae at the time ye werenae long in gettin' one…
> (Mr G) There were nae question o' you gettin a job – you got a job. The job was there waitin' on you.[39]

On reaching the age of fourteen, therefore, the vast majority of children in the village went into the Mill more or less automatically and more or less immediately. There was no period of grace between being a child at school one day and the next day, literally the next day, being a young worker. As a rite of passage into the adult world this was brutally abrupt and there was nothing provided at school – certainly no career guidance – to prepare one for the transition.

> Was the first job, or the only job you got right from the age of fourteen straight into the Mill?

(Mrs B) Straight from the school one day and into the Mill the next day.

As quick as that....?

(Mrs B) Yes. Ye never got a spell to think aboot it.

(Mrs C) Ye didnae get a chance.

(Mrs B) I was actually – my birthday was in May and I didnae start in July.... I didn't start work til July because there was no... I didnae start workin' then til July because I had missed the leavin' date y' see which was in April and my birthday was on the sixth of May so I got another two or three months grace before I went into the Mill but I left the school on the Wednesday and was in the Mill on the Thursday. I know it is unbelievable to the young ones noo.[40]

Although this generation, especially the women, were more likely used to working in the house than following generations, and many boys may have had milk rounds and so forth, and they all remember school as being strict, the shock of Mill life was still real. This is partly indicated by an ex-foreman who recalled that his most difficult task was disciplining the young fourteen-year-old girls who, when they first started, worked in groups as 'shifters'.[41] More directly, the 'subjective' memories of the women themselves leave no doubt about the trauma they experienced. One women recalled how she had not wanted to work in the Mill and how she cried every night for six weeks after starting.[42]

No one interviewed recalled looking forward to working in the Mill. Everyone remembered that, for one reason or another, they did not want to go there. Some women came to terms with the job, and one woman positively enjoyed her work, but for others the sense of waste and resentment remains. Mrs B: 'And I used to stand and say to maself when I was workin'. "Is this really what we got a brain to do – stand here and do this?" I used to say that every day.'[43] Whatever ambitions the girls may have harboured, they were dashed by the reality of work in the Mill:

(Mrs B) Why I didna like Prinlaws workin' wiz because I wanted to be a nurse and I thought, 'Well, I'll go til I'm sixteen and maybe I'll get away when I'm sixteen'. Ah, but sixteen came and went and I says, 'Well, maybe I'll get away when I'm eighteen' [laughter]

(Mrs D) There wasnae any...

(Mrs C) No, didna get nothin'.

Do you think girls like you, when they were goin to leave the school, that they had ambitions to be something else, or.[...]?

(Mrs B) Oh, yes, Definitely.

(Mrs C) Certainly.

(Mrs B) Circumstances were against them – that was the only thing.

(Mrs C) There's nane o' us dunderheads, de ye ken, dull or onythin like that but yet ye had to go to the Mill to work that nae matter what ye wanted to dae, if ye wanted to better yerself ye'd had it.

(Mrs B) It was just taken for granted.

(Mrs C) You went to Prinlaws Mill, no matter how clever...

(Mrs B) An' ye never thought o' defyin' yer parents at that time. Ye never thought about it. Ye just hoped they would allow ye to do a thing but never....[44]

Mrs B said more about her desire to be a nurse on a later occasion and how it was circumscribed by the material needs of the rest of the family. Her statement came in reply to a question I asked about Prinlaws wanting to retain those women who had been trained on the job:

Oh they did because I mean you had to train somebody else obviously to start the work but they always had an ongoing thing because I mean the young ones just automatically went intae the Mill. I wanted tae be a nurse but I knew perfectly well that I had to help tae bring up the other three below me so I jist had tae abandon a' these ideas. I would have loved to go intae nursin'. But there it was, ye jist had tae go where the work wiz. Of course it wiz difficult tae get intae nursin' at that time.[45]

WORK AND FAMILY

Once they started in the Mill the girls were set to work as 'shifters', i.e. they lifted or shifted the bobbins for the spinners: empty ones on to the frames and full ones off.

(Mrs B) Well, the little bobbins I was speakin' about were put on frames an' the stuff was brought from big, thick, as thick as yer finger, rollers – down and it was spun on to thur wee ones. Well they had abut ten girls used to go round a' these frames an' shift a' these bobbins. Take the full ones off and put the empty ones on an' they called them shifters an' that was yer first job was doin' that an' yet every so often once these frames were a' changed an' ye had a wee rest an' then it was time to go an' do them again once they got filled up an' they did that a' day.

(Mrs C) Roond an' aroon'.

(Mrs B) Borin'. [Laughter][46]

(Mrs G) I mean I started as a shifter. I had to pit the fu' pins aff an' pit the empty ones on. The auld type o' frame an' that went on fur twa or three year. Ye went fi there, as I say, tae the Misses shiftin' an' then the piecers an' then efter, if a frame come vacant, if anybody retired 'n they had frames ye got a frame an' then you were a spinner an' then the shifters come in an' did that wi' your frames if ye ken what I mean...[47]

Apart from the new discipline of factory work itself there was also the length of the working day for young people to contend with. There was some confusion among interviewees over exact starting and finishing

times, partly due to the enforced shortening of the working week in 1935/
6. This circumstance was particularly clear in one woman's mind because
she started work towards the end of 1935.[48] Mrs D: 'I was lucky my birthday
was in October and I was lucky compared to them because they worked fi
six o'clock in the mornin' to six at night but I only did that October,
November, December and then in January they started startin' at a quarter
to eight in the mornin' to half past five at night.'

There is no doubt that prior to 1935/6 the starting time at the Mill was
six a.m., though it is unclear whether the working day finished at five or six
in the evening. There were two breaks during the day – for breakfast and
lunch.[49] Mrs G: 'Aye. when I started work it was six o'clock in the mornin'.
Six to nine then we had an hour for breakfast and then fi ten to one an' then
we had an hour for dinner an' then two to five an' then they altered the
'oors.'

This was a long day by anyone's standards – though interviewees were
aware that they worked shorter hours than their parents – and the firm took
precautions against anyone sleeping in:

(Mr G) Ye had tae be doon at the Mill at six o'clock in the mornin' and'
they blew the Mill horn...
(Mrs G) Aye they blew it twice. At six in the mornin'. They blew it at
twenty minutes to six. This was fur ye tae get up. An' then...
For the whole village?
(Mr G) Aye the whole place.
(Mrs G) Ye heard Prinlaws horn for a long time. An' the six o'clock
one was fur ye tae start....
(Mr G) You had to be there fur six o'clock fur the second one goin'...
But everybody got their alarm call at twenty to–
(Mr G) Aye, ye would dash doon the hill when the second blew, ye
had to go some.
(Mrs G) We got – I had to get up at the back o' five o'clock to start –
when I started at fourteen year old.[50]

The added necessity of household chores, particularly for girls, made
the day even longer.

(Mrs B) Oh, we worked from mornin' to night. When my mother
used to do her blankets we worked in the Mill and we were up to four
o' clock in the mornin' helpin her do the blankets. Before we went
and started at six o'clock til nine...
(Mrs C) And there was nae washin' machines when it come to
blanket time. Wi had to tread them.
(Mrs B) Tread them. We went in the tub an' thingme'd them wi oor
feet.
(Mrs C) And ye stamped them wi' yer feet.
(Mrs B) An' then they went through the mangle.
(Mrs C) Tread them doon an' through the mangle then inti the rinse.
All the children helped?

(Mrs B) Oh yes. Everybody had their job. As everyone came up to work the one that was oldest at school had to do all the boots in our house, a' the boots an' then once they went to work they got off wi' that chore but the next one comin' up had ti do it. And my father he worked, ye know wi' lime an' a' that sort o' thing, and ye used to get a' the lime covered wi' blackenin' and ye use to drop them an' the lime fell off an' they were a' white again and ye had to go an' do them again. [Laughter] Aye, they wiz the sort o' thing ye had to put up wi'. And then the girls had to help. They had a' their chores to do.

...Oor brithers just used to disappear – away roamin' the hills an oot playin' football an' we had to work so hard.
Did the men do anything in the house?
(Mrs B) In the house? Did they hang! They never did a hand's turn. They kept their gardens....[51]

The financial reward for all this toil was not great: at 14 the girls were paid 9s 4d per week in the Mill; at 15 their wages went up to 12s and there were further increments after that. When a girl eventually graduated to become a reeler or a spinner her wages became significantly larger; e.g., Mrs D, a spinner who operated two frames, was paid £1 8s 9d per week. For boys the wages were much the same; Mr H recalls his first wage being 9s per week when he started in 1926.[52] Like the girls, there was an annual increase until they reached nineteen, at which point most of the 'boys' were paid off since they were now entitled to a 'man's wage' or a 'journeyman's wage'.[53]

These wages were not, however, the exclusive property of the young workers. They were an integral part of the family's income and were expected to be surrendered to their parents. One man worked for ten months in the Mill when he was fourteen while he waited for an apprenticeship with a local joiner.[54] Mr A: 'Well, when I started work my mother said, "You'll start payin' your way now." I had nine shillings a week so probably give her aboot five shillings, something like that and I would hae the rest tae masel.' Possibly because he was a boy or, more likely, because he was the youngest of the family with a brother and sister already working, Mr A was actually being allowed to keep a relatively large proportion of his wage. His wife was in no doubt that 'he was better off then me', since she got only one shilling a week pocket money, and that when she was sixteen. However, there was no sense of any resentment in her recollection. She simply understood that the money was needed by her family and that she was still a child in her parents' house. Mrs A: 'I gave my mother my wage because my mother needed it but if I needed anything my mother always bought if for me. I didn't have to want for anything... I always gave it to my mother and I got my pocket money...'[55]

That the money they were allowed to keep for themselves was called 'pocket money' shows just how young they were. This was brought out well in conversation with one woman who recalled that she was allowed to keep her very first wage – all 8s 9d (she was also a youngest child). After that, however, she handed everything over to her mother and got 1s pocket money which was spent on: going to the pictures, 3d; a poke of chips, 1d; a bag of sweets, 1d; a comic, 1d and 6d left over.[56]

It does not appear that boys were treated any differently from girls in this respect; any differences were a result of differing family situations. Thus, one man who started work in a mill in Dundee in 1916 recalled, 'When I started first of all I was lucky if I got a penny.'[57] He was also the youngest of the family, but his mother was a widow and the family's situation fairly precarious. Another man, who started work in Prinlaws in 1940, recalled getting 2s 6d, but he was an only child whose parents could even afford a holiday.[58] Another man, more or less the same age as the second but from a large family, remembered having to 'work' before he had left school. Mr K: 'Before I left the school I worked wi, I delivered milk in the mornin' an' I delivered messages at night an' I think I got five shillins for the milk an' I got seven an' six for deliverin' an' I handed a' a that over, I mean it wisnae mine's, it wiz ma mither's. Ye ken there wiz eight o' us in the hoose, ye ken.'[59]

It was, therefore, laid out at the very beginning that their wages were not their own. As they got older, however, things gradually got more relaxed and they either retained more money or had more money given to, or spent on, them. It would appear that so long as children remained at home the final word went to their parents; parents, in turn recognised that their children were entering an adult world which demanded money. Of course, as they got older they were also earning more so, proportionately, their pocket money may simply have remained the same.

(Mrs C) We gave up wur wages, Oh yes.

(Mrs B) Every penny till the day we were married.

(Mrs C) We didnae pay fur nae food or nuthin' like that.

(Mrs B) There was nothin' like that then an' nobody went away and got a flat on their own or anything like that.

(Mrs C) ...I mean if ye were needin' clothes yer folk bought them tae.

(Mrs B) Aye, til ye were aboot gettin' married. Aye. Ye began to get a wee bit choice – no much – a wee bit. If it was too dear ye were told in no uncertain manner that ye werenae gettin' it and that was it.[60]

All the people interviewed recalled that their upbringing had been strict, yet even where parents had meted out corporal punishment, no-one felt that they had been treated cruelly or unkindly. Parental discipline was simply not questioned and was seen as being 'hard but fair' or as evidence of parents' protectiveness towards their children. 'We used tae think it wiz terrible – funny how the other ones get to go about and yet he'll no let us go. I suppose it's like everything else – it's just the mother and father sort o' shelterin' their family'.[61] The emphasis placed upon discipline and respect was a constant feature of young people's lives, not only at home but also at school and at the Mill.

(Mrs C) Ye went – ye respected yer teacher – ye respected the
Heedmaster. When ye met him, 'Good morning Sir!' And the laddies
doffed. They did ... ye had tae dae it. And it wiz the same wi' the
bosses doon in, the heid yin doon at Prinlaws Mill. Ye know the men
doffed their hats but when Mr Porter or Wylie or ony o' them showed
up – 'Here's the maister comin.' They doffed their hats.[62]

At such a point strictness enforced social subordination. There is no
recollection whatever of Prinlaws Mills ever experiencing a strike or
anything even remotely approaching an industrial dispute. Maintaining
discipline on the factory floor was the responsibility of the foremen or
'gaffers', the owners and managers being far too remote to play a direct
role. All the gaffers were men, although, interestingly, there was a memory
of a woman gaffer during the First World War. Even among women who
did not start work in the Mill until well after the War there was a clear
recollection of this woman and that she had been 'a good gaffer'.[63] However, she was replaced once the War was over. Again, there was common
agreement that the gaffer himself played a big role in determining how
pleasant or otherwise were the working conditions since he had the power
to allocate 'good work' to those who were 'his favourites' or 'rotten work'
to those he did not like. One man in particular was remembered, even fifty
years later, as 'a cruel man', and women who had not worked in the Mill
knew of him through their families and by reputation.[64] One young girl in
particular felt persecuted by this gaffer but knew there was little or nothing
she could do about his behaviour since there was no procedure for voicing
grievances or complaints to the managers. Recollection of incidents like
this brought out a slightly different perspective on the virtues of obeisance.

(Mrs C) But y' see at that time ye didni talk back.

(Mrs B) Ye widnae dare.

(Mrs C) You were feart to talk back.

(Mrs B) You would have been out.

(Mrs C) No' like hoo they are now. They'll tell them where to go.

At the same time this was not simply a question of attitude. Behind it lay
the threat of unemployment. Girls may have been needed by the Mill but
none of them were indispensable, 'Because bad as the jobs were there were
people always standin' waitin' fur your job, y' know.'[65] Although the
young women had no means of gaining redress by themselves, the power
of the gaffer did not go completely unchecked. In this instance the girl was
eventually given peace once her mother decided to act. Mrs C: 'I said, "I'm
no goin' back. That's me finished. I'm no goin' back." I couldna face that
man ony mair, because he was so cruel. So my mother just oot the door and
she caught him. He lived on an ootside stair an' she pinned him against the
wall and she tore into him. She did indeed and he flew awa into the hoose.
He was terrified.'[66]

The significance of this incident is that it shows the continuing strength
of the child-parent relationship: if the young worker really had been an

independent actor she would not have needed her mother's intervention. In this village, moreover, the link between home and work was especially close due to the 'tied' nature of mill-workers' houses. All the houses in the village were owned by the company and were only let to families on condition that they provided labour to the mill. Specifically this meant girls. One ex-foreman informed me that in order to get a company house people had to sign a missive that their daughters would work in the mill.[67] Prinlaws houses were remembered as being basic and lacking in modern amenities but, nevertheless, there was a constant demand for them since there was no alternative source of quality housing; the rents were cheap and were deducted directly from wages, and being in a company house meant that one's daughters were likely to get employment. That it was young women's labour that was most demanded by the Company is shown by the experience of one family:

> (Mrs L)…We were all born at the East End [of Leslie] … then when we were beginning to grow up – well ma Dad got to Prinlaws Mills, ye see? Well, ye jist got a house if ye had girls comin' up so' they would get intae the Mill. That's how we managed t' get a house. We had three girls ye see? So that's why we had t' go t' the Mill t' work because we had got a house down in Prinlaws… I would be about twelve years old when we flitted to Prinlaws but these were the conditions you got the houses if you had girls that would work in the Mill, you know?[68]

The nature of the Prinlaws labour market encouraged families with daughters to come to the village as well as women who were single or left to bring up their children on their own. In 1891 the proportion of female heads of households in Prinlaws was 43.4 per cent whereas in the wider district only 24.6 per cent of households had a woman as head.[69] Furthermore a higher proportion of female heads of household in Prinlaws were single, unmarried women: 38.5 per cent as compared to 28.8 per cent in the wider district.[70] However, this preponderance of women both in the mills and in the community does not explain the lack of industrial organisation or militancy. As Walker has commented on Dundee and the jute industry, 'to the extent that organisation was poor, the explanation may lie not in the number of females in the industry, but in circumstances which were bound to weaken organisation among males and females alike.'[71] If Dundee textile workers were disadvantaged in their efforts to unionise in comparison to the cotton workers of Lancashire,[72] it is not hard to see how much more difficult it must have been for workers in a 'feudal' environment such as Prinlaws.[73]

The authority the company enjoyed through its double control of housing and employment ensured a largely quiescent workforce. In the case of the behaviour of the gaffer referred to above it is clear that there were limits beyond which parents were not prepared to let their children suffer, but given the responsibility which the girls had to their families –

their continued employment being necessary to secure the house – it is hardly surprising that there were few outward signs of militancy. It is interesting that the women who lived in the village recalled the girls who travelled to the mills from the mining villages as having a completely different attitude to the bosses:

> (Mrs B) They got young girls in and brought them in on buses from Ballingry and Glencraig and Lochore of all places and Methil and they didn't stand that nonsense. They were real tartars... They could swear like men and they didnae give a hang for them... They came from the right places, y' know where the miners, where the unions were strong and they thumbed their nose at the bosses and, eh, they were brought up the same.[74]

CONCLUSION

What historical work there has been on young women workers generally falls into two separate camps: that which emphasises the link between work and home in terms of continuing parental control and authority, and that which sees girls at work enjoying a brief flirtation with freedom, a period of carefree self-indulgence. These two positions have their own gender division. The former is argued by women authors whose research is largely based upon the direct oral testimony of working women themselves;[75] the latter is argued by men who tend to rely on contemporary evidence collected by middle-class (and mainly male) social investigators.[76] The view of young women regarding their early working life as a short moment in which they were free to please themselves and enjoy life to the full is well expressed by Standish Meacham:

> The great majority of young factory girls, if they did not look upon work as a lark, viewed it as a daily penance to be accepted as natural, and endured uncomplainingly as payment for the pleasures it provided. To hand over even as little as a shilling or two as her own contribution to the family's weekly earnings and to spend all that remained on whatever struck her fancy: the gratifying self-importance implicit in both these delightfully adult-seeming actions left the factory girls without much need for further ambitions or goals.[77]

Meacham is aware that such a carefree outlook was not possible for other girls employed in domestic service or as shop assistants.[78] Yet it must be asked just how realistic a description of factory girls' experience is it. Elizabeth Roberts flatly contradicts Meacham's account of how the independence young workers gained through their earning power led to an inverted state of affairs in which parents became dependent upon their children.

> The oral evidence would seem to offer a different interpretation; there is no evidence of parents feeling dependent upon, or beholden to, their offspring. Standish Meachams's interpretation overlooks the immense moral authority which parents continued to wield, and

the great respect their children continued to show well into adult life, in most cases until the death of the parents. It was this all-pervading moral and ethical climate which ensured that in all but the most prosperous working-class families, young people's wages were handed over intact to their parents (almost invariably to their mothers), and their financial independence voluntarily given up.[79]

This view of the continuing power and reality of parental authority is supported by the work by Bornat and also by the evidence collected in the current study. At the same time we have to be aware that where women are looking back – over half a century or more – with the hindsight of (in most cases) having brought up families of their own they may have exaggerated, understandably, the degree of authority and control they experienced and their own meekness and obedience. Yet the memories and descriptions of the women in the village were consistent with one another and clearly based on actual experience. However, the relationship between young people and authority was more subtle than immediate impressions might suggest, and is well expressed by one woman's comment, 'No, no, ye didnae step oot o' line unless ye did it very discreetly if ye did.'[80]

Once conversation had moved on to descriptions of how, as young people, the women had enjoyed themselves, then cracks began to appear in the structure of this apparently authoritarian community. Despite the demands of work, both in the Mill and at home, the young women still had the energy and compunction to enjoy themselves in a relatively spontaneous and unrestricted fashion; more than one woman described herself as having been 'dancin' daft'.[81] Dances provided the perfect opportunity for going out with girlfriends or in larger mixed groups and, of course, for meeting boys. The young people of the village might venture as far afield as Dundee or Edinburgh to visit one of the big Dance Halls such as the Fountainbridge Palais but, more usually, they went to a local hall or walked to a dance in one of the nearby villages. Certain ruses and stratagems might be needed in order to get to a dance, such as pressing a sister to act as chaperone or pretending to go to the Choir while smuggling out the dancing shoes. Not everyone was keen on 'the dancin' but those who were remembered it with great enthusiasm:

> I thoroughly enjoyed ma life at that time. My father – we were goin' too often though – he put his foot down and put a stop tae us goin' so often. Of course sometimes ye were goin' three times a week, you know. It was ridiculous because ye were workin' long 'oors in the Mill and I've seen us goin' out to a Friday night dance, of course ye were loathe tae get up in the mornin' tae go tae yer work as he cried, 'If ye can dance a' night ye can work.' And that was us. [laughter] Ye were standin' there half sleepin'. But, oh, we had great times then…[82]

It is important to a full understanding of the lives of these women that such vivid memories of pleasure and enjoyment be given recognition. However, they hardly support Meacham's view that this period in a young girl's life was one of carefree gratification. If we need to be aware of the natural distortions of recollection we must also be wary of the biases inherent in the contemporary sources. It is clear that many middle-class observers were shocked by the independent spirit displayed by working girls, be it displayed in their clothes or even in how they walked and talked. Meacham provides many examples of this type of reaction; one commentator on girls in the East End of London, for instance, remarked about their interest in fashion, that 'It is a pathetic little outburst of vanity in most of them... After marriage they relapse into the hopeless slatternliness of their childhood.'[83] It is not that Meacham is unaware of the subjectivity of such sources – but an over-reliance on such witnesses nevertheless leads to a badly focused image of what young working women were really like. In the case of the women described in this article it is very likely that a middle-class social investigator observing a group of girls walking home after midnight in the company of boys after a night's revelry at a dance might find his or her sensibilities outraged, especially if the next day was a working day.

The experience of full-time employment after school represented a mixture of freedom and responsibility for young women. The fact that they were earning a wage did not make them independent; they continued to live at home and remained under their parents' authority. There was no contradiction in being expected to go out to work and still being regarded as a child – their own parents would have started work even earlier than fourteen. The majority of women stopped work when they married but this does not mean that they had gone to work simply to fill in time before marriage. Certainly, in a textile village such as this, marriage was a possibility, whereas working in Prinlaws Mill was more or less a certainty. Mill work was not looked forward to by girls but was understood by them as an unavoidable necessity. It is easy to isolate this period from the rest of women's lives and divest it of any meaning but, whether the time spent at work was good, bad or indifferent, it was, nonetheless, an integral part of each woman's life experience.

NOTES

1 The recent excellent overview by Elizabeth Roberts, *Women's Work 1840–1940* (Basingstoke & London, 1988), has a separate chapter on married women but no specific treatment of young women.

2 T. Ferguson & J. Cunnison, *The Young Wage-Earner: a study of Glasgow Boys* (London & New York, 1951); see also C. E. B. Russell *Manchester Boys* (Manchester, 1905).

3 J. Treble, 'The Characteristics of the Female Unskilled Labour Market and the Formation of the Female Casual Labour Market in Glasgow, 1891–1914', *Scottish Economic and Social History*, Vol. 6 (1986), 33–46, 35.

4 The Women in Scotland Bibliography Group, *Women in Scotland:*

    an annotated bibliography (The Open University in Scotland, Edinburgh, 1988), 21.

5 *Women in Scotland*, op. cit.

6 A. J. Durie, *The Scottish Linen Industry in the Eighteenth Century* (Edinburgh, 1978), v.

7 *Census of Scotland* 1891.

8 *Census of Scotland* 1901.

9 A number of books spring readily to mind which deal with mining and miners in Fife both on their own account and as part of general studies of the coal industry: R. Page-Arnot, *A History of the Scottish Miners From the Earliest Times* (London, 1955); B. F. Duckham, *A History of the Scottish Coal Industry, Vol 1, 1700–1815* (Newton Abbot, 1970); S. MacIntyre, *Little Moscows* (London, 1980); I. McDougall, *Militant Miners* (Edinburgh, 1981). There is no specific study of the Fife linen industry although Fife is covered by Durie, op. cit. The recent collection of essays on Scottish textiles by Butt and Ponting has no contribution on Fife and linen; J. Butt & K. Ponting (eds), *Scottish Textile History* (Aberdeen, 1987).

10 Census Report, 1921; 3rd Statistical Account.

11 *Census of Scotland 1951*.

12 G. P. Bennet, *The Past at Work*, (Markinch, n.d.), 66.

13 Ibid.

14 A. Hunter, *The Auld Toon o' Leslie* (Leslie, 1957), 67.

15 The whole question of the paternalism of industrial employers in Fife is dealt with by Smyth & Morris, 'Paternalism as an Employer Strategy', Social Change and Economic Life working paper ESRC/ 30 No. 11.

16 One estimate (by Naismith) for the 1780s gave a figure of 170 000 women who were mainly employed in spinning yarn. Cited in Durie, op. cit., 159.

17 M. Berg, *The Age of Manufactures 1700–1820* (London, 1985), 239.

18 *Statistical Account of Scotland*, 1978 edition, 'Parish of Leslie', 580–1.

19 Durie, op. cit., 95–6.

20 Ibid., 96.

21 PP 1839 (41) XLII, *Returns Relating to Factories*.

22 *Census 1851*, 'Houses in populations of Parishes'.

23 *New Statistical Account Vol IX* (Edinburgh & London, 1945), 'Parish of Leslie', 119.

24 All the oral testimonies refer to the mining girls walking to Prinlaws. By the later 1930s there were bus services operating between the villages.

25 Population figures for the Parish taken from *Census 1891* and for Prinlaws; all figures extracted from the manuscript schedules held in New Register House.

26 Bennett, op. cit., 56.

27 PP 1839 (41) XLII).

28 The format of the Tables follows the information provided for 1839.

29 Board of Trade Labour Department, *Changes in the Employment of Women and Girls in Industrial Centres. Part 1 – Flax and Jute Centres* (London, HMSO, 1898), 15, 20–1.

30 Factory Commission on the Employment of Children in Factories, Minutes of Evidence, Vol 1, PP 1833 (450) XX. James Aytoun, who

owned two mills in Abbotshall was 'of [the] opinion that unless children begin to spin at or before twelve years old, they never become good spinners'. James Peter, manager of the Kirkland works: 'Spinners are never so expert or dexterous who do not begin early; at all events before twelve years old.' William Punt, overseer at Fergus's mills, 'is satisfied that women will not be good spinners in their lifetime unless they begin at the age of from nine to fifteen years of age'. Alexander Boswell, one of the owners of Boswell & Co's mill at East Prinlaws: 'Spinning can never be well learned but by young people, not more than twelve years old.'

31 M. Cruikshank, *Children in Industry* (Manchester, 1981), 174; Board of Trade, Labour Department, *Statistics of Employment of Women and Girls* (London, HMSO, 1894), 16.
32 Cruikshank, op. cit, 175.
33 William M. Walker, *Juteopolis: Dundee and its textile workers 1885–1923* (Edinburgh, 1979), 35.
34 In living memory in Prinlaws there had only ever been one woman 'gaffer', but this occurred during the First World War and the woman had been forced to give up her position after the armistice. See p. 108.
35 *Census of Scotland* 1891.
36 *Census of Scotland* 1921.
37 Inter 2. The interviews on which this chapter is based were conducted under the aegis of the ESRC Social Change and Economic Life Initiative. This work represents part of the project undertaken by the research team at the University of Edinburgh which was a study of family life and labour in Kirkcaldy District over the past one hundred years. Interviews were conducted with men and women from two specific communities who (mostly) entered the labour market during the 1920s and 1930s. In all over forty interviews were made.
38 Inter 1.
39 Inter 4.
40 Inter 2.
41 Inter 17.
42 Inter 3.
43 Inter 2.
44 Ibid.
45 Inter 5.
46 Inter 2.
47 Inter 4.
48 Inter 2.
49 Inter 4.
50 Ibid.
51 Inter 2.
52 Inter 7
53 Ibid.
54 Inter 1.
55 Ibid.
56 Inter 3.
57 Inter 7.
58 Ibid.
59 Ibid.
60 Inter 2.

61 Inter 6.
62 Inter 2.
63 Inter 2.
64 Ibid.
65 Ibid.
66 Ibid. This cruelty was not restricted to girls but was also practised on boys. The same gaffer humiliated a cousin of this girl by putting his head down a toilet pan. Summing up this man, Mrs C made the damning remark, 'He wouldna face another man up – boys and lassies.'
67 Inter 17.
68 Inter 9. This woman already had an older brother working in the Mill as well as her father but the family only got a house once the girls were almost of working age.
69 Census manuscript schedules, 1891, County of Fife. The district in mind is the area which conforms to the current boundaries of Kirkcaldy District.
70 Ibid.
71 Walker, op. cit, 36–7.
72 Ibid.
73 More than one respondent used the word 'feudal' to describe the control over the village enjoyed by the owners.
74 Inter 2.
75 See Elizabeth Roberts, *A Woman's Place: an oral history of working-class women* (Oxford, 1984); Joanna Bornat, '"What about that lass o' yours being in the Union?": Textile Workers, and their Union in Yorkshire, 1888–1922', in Davidoff & Westover (eds), *Our Work, Our Lives, Our Words: women's history and women's work* (Basingstoke & London, 1986).
76 See Standish Meacham, *A Life Apart: the Engish Working Class 1890–1914* (London, 1977); Peter Stearns, 'Working Class Women in Britain, 1890–1914', in M. Vincinus (ed.), *Suffer and Be Still: Women in the Victorian Age* (Bloomington, 1972); see also *Lives of Labour: work in a maturing industrial society* (London, 1975).
77 Meacham, op. cit., 183.
78 Ibid., 189.
79 Roberts, op. cit., 42.
80 Inter 2.
81 E.g. Inter 1.
82 Inter 5.
83 Helen Bosanquet, *Rich and Poor* (London, 1896), quoted in Meacham, op. cit., 190.

SELECT BIBLIOGRAPHY

M. Berg. *The Age of Manufactures 1700–1820*. London, Fontana, 1985.

J. Bornat. '"What about that lass o' yours being in the Union?": Textile Workers and their Union in Yorkshire 1888–1922'. In Davidoff & Westover, eds, *Our Work, Our Lives, Our Words: women's history and women's work*. Basingstoke and London, MacMillan, 1986.

M. Cruikshank. *Children in Industry*. Manchester University Press, 1981.

A. J. Durie. *The Scottish Linen Industry in the Eighteenth Century.* Edinburgh, John Donald, 1978.

S. MacIntyre. *Little Moscows.* London, Croom Helm, 1980.

S. Meacham, *A Life Apart: the English Working Class 1890–1914.* London, Thames & Hudson, 1977.

A. Pollert. *Girls, Wives, Factory Lives.*London, MacMillan, 1981.

Elizabeth Roberts. *Women's Work 1840–1940.* Basingstoke and London, MacMillan, 1988.

Elizabeth Roberts. *A Woman's Place: an oral history of working-class women.* Oxford, Blackwell, 1984.

T. Ferguson & J. Cunnison. *The Young Wage-Earner: a study of Glasgow Boys.* London & New York, Oxford University Press, 1951.

C. E. B. Russell. *Manchester Boys.* Manchester 1905.

J. Sarsby. *Missuses and Mouldrunners: an oral history of women pottery-workers at work and home.* Open University Press, Milton Keynes, 1988.

P. Stearns. 'Working Class Women in Britain, 1890–1914'. In M. Vincinus, ed., *Suffer and be Still: Women in the Victorian Age.* Bloomington, Indiana University Press, 1972.

P. Stearns. *Lives of Labour: Work in a maturing industrial society.* London, Croom Helm, 1975.

J. Treble. 'The Characteristics of the Female Unskilled Labour Market and the Formation of the Female Casual Labour Market in Glasgow 1891–1914'. In *Scottish Economic and Social History* Vol. 6 (1986): 33–46.

W. M. Walker. *Juteopolis: Dundee and its Textile Workers 1885–1923.* Edinburgh, Scottish Academic Press, 1979.

6

IN BONDAGE:
THE FEMALE FARM WORKER IN SOUTH-EAST SCOTLAND
BARBARA W. ROBERTSON

THE WORKING AND LIVING CONDITIONS OF THE BONDAGER

There was a lot of female labour on the Border farms at that time, and some of it was free and jolly and some of it was rather coarse. But Mrs Graham was a dignified old lady with small hands. Although she spoke the Border dialect and although I always saw her dressed in working clothes, yet there is no other way in which I can describe her. She had such extraordinary grace and poise. They said she was seventy at that time, yet except for her furrowed face and her white hair she looked quite young. Her waist was gimp [slender] as any maiden's although she had borne three children, her step was firm and very light, her blue eyes set in her brown face looked proud and unafraid. She wore a wide hat trimmed with artificial poppies, a grey blouse with white pearl buttons, a grey cloth skirt that came just below her knees, black stockings and elastic-sided boots... I always felt in the presence of nobility when I spoke to Mrs Graham.[1]

This passage describes the harvest-field scene on a Berwickshire farm in the year 1916. The opening sentence could apply just as accurately, however, to the same farm scene in 1866. Or perhaps even in 1826. For women out-workers, or bondagers, as they were called, were a feature of the farm workforce throughout north Northumberland and the south-east counties of Scotland from early in the nineteenth century to well into the twentieth.

Who were these bondagers, what work did they do and what was their status in the agricultural community of their times? 'Bondage' originally denoted serfdom, or service due from a tenant to his superior; a bondager, therefore, was one who performed bondage service. In the early nineteenth-century agricultural scene of the Border counties it was the responsibility of the farm servant, or hind,[2] to provide a woman out-worker, or bondager, to work on the master's farm. The bondage system, as it was called, had evolved following the radical agrarian reforms of the previous century. Many of the arable farms of south-east Scotland were in the forefront of the Improvement Movement and saw the development of new crops, grasses and rotation systems. As the land was worked more and more intensively under the new methods not only a large and stable workforce but also seasonal labour, for peak periods of activity such as grain harvesting, were required.[3] There were few villages in the Borders at this time; the farm workers, therefore, came from the cottages on the farm itself.[4] With a limited number of dwellings on a farm, each house had to provide more than one worker.

Part of the hiring bargain struck for the year between hind and farmer was an agreement that in lieu of paying rent for his cottage the hind would provide a woman worker to help at harvest time.[5] The woman worker would receive no pay from the farmer other than victuals. There was also work for her at other times of the year, however, and this would be paid for by the farmer at a daily rate. Provision of a female worker was thus part of the bond made between hind and farmer, and farmers as a result had a ready supply of male and female servants at hand to ensure that all the tasks of the improved farming were carried out over the entire year.

Fenton describes the post–Agricultural Revolution farm scene, and the broad pattern of the year's work:

> The shaping of the new farms, neatly enclosed and with fenced fields worked in an established rotational cycle, led to an annual farming rhythm that did not differ so much from that of the old community, except that it was more structured in the terms of management and had a definite market orientation. It was a rhythm that involved winter ploughing, the daily feeding and cleaning of animals, the weekly driving of stacks to the barn for threshing, an intensive round of ploughing, harrowing, sowing and rolling in spring, the driving of muck to the fields, the opening and mucking of drills for turnips and potatoes, the hay and corn harvest, and the long-drawn-out pulling of turnips in the cold days when the beasts were again indoors.[6]

In many of the tasks associated with this farming year both men and women took part, the women being particularly adept, for instance, in the use of the sickle, a grain-cutting tool which was later superseded by the scythe. This latter, being larger and heavier, was a man's tool.[7] The areas of work where the management of horses was involved were male-only areas, and this was a basic pattern of labour division which lasted well into the twentieth century. In all other farm activities, however, ranging from the spreading of muck in the fields and the weeding and singling of turnips, to the gathering-in of the harvest, the women worked alongside the men throughout the year, in all kinds of weather.

As a means of obtaining labour in the early decades of the nineteenth century the bondage system was certainly advantageous to the farmer. For the hind it worked reasonably well when he had a female member of his own family – either his wife or daughter old enough to work. But for any hind with, for instance, small children and a wife not free to do the required outside tasks, including the vital harvest work which represented the rent payment for the cottage, the situation was more difficult. In order to complete his own bond with the farmer, the hind was obliged to engage a female worker for the year – that is, one farm servant had to hire another. The female worker had to be paid by the hind at an agreed yearly rate as well as housed by him; the hind, in turn would be paid by the farmer at a daily rate of pay for the days the bondager was actually employed in farm work. In short, every hind had to 'supply a female labourer, his wife, or daughter, or hired servant, to be employed in the work of the farm for daily pay, except during harvest when her work is given as for rent of the house which he occupies'.[8] The bondage system, it was noted by another writer, was 'found convenient, and even necessary, to the various operations of a farm in thinly peopled districts'.[9]

These statements, written in the 1830s by contributors to the New Statistical Account,[10] give a matter-of-fact précis of what in human terms was a far from simple situation. The bondage system served the needs of the land well; it appeared to be generally accepted; but it had created two different kinds of female bondager, one being a family member and the other a problematical non-family addition to the hind's home. Three such problem areas are immediately obvious: finances, housing, and social and moral questions arising from this latter.

A detailed account of the financial arrangements between master and hind given in the Fogo, Berwickshire, parish account indicates the potential economic problems:

> Hinds or yearly servants working a pair of horses, receive 14 bolls of grain, a cow summered and wintered, ground for planting half a boll of potatoes, producing 10–12 bolls; £4 in money; four double carts of coal (48 bolls) driven, and a dwelling house and small garden for vegetables, of the value of £2 – for which last they find a shearer in harvest, the tenant (farmer) furnishing victuals, as he does to all his labourers in harvest. A hind's gains are estimated at £30. If he has children above ten, they are employed and paid for work in the fields, which adds to the income of the family. The hind is also bound to keep a bondager for out-of-door work at the master's call, who pays for the bondager, when employed, 10*d* a day.[11]

Payment in kind – an arrangement which, with modifications in the items included, lasted into the twentieth century – was an important and valuable part of the hind's livelihood, his actual cash payment of £4 being a small proportion of the overall gains 'estimated at £30'. The hind without a female family member available for work, however, had to pay out '£6.10s to £7' a year to a hired bondager; in return for her work on the farm he would receive from the farmer 'from 8*d* to 10*d*' for any day she worked (excepting harvest, as described above). At 8*d* a day the bondager would have to have 195 days of paid work from the farmer before the hind recovered his £6.10s; there might be occasions therefore, when he was out of pocket.[12] In addition, of course, the hind was giving his bondager board and lodging for the full year. As the Morebattle parish account reports, there were complaints from the hinds and allegations that the incoming cash from the farmer barely balanced with the outgoing cash to the bondager and that therefore they, the hinds, were giving the bondager 'victuals for nothing' for the whole year.[13] This complaint from the hinds was ultimately to be one of the factors which led to the abolition of the bondage system in the 1860s.

Throughout the New Statistical Account there is no indication of what the bondager herself felt about her work and wages in the 1830s and 1840s, or of how she used the money she earned. There is an occasional comment on 'the dress of the female peasantry' which, in the opinion of one parish minister, was 'in many cases too gaudy and expensive for their station'. 'The straw bonnet' he added, 'of various shapes and hues, is very general'.[14] Can it be inferred from this that the average bondager spent all her £6.10s on dress and frivolity? Perhaps some did, but it is equally possible that at least some of the bondagers, after any expenditure on working clothes, would have given their earnings to help parents with younger children to bring up. Others may have saved some money in the local Savings Banks, perhaps towards the day of their marriage.[15]

Clearly the main beneficiary, in economic terms, of the bondage system and the exploitation of the women workers as cheap labour was the farmer. Women on farms were not of course alone in being thus exploited: society in general throughout the nineteenth century regarded women, whether wives or daughters, as dependents who were not entitled to the same rate of pay as their male counterparts. The Border hiring system, 'which combined in an effective working relationship, a corps of skilled plough-men and large numbers of low-paid women'[16] was a reflection of this attitude.

If the women, and at times the hind, lost out economically in the work situation, was there perhaps recompense in their housing conditions? The answer is no. One writer of the period describes their dwellings, with some justification, as 'hovels';[17] a more restrained report admits that, while farm houses and farm buildings had been greatly improved by the 1830s, there was 'still great room for improvement in the houses of the hinds'.[18] This is indeed somewhat of an understatement. The majority of hinds' dwellings in the first half of the nineteenth century consisted merely of one room, with a floor of beaten clay, and lacked even the barest of fitments; the farm servant had to bring his own kitchen grate bars and swee (rod for hanging cooking vessels over the fire) for instance. Box beds formed a partition of sorts between kitchen and room-end. The task of making the house habitable lay entirely with the occupant, who started off with an almost bare structure and had to transform it, as best he could, into a dwelling place for himself and his family.[19] In many cases the worker lived in conditions less comfortable than those of the animals he tended throughout the day.[20] Two possible reasons for the low standard of housing are spelled out in the Whitsome parish account: non-resident landlords; and the mode in which 'an incoming tenant takes all the buildings off his predecessor's hands, who is merely under the obligation to leave the cottages *habitable*, a term which needs no comment'.[21] This, then, was the kind of accommodation which housed the hind, his wife, his family of all ages, and a non-related female bondager.

In view of the crowded conditions in the majority of hinds' cottages it is a little surprising that the minister-reporters of the 1830s parish accounts in the NSA have so little to say about the social and moral aspects of the bondage system. Their comments on the home life of their farm-worker parishioners tend to relate to material factors rather than moral ones. They commend, for instance, the standards of cleanliness in many cottages, the possession of books and the educational achievements of their parishioners, and write with approval of the 'sober, industrious, contented character' of the workers.[22] Nowhere, it is averred, can be found a 'more intelligent, moral and well ordered peasantry than our own agricultural population',[23] though one more realistic voice adds that 'some, as in every community, are of a different character'.[24] The outspoken comments in 1841, however, from just over the Scottish border in the north Northumberland parish of Norham, where a similar bondage system operated, give a much more down-to-earth appraisal:

> How common decency is preserved, how unutterable horrors are avoided, is beyond all conception... It shocks every feeling of propriety that ... civilised beings should be herding together without a decent separation of age and sex. So long as the agricultural system, in this district, requires the hind to find room for a fellow-servant of the other sex in his cabin, the least that morality and decency can demand, is, that he should have a second apartment, where the unmarried female and those of tender age should sleep apart from him and his wife.[25]

Civil registration of births was not introduced until 1855; prior to this date any such information was recorded in the parish records. The accuracy of these varied considerably, however, and a true picture of any population increase, whether legitimate or illegitimate, is not always possible to construct.[26] Yet from the population figures included in the individual NSA accounts some indication of the 'moral' standards can be gleaned. Legerwood parish, for instance, with a population of 565, an average number of births over the previous seven years shown as almost fourteen, and some eight illegitimate births in the preceding three years, thus had a ratio of illegitimate: total births approximating 1:5.[27] For Bunkle parish, however, with a population of 740, the report states that there was 'only one illegitimate birth for several years'.[28] And Whitsome, with a population of 664, also reports a low number of illegitimate births, making the ratio there approximately 1:18.[29] Many of the parish accounts make no mention at all of illegitimacy. Indeed, in several of the reports, the word 'moral' is used not in relation to female chastity or the lack of it, but in association with activities such as smuggling or poaching.[30]

These, then, were some of the views and comments by outsiders on the social and moral aspects of the peasantry's living and working conditions in the early decades of the nineteenth century. The thoughts and feelings of the hind and his family on the subject, however, or of the bondager housed with them, were not to be openly articulated and willingly heard until some years later.

The picture thus presented of the lives of these male and female farm servants of south-east Scotland during the years in which the bondage system tied them not merely to the farmer but to the land itself, is not only one of hard work and poor living conditions but also one of great endeavour to bring about change. The workers on the land were still in a feudal relationship with the farmers but so also, to a certain extent, were the tenant farmers to the landlord.[31] A class system was emerging or indeed had emerged, with a pecking order of landlord, tenant farmer, farm servant and, apparently at the bottom, the hired female bondager. Life revolved around the farm, for although the worker was no longer faced with the possibility of starvation as his forebears in pre–Agricultural Revolution days had been, his way of life and his very income were governed by the land. Deprivation there undoubtedly was, but compared with conditions that prevailed in the bothy system counties north of the Forth or in the lives of many urban workers, the Border farm servant, whether male or female, was certainly better off. As Smout points out, it was indeed a 'hard, tough life, but the hind of south-east Scotland was the best paid and best fed of Scottish farm workers of the 1840s'.[32]

There was also the variety and companionship of farm work; the social life of the often highly populated farm itself; the satisfaction of bringing in a good harvest balanced against the misery of other tasks on the farm such as cutting turnips on cold frosty mornings. Life was all of a piece: work and home were interwoven and though work was often dirty and unpleasant, and home life was far from comfortable by present-day standards, the alternative occupation for the daughters of the farm servants – domestic service – was not necessarily any better, and at times might even have been worse. Robson writes;

> Impromptu and everyday pleasures, like the smell and taste of oatmeal porridge bubbling ready for the hungry labourer, an evening dance in the farm kitchen to the music of the hind's fiddle, the fresh milk produce, or just a fine spring morning in the country, made life much more tolerable, and it is certainly not possible to accept that the life of a Border farm worker prior to, say, 1850, was one of downtrodden misery, drudgery and squalor.[33]

AGITATION AGAINST THE BONDAGE SYSTEM

By the mid-nineteenth century agriculture in south-east Scotland was not only thriving but was acknowledged throughout the country as representing the best in modernised farming. This prosperity was to continue over the next two or three decades.[34] The part played by the workforce in achieving this laudable state did not go unnoticed, however, and the injustices inherent in the bondage system began to be more openly highlighted, with the argument invariably returning to the need for more and better housing for the hinds and their families. The various strands of anti-bondage activities were to interconnect and gradually tighten around the system, making its demise assured by the last quarter of the century. Among the agents of change were the Highland Society, the Church, the Registrar General, the farm people themselves and, in the 1860s a Royal Commission on female agricultural labour.

The Highland and Agricultural Society had originated at the end of the eighteenth century primarily to help and advise landlords and farmers in matters agricultural; by the early decades of the nineteenth century it had widened its remit to include the welfare of the work force. By the 1840s the subject of workers' housing had been taken up, and architects were producing designs for cottages and submitting them to this 'ever active Society' in the hope of winning a premium.[35] Ploughing matches and harness competitions, at which prizes and inscribed medals could be won, were introduced and became part of the ploughman-hind's way of life, continuing not only throughout the nineteenth century but also into the twentieth.[36]

In 1853 a voice from the Church spoke out on behalf of the agricultural labourers and their social conditions; the Reverend Harry Stuart delivered an address to the Forfarshire Agricultural Association in which he attacked both the bothy system and the bondage system, spelling out the 'debasing' situation of a (non-family) bondager: 'Picked out at random from among hundreds that are offering themselves as bondagers in a public market, by a man they likely have never before seen or heard of, and that man himself but a servant on the lowest scale.'[37]

In his lengthy and wide-ranging paper, Stuart comments that hinds themselves are anxious to get rid of the system. He quotes Adam Smith in support of the view that country labourers cannot combine to complain as those in town can, and argues that the emigration lists bear witness to complaints made 'in the ploughman's own way, viz. leaving in dogged silence when aggrieved'.[38] The solution he advocates for many of the wrongs is the building of more and better cottages. Not only would this do away with the bothy system, he argues, but in the south-east it would relieve the overcrowding in cottages by allowing earlier marriages; there would thus be more families on each farm, but 'less immorality, and families [would be] grown up and able to look after themselves by the time parents were old'.[39]

A few months after the delivery of this paper, an Association for

Promoting Improvement in the Dwellings and Domestic conditions of Agricultural Labourers in Scotland was formed 'to stimulate exertion towards the required improvements' and to 'cooperate cordially with local agricultural and cottage societies, and especially with the Highland Society'.[40] The Chairman of this Association was the Duke of Buccleuch, one of the Border landlords already in the forefront of the movement for improvement to buildings; the Honourable Secretary was the Reverend Stuart. The 'social conditions' of farm servants throughout lowland Scotland had become a matter of concern and demanded remedial action.

The third quarter of the nineteenth century was to witness a vast improvement in much of the south-east farm workers' accommodation and even by the 1860s some farms had implemented major changes.[41] In the early fifties further 'relief came in the form of a rent-free house', making it possible – theoretically – for men to find engagements without having to furnish a woman worker to do unpaid harvest work in lieu of cottage rent.[42] Those who had a female outworker, however, were at a great advantage in the hiring market; they remained thus until the end of the century and, indeed, well into the twentieth.

A national, as opposed to agricultural, factor which further contributed to the routing of the bondage system was the publication in 1858 of the Registrar General's statistics relating to illegitimacy rates throughout Scotland. Two unexpected points in these statistics were that rural areas showed a much higher ratio of illegitimate births to total births than did urban areas and that there was great variation in this ratio throughout Scotland. In the south-east, the county of Berwickshire, though by no means the worst, was among the higher grouping.[43] Questioning of the home and working conditions of the rural workers increased.

By the 1860s the workers themselves had become more vociferous against the bondage system and in this they were supported by some of their employers. An influential Kelso farmer, John Clay, writing in the Kelso Chronicle of January 1866 strongly advocated an extension of the family system of employment 'by getting our landlords to build more servants' cottages', adding that 'as a farmer I would advise the farm servants to get the grievance of the bondage system done away'. That a measure of success was achieved, at least in the Kelso area, is indicated by the statement in the Rutherford Directory for that year that the bondage system had greatly altered for the better. This was possible, the Directory explains, 'because the peasantry of the district began in earnest to agitate for its removal, and with a great amount of ability and prudence have not only carried their purpose, but have, as a rule, carried with them the sympathy of the public, and the good will of the farmers in the change.'[44]

This 'agitation' was not confined to the Kelso area but had supporters throughout the bondager counties. Indeed the bondage system was even given mention in an 1866 London 'Field' on the occasion of a prize being offered by the Reverend John Thomson of Hawick for the best essay 'by farm stewards, shepherds, ploughmen and their sons and daughters, in the counties of Roxburgh, Selkirk and Berwick, on the Evils of the bondager system, and suggestions for their removal'. The first prize, £30, was won by a Berwickshire shepherd, whose essay was reviewed in glowing terms in the London paper.[45] His primary argument concerned the economic hardship of the hind. The writer of the second-prize essay, however, Mrs Williamson from Galashiels and 'for many years a bondager' argued her case from a different standpoint.She began by pointing out that 'remains of serfdom of the middle ages' were still lingering in the form of the bondage system, went on to discuss the Money View briefly, and then wrote feelingly of the Home Circle, and of the problems of jealousy – Illegitimacy – Hind Loving his Bondager: 'We are aware we are venturing on delicate ground, but had it not been that we speak from personal observation, we would not have cared for bringing forward the subject at all.' She stressed the lack of family privacy for a hind with a bondager ever present (Bondagers Tell Secrets), and deplored also the typical situation in which a mother had to do the bondager work in order to avoid hiring a non-relative into the home circle. But bondagers also felt the evils of the system: they sometimes had to put up with poor food, or with rude and ill-governed children, while 'the husband may be vicious, and base in language and manners, and very unfit company for an inexperienced young girl'. As did Stuart some ten years earlier, Mrs Williamson advocated the building of more cottages for families, and noted that some landlords, at least, were building or had already erected comfortable and good-sized cottages on farms. 'This shews that there is a feeling of consideration for the state of the labourer abroad.'

Why should there not be an appeal to the Legislature, she then asked, pointing out how other enslaving work conditions had been altered by this means; the lot of women in mines and children in factories had been improved; changes had been made to the infamous truck system; legislation had recently been introduced to 'protect the women and children employed in the bleachfields'. Her final plea was to the hind to shake off his apathy, even though this was an apathy she could appreciate from his point of view; and she emphasised that it was not the pocket alone that was affected by the bondage system but the hind's 'social standard' as a whole. The concept of citizenship was not in current use in the mid-nineteenth century – even the male rural worker was not enfranchised until 1884 – but the writer was here making the point that every subject in the land had equal basic rights. 'Ploughmen, for the sake of your wives, for the sake of your daughters growing up to take their places as wives of hinds, seek for [the bondage system's] removal, and leave it not as an evil inheritance to your children.'[46]

Not only in the Kelso, Hawick and Galashiels areas did the farm servant voice his grievances, but in the Jedburgh district as well. Here, the discontent crystallised into the formation of a trade-union-like organisation in the early 1860s. Trade unionism among farm servants at a national level was not to appear until much later, in 1912, and the few attempts at combination in the nineteenth century by the male workers were of short duration and of little apparent success.[47] However, the Jedburgh-based Border Farm Servants Protection Society, set up in 1865, did survive for a few years. Its aim was, first, to abolish the bondage system and second, to extend the franchise. The Society gained its first objective, but thereafter membership fell off.[48] The timing of its emergence, however, was opportune in that its voice was heard at a national level by means of the Royal Commission set up in 1867 to look into the 'Employment of Children, Young Persons and women in Agriculture'.

The evidence of this Royal Commission makes fascinating reading; in their *History of British Agriculture,* Orwin and Whetham review the Commission's findings and compare Scottish with English farm conditions. They note, for instance, that in the northern counties of England (where the farming system was similar to that of south-east Scotland) the picture was brighter than elsewhere in England; in Northumberland, for example, married men still received much of their wages in kind, daughters worked in the fields, and the unpopular 'bondage system' was dying out. Orwin and Whetham comment on the 'infinite variety' of conditions in Scotland, and refer to the testimony of 'ministers, school masters, farmers, workers, labourers, women and children, ... from which a composite and very human picture of the social scene emerges'. A comparison of education in the two countries showed Scotland to advantage:

> In the rural districts of England the farmers are too often opposed to education; the labourers, and sometimes the landowners themselves, are indifferent about it... In Scotland the feelings of the people on this subject are totally different. There, all classes, farmers and servants, ministers and laymen, are unanimous in their conviction of the importance of education, and are willing to cooperate for the purpose of securing it.

But the need for better housing in rural areas is noted:

> The shortage of cottages and the inadequacy of most of them was a complaint throughout the whole country. Conditions are slightly better in the south than in the north, but the prevailing type is still one-roomed with built-in box beds, though some had two rooms. Clearly public opinion was concerned at the state of housing, and farmers testified that they got better workers, who settled down and stayed with them, on farms where there were good cottages.[49]

Although Orwin and Whetham's précis of the Royal Commission evidence is useful, the actual testimony of those who worked on the land, particularly with regard to the bondage system, gives a clearer indication of their day-to-day situation and their attitudes in general.

Ploughman's wife, Eccles, Berwickshire:

> We have four children; the eldest, 12 years old, is still at school; we

always keep them at school as long as we can afford. We bake barley and barley and peas bannocks, and kill two pigs in the year, and we've a good cow. The father and the two youngest take their porridge night and morning, but the others dinna care for them.

They say the bondage is *waur* than ever, and some of the women's asking £9 5s for the summer half-year, and I'll warrant they'll ask £5 for the winter. We're comfortably off i' the hooses, there's as much room as labouring folk want.[50]

There is no suggestion here that this family had to supply a woman outworker; it seems clear that the bondagers in the area were not meekly accepting what was offered by the ploughman-hind, but demanding a better financial deal for themselves. '*Waur* than ever' implies that they had been making these demands for some time.

Bell Fortune, a retired bondager Dunse parish:

I have a cot house from Mr. Wilson to keep a woman worker. I have what the girl wins [earns], and I have a cottage and garden free, my coals led (say four tons), 1,300 yards of potatoes, and three bushels of barley. I believe cottars used to have peas and the barley is in place of them.

I pay my girl £7 for the summer half and £4 for the winter. I can't just tell what she costs me to meat her and wash her.

I can't do much at outwork now, you may say, next to nothing; I'm 67, but I worked full work till I was 65.

The girls are much better off now than they used to be, but they dress so fine; the merchants get a good deal out of them. There was no such thing in my young days.[51]

The Commissioner adds a footnote here to the effect that 'this old woman gets her cottage and like privileges for keeping the woman worker'. The girl was not related, but was the daughter of 'well-to-do' parents, her father being the steward on a neighbouring farm. The cottage was 'very neatly kept, and both the young woman and old bear excellent characters'.

Farm steward, Coldstream parish:

I think it would be a great misfortune to the county if our young women were to give up field work, and oblige farmers to keep Highland or Irish girls in bothies. It's a great matter both for moral and religious training, to keep families together.

A labourer should begin to save money as soon as his children get out to work, and young men and women may easily save.

As to the family purse, my daughter, for instance, who is out at service, brings her money to me, and I invest it for her.[52]

There are two points to note here: first, the stress laid on keeping the family together; and second, the father's apparent control of the purse strings, at least where the daughter's earnings were concerned. The money thus laid aside would probably be for her 'bottom drawer', i.e. for use when she married and set up house.

In the following extract it is the mother who sees to the laying-out of the family income. This was the more usual arrangement, lasting into the twentieth century. The speaker, who has two daughters at home doing field work, is the wife of a hind in Ladyrig, Kelso:

> My husband is a hind, but he's no bund to keep a worker; the lasses like to stay at home and work, and it helps to school the others; they give me all they win [earn] and I buy their clothes for them; most everybody does the same in this quarter.[53]

A footnote to this account adds that the two girls, being in for their 'dinner time', were sitting near mending their clothes, while their mother was giving her evidence.

The evidence of a Bunkle farmer reveals another aspect of the bondage system, i.e. that a hind with 'surplus' daughters could 'benefit' financially, and was free to do so:

> One of my men has three daughters, only one of whom is bound to serve me, one is now away as a bondager, and the other is not bound to serve me because her father wishes to get her out as a bondager elsewhere on account of the board.[54]

A final comment, from a labourer's wife at Fairnington, Roxburgh, not only sums up the three main possibilities in women's work very matter-of-factly, but reveals prevailing attitudes to 'the bondage'. The speaker has three daughters: one in domestic service, one doing field work at home as part of her father's bond, and one doing field work as bondager to a non-relative.

> Girls in service get less than they do working out, but it takes less to keep them. Some of them incline to service in the house, but I daresay most of them likes field work better. They that have them within themselves [i.e. daughters of their own] like best to keep them at home, though I think the bondagers are just as well looked after as house servants; maybe they are not subject to such strict rules, and that's why they like it better.
>
> Young married people lose by the bondage; but I don't see that it's any injury to families, and it keeps them together to help one another.
>
> There's only two women hired into houses in this toon [farm village] though there's more than 20 bondagers [female field workers], the rest are the daughters and sisters of cottars and ploughmen.[55]

Note that this interviewee used the term 'bondager' to include both the female family member and the non-family female worker. She too stressed the family aspect. She lived on one of the largest farms in Roxburghshire, hence the large number of bondagers employed.

And what did these women workers/bondagers actually do at this time? According to one Berwickshire landlord, farm work of all kinds, with the exception of work connected with horses and heavy spade work. The various tasks would include filling and spreading manure, singling and hoeing root crops, trimming and slicing turnips for sheep, barn work, cutting and binding corn, and occasionally driving carts between the farm offices and the fields.[56] Normally, everyone worked nine hours a day but at harvest time these were extended to ten hours and to 'as long as light will allow when carrying in the harvest'.[57] The numbers employed related to the number of ploughmen on the farm: generally, one bondager per pair of horses, i.e. per ploughman, or as another Berwickshire farmer stated, 'in the proportion of $1^1/2$ women to 100 acres of arable land on farms suited for turnip culture'.[58]

Throughout the evidence there runs matter-of-fact acceptance of the fact that women did this, at times very hard, work. One landowner, however, did voice some reservations: 'I think that the turning of dung with heavy graips [forks] is rather severe work for young females; but I never heard of any injury having occurred to them in consequence.' It seems that he had other reasons for disapproving of 'roughwork' for women:

> There can be no doubt that the rough agricultural work females do
> is very prejudicial to their fitness for domestic duties, except in their
> own cottages. Their morals also must suffer: I have heard that when
> in the fields they are exposed to very foul language and improper
> liberties. I should be glad to see a restriction on female agricultural
> labour, so as to force women into other occupations more congenial
> to their sex.[59]

The most readily available other occupation 'more congenial to the female sex' would be domestic service.

Despite this landlord's concern about the effect that agricultural work might have on the morals of females thus employed, there is little if anything in the interviews with workers to show what they themselves felt on the subject. Views were sought from doctors and others outside of agriculture, however, and these at times were bluntly and emphatically expressed. One doctor described the morals of the females in agriculture as loose in the extreme, and saw this as arising from overcrowding in the hinds' cottages, whilst another medical interviewee from the same area thought differently and considered that the said morals compared favourably 'with the same class otherwise employed'. This latter view was also held by a Coldingham farmer and a Dunse landowner.[60]

The Sheriff Substitute of Berwickshire, however, drawing on 'disclosures in filiation cases in my court' put the blame in such cases on the women.[61] All of the above were male interviewees.

In his summing-up on the Morality of the Labouring Classes, the Commissioner for the Border counties suggested that their attitude towards the unwed mother should be kept in mind. 'Among her own class there is no feeling of indignation regarding her lapse from virtue' he wrote, and any such lapse 'is looked at merely as a "misfortune" because she is for a time incapacitated from earning her daily bread, but the "misfortune" is no impediment to her after-marriage, either with the father of the child or some other man'.[62]

The views of a Chirnside farmer, staunchly supporting the farm workers' character generally, are probably more representative. He pointed out that there were scarcely any serious crimes committed by the peasantry, that intemperance was exceedingly rare among them, that the only blot on their character was that 'ten per cent of the births in Berwickshire are illegitimate'. In justice to the people he knew so well he felt that other factors should be kept in view 'before disparaging the character of our community'. First, there was no prostitution; secondly, conjugal unfaithfulness was nearly unknown; thirdly, there were no manufactories or mines to absorb the increasing population, and the supply of farm cottages was such that young people had either to defer marriage until an opening with a cottage occurred for them, or leave the district. 'And in my humble view the true cause of it [illegitimacy] is the impediment to early marriage, to which I have referred.'[63]

While much blame for the high illegitimacy rate of Berwickshire, only recently made public, was being placed on the bondage system, crowded cottages, and/or the bondagers themselves, the argument collapses when the national statistics are analysed. These show that in 1861 much higher illegitimacy ratios existed in Banff (16:62), Wigton (15:56) and Perth (10:87), and none of these counties had a bondage system in operation. The causes of variation throughout Scotland were complex and discussion as to the possible causes still continues today.[64]

Although the term 'bondager' was used throughout the Royal Commission evidence it is clear that by the late 1860s the 'true' bondage system whereby hinds hired women from outside the family was well on its way out, and that a family hiring system had taken its place. Commissioner George Cully summed up the situation thus:

> What proportion of the women workers are hired by the hinds I have not the means of knowing; but I am inclined to think the proportion is very small and is gradually diminishing as the supply of cottages increases. On many farms the bondage system is entirely given up, while on others, where the hinds are still bound to provide a [woman] worker, the supply is pretty nearly provided by the families of the hired servants.[65]

THE END OF BONDAGE

By the last quarter of the nineteenth-century the bondage system had evolved into a purely familial hiring system; family togetherness, stressed so often during the nineteenth-century, continued to be the underlying leitmotif in Border agricultural life well into the twentieth-century. Farming itself changed relatively little over these decades and still required the labour of many men and women throughout the year. The family hiring system provided this. Habits die hard in rural communities, however, and though these women workers were now always members of the hind's own family, they continued to be referred to as bondagers as late as the 1930s. And, in the eyes of one observant onlooker – the leader of the Scottish Farm Servants Union, formed in 1912 – the women outworkers were still being used as cheap labour.[66]

But how did these twentieth-century women see their status? Did they feel that 'family togetherness' equated with security, or with 'bondage'? Were they content to be farm workers alongside their fathers and brothers or did their aspirations, and indeed their abilities, suggest to them that other, wider opportunities were their entitlement?

The answers are as varied as the women themselves, as a few brief examples show: 'Ah never wanted tae dae onything else: it was a grand life, an' there was aye some kind o' banter going on. There's nothing like it today – the neighbourliness and the cheeriness seem to have gone.'[67] The speaker was the holder of a Long Service Certificate from the Highland and Agricultural Society; on the farm where she lived, and where she had lived for most of her life, only two of the eight cottages were now occupied.

Margaret, another farm worker, had been in domestic service at first, but found the outside life more appealing: the fresh air, the company, and the variety of jobs throughout the year were much preferred to the inside life of a domestic servant or 'the monotony of mill work'. And at the end of the day 'ye saw something for your labours ... and had the satisfaction of seeing the end product ... of the year's work'.[68]

Jean passed all her exams for High School, in the 1920s, 'but there was all the books an' things – and we just couldna afford them. Besides, I was needed at home as my sister who worked out was getting married and faither had to have a bondager or else move to another ferm.... Looking back, ye wonder ... but at the time it just seemed ye had to do it.' She spoke of the 'hard labour' that was required at times, and of the differences between farmers in the way they treated their workers. Further conversation revealed that her mother, too, had been bright at school and had wanted to stay on 'as a pupil teacher' but, like the speaker, had been obliged to help out the family and be a bondager instead.[69] No bitterness was apparent in her disclosures about this lack of choice; whether she had felt differently in her youth is another matter. But to the observant onlooker in the Trade Union of the day, this woman was one of the 'Women in Bondage' he described in 1937 as still being 'sacrificed to the family'.[70]

With the outbreak of World War II came the beginning of tremendous change; the war years themselves were a kind of watershed between what could be termed a traditional way of life on Border farms and the emergence of a new industrialised one. Lessons learned from World War I concerning the importance of both agriculture and of the agricultural worker in wartime were applied immediately, and the farm worker's role was acknowledged at national level to be every bit as important as that of the members of the Armed Forces. Mechanisation increased rapidly during the war years, transforming much of the previous horse-power into tractor-power, and by the early 1950s the traditional Border farm scene of men with horses (and with attendant women workers) was giving way to a lonelier picture of one-man-with-machine.[71] Farm population and its associated social life of the past was changed dramatically.

And the womenfolk on Border farms? They were of course more important than ever during wartime, and the female workers who were still at home – for many took the opportunity to 'escape' from farm life and go into the Armed Forces – were joined by members of the Women's Land Army, many of whom, in turn, were 'escaping' from town and city. These 'incomers' brought with them new and different values – urban values; many were to remain in the country once war had ended, marrying into the local community and further making their contribution to social change in the countryside. For the post-war years brought many changes: a falling farm and rural population led to the closure of many small country schools and thus to the education of rural children becoming centralised in towns; travelling for pleasure replaced the earlier work-associated mobility pattern; media influence spread more rapidly throughout town and country, and so at an early age the young people on farms acquired urbanised attitudes and goals. Farm encapsulation was over, for all time: indeed, there no longer was employment on farms for sons and daughters, and so, if they wished, both could and did go on to higher education, to college and university, and to work in towns and cities.

The Agricultural Revolution of the eighteenth century created many changes throughout the land, but the effects of the mid-twentieth century Industrial Revolution in agriculture were possibly even more far-reaching. As machinery on farms increased, so did the work force decrease; the 'hard labour' was taken out of much of the agricultural work itself, and the 'farm servant' became an 'agricultural employee' with, as in other industries, nationally agreed wages and work conditions. Men and women of the Border farms were no longer 'thirled' (bound) to the land as their forebears had been; their daughters, no longer sacrificed to the family's needs, could participate in and make use of the same opportunities as their urban-bred sisters.

The bondager had become a figure in history.

NOTES
1   Allan Fraser, *Hansel Craig* (London and Edinburgh, Chambers, 1937), 53. For a detailed account of the bondager dress, see Anne M. Scott, 'Women's Working Dress on the Farms of the East Borders', *Costume* no. 10 (1976), 41–8.
2   Hind, or ploughman, or ploughman-hind. For the purpose of this essay, the terms are interchangeable.
3   For more details of what was a long and complex period in agricultural history, see J. A. Symon, *Scottish Farming Past and Present* (Edinburgh, Oliver and Boyd, 1959) chapters 7, 9.
4   Michael Robson, 'The Border Farm Worker', in T. M. Devine (ed),

Farm Servants and Labour in Lowland Scotland 1770–1914 (Edinburgh, John Donald, 1984), 72, 76.

5   Hiring Fairs provided the market place for the selling and buying of the farm servants' labour. Reasons for their geographic mobility are given in B. W. Robertson, 'The Border Farm Worker 1871–1971: Industrial Attitudes and behaviour', *Journal of the Agricultural Labour Society* (later became *Agricultural Manpower*), vol. 2, no. 2 (December 1973) 80–1.

6   Alexander Fenton, *Country Life in Scotland* (Edinburgh, John Donald, 1987), 46–7.

7   T. M. Devine, 'Women workers, 1850–1914', in T.M. Devine (ed), *Farm Servants and Labour in Lowland Scotland 1770–1914* (Edinburgh, John Donald, 1984), 101–2. The change from sickle to scythe changed the female role in the harvest field from that of grain-cutter working alongside the men to that of grain-gatherer, working behind the men, thus introducing a sexual division of labour. See William Howatson, 'Grain Harvesting and Harvesters', in T. M. Devine (ed), *Farm Servants and Labour in Lowland Scotland 1770–1914* (Edinburgh, John Donald, 1984), 139.

8   The New Statistical Account of Scotland, hereafter referred to as NSA (Edinburgh, 1842), Berwickshire, 353.

9   Ibid., Berwickshire, 78.

10 The ministers of the respective parishes.

11 NSA, Berwickshire, 227.

12 Ibid., Berwickshire, 173. In today's currency £6.10s is £6.50 and 8*d* is $3^1/_3$ pence.

13 Ibid., Roxburghshire, 453.

14 Ibid., Roxburghshire, 292.

15 Ibid., Berwickshire, 79.

16 Devine, op. cit., 101.

17 W. S. Gilly, *The Peasantry of the Border … an Appeal on their Behalf* (First published 1842. Reprinted Bratton Publishing Limited, Edinburgh, 1973), 16.

18 NSA, Roxburghshire, 451.

19 R. Shirra Gibb, *A Farmer's Fifty years in Lauderdale* (Edinburgh, Oliver and Boyd, 1927), 16–7; Michael Robson, op. cit., 76–7; For an overview see Alexander Fenton, 'The Housing of Agricultural Workers in the Nineteenth Century' in *Farm Servants and Labour in Lowland Scotland 1770–1914*, ed. T. M. Devine (Edinburgh, John Donald 1984), 188–212.

20 Gilly, op. cit., 6.

21 NSA, Berwickshire, 175.

22 Ibid., Berwickshire, 155, 277, 183.

23 Ibid., Berwickshire, 198.

24 Ibid., Berwickshire, 44.

25 Gilly, op. cit., 19–20.

26 NSA, Berwickshire, 139, 238, 305.

27 Ibid., Berwickshire, 353.

28 Ibid., Berwickshire, 119.

29 Ibid., Berwickshire, 172

30 Ibid., Berwickshire, 208.

31 Christabel S. Orwin and Edith H. Whetham, *History of British Agriculture, 1845–1914* (London, Longmans Green, 1964), 164–7, 170–7, 298–300. See also John Clay, *John Clay, a Scottish Farmer* (Chicago, privately printed, 1906), 70–82, 91–116.

32   T. C. Smout, 'The social condition of Scotland in the 1840s.' The Dow Lecture. (University of Dundee, 1981), 10.

33   Michael Robson, op. cit., 88. ('Farm worker' of course includes the bondager).

34   Symon, op. cit., Chapter 11, 176–189.

35   Fenton, op. cit., 1984, 198.

36   Alexander Fenton, *Scottish Country Life* (Edinburgh, John Donald, 1976), 217–8.

37   Rev. Harry Stuart, *Agricultural Labourers, as They Were, Are and Should Be, in their Social Condition* (Edinburgh, Blackwood 1854), 25.

38   Ibid., 58.

39   Ibid., 34.

40   Ibid., Appendix.

41   Fenton, op. cit., 1976, 188.

42   John Wilson, 'Half a Century as a Border Farmer', Transactions of the Highland and Agricultural Society in Scotland, 5th ser., XIV, 1902, 38.

43   Christopher Smout, 'Aspects of sexual behaviour in nineteenth-century Scotland' in *Social Class in Scotland: Past and Present*, ed. A. A. MacLaren (Edinburgh, John Donald, 1976), 63.

44   J. and J. H. Rutherford, *Southern Counties Register and Directory* (London, Longman, and Edinburgh, Menzies, 1866), Addenda, 'The Bondage System', 744.

45   London Field of March 10, 1866. Quoted in Rutherford, op. cit., Addenda, 745.

46   Mrs Williamson, 'Essay on the Bondage System' in *Voices from the Plough* (Hawick, Robert Black, 1869), 29–49.

47   Barbara W. Robertson, 'The Scottish Farm Servant and his Union: from Encapsulation to Integration' in *Essays in Scottish Labour History* ed. Ian Macdougall (Edinburgh, John Donald, 1978), 90–2.

48   *Royal Commission on the Employment of Children, Young Persons and Women in Agriculture, Fourth Report. Parliamentary Papers 1870, XIII* (hereafter *Fourth Report on Women in Agriculture, 1870*), App. Part I, 56 fn.

49   Orwin and Whetham, op. cit., 210–20.

50   *Fourth Report on Women in Agriculture, 1870*. App. Part II, 127.

51   Ibid., App. Part II, 126.

52   Ibid., App. Part II, 125–6.

53   Ibid., App. Part 1, 56. Note that the interview took place in the interviewee's own home. The 'dinner time' referred to would be two hours – a long break *so as to give the horses a rest*. The 10-hour day of the Scottish system is compared with the shorter English working hours in App. Part I, 46–7.

54   Ibid., App. Part II, 123.

55   Ibid., App. Part I, 56.

56   Ibid., App. Part II, 124, 127.

57   Ibid., App. Part II, 124.

58   Ibid., App. Part II, 124.

59   Ibid., App. Part II, 121.

60   Ibid., App. Part II, 122, 123, 125, 126.

61   Ibid., App. Part I, 81, fn.

62   Ibid., App. Part I, 80.

63   Ibid., App. Part II, 124–5.

64   Ian Carter, 'Illegitimate Births and Illegitimacy Inferences', Sc. J.

Sociology, vol. 1, No. 2, April 1977, 125–35; T. C. Smout, 'Illegitimacy – A Reply', Sc. J. Sociology, Vol. 2, No. 1, Nov. 1977, 97–104.
65 *Fourth Report on Women in Agriculture, 1870*, App. Part I, 56.
66 J. Duncan, 'Women in Bondage', Journal of the Scottish Farm Servant, IV, No. 34, Jan. 1916, 13.
67 Oral evidence: S(1) b. 1905 (based on interviews carried out in the 1970s).
68 Oral evidence: M(1) b. 1910.
69 Oral evidence: (1) b. 1915.
70 J. F. Duncan, Discussion on paper by R. Henderson, 'Some Sociological Aspects of Farm Labour', J. Agricultural Economics, IV, No. 4, April 1937, 320.
71 Robertson, op. cit., 1978, 100–2.

SELECT BIBLIOGRAPHY

There are very few secondary sources on the bondager system. A major primary source are the parliamentary papers: *Royal Commission on the Employment of Children, Young Persons and Women in Agriculture.*. Fourth Report. Parliamentary Papers. 1870, XIII.
Secondary sources:
T. M. Devine, (ed.) *Farm Servants and Labour in Lowland Scotland 1770–1914*. Edinburgh , John Donald, 1984.
Alexander Fenton, *Country Life in Scotland*, Edinburgh, John Donald, 1987.
Allan Fraser, *Hansel Craig* London and Edinburgh, Chambers, 1937.
R. Shirra Gibb, *A Farmer's Fifty Years in Lauderdale*, Edinburgh, Oliver and Boyd, Edinburgh, 1927.

7

RURAL AND URBAN WOMEN IN DOMESTIC SERVICE
LYNN JAMIESON

Domestic work has been part of the working day of vast numbers of women for centuries. Since the Victorian era 'domestic service' has come to mean paid domestic work performed by women under particular conditions: living in the house of their employer and being at the beck and call of their 'master' or 'mistress'. Prior to the nineteenth century, 'living-in' servants were not predominantly women doing domestic work but men and women performing a variety of indoor and outdoor tasks which contributed to the household economy. Moreover, servants and other household members were not a 'class apart', as all worked for the household economy under the supervision of the head of household. It is likely that something of this tradition persisted throughout the nineteenth century and even into the twentieth, albeit in diminished proportion and increasingly unrecognised as 'domestic service' became the norm.

Historians generally agree that by the end of the nineteenth century it had become rather difficult to recruit domestic servants and that this was an important factor, if not *the* important factor, in the decline of service.[1] Several authors have noted that service became a stigmatised and disliked occupation.[2] Higgs has been particularly careful to distinguish between the experiences of urban and of rural women, arguing that domestic service was only stigmatised among the former;[3] hence, he links the decline of service to the drying up of the pool of rural recruits as urbanisation advanced.

The main reason given in the literature for the increasing unpopularity of domestic service is the increase in the availability of more attractive work. While better pay, shorter hours and more freedom have been cited as giving an advantage to other types of work, the most emphasised differentiating factor is the absence of the subservient and demeaning relationship to the employer. But without a relative or friend in the city to 'speak for you' and provide accommodation, many other types of work may have been closed to rural women.

While not wishing to defend domestic service, which clearly was (and is throughout the world) work typically involving poor conditions, low pay and the patronage of the employer, the question of how and when it became 'disliked' seems to require further attention. For example, were vestiges of other systems of service left even into the twentieth century, or was it exclusively a matter of the 'well-to-do' using their superior economic position to patronise and buy service from the rural poor? Did those who employed servants always consider themselves as 'above' the work they expected of their servants? Was service always entered into as the result of lack of other work, or was it sometimes 'chosen'? Where and when, if ever, did it have redeeming features? To put it bluntly, was 'domestic service' nothing other than a system whereby one class paid women from another to do their dirty work, treating them as lesser human beings in the process, and was it generally recognised as such?

Although there are a number of studies of domestic service in England and Wales, little has been written about domestic service in Scotland. This is despite the fact that for almost a century between one in four and one in five of all Scottish women officially recorded as in employment were domestic servants. In 1976 and 1977 I interviewed Scottish men and women born around 1900, sixteen of whom were brought up in households with one or more resident servant and twenty-one of whom went 'into service'. This chapter offers some sense of the variation of experience of those 'in service' in Scotland at the beginning of this century. It explores the issue of how and when service was liked or disliked by contrasting the experiences of urban and rural women in service. Defining rural communities as those with populations of less than 10,000, of the interviewees who had been in service twelve came from a rural background, seven from an urban background and two from mixed backgrounds (see Appendix).

Some of the women quoted talk about service before the First World War, some about service during the war and some the inter-war period. It may not be correct to lump these together, since the economic context of these periods – as reflected, for example, in availability of employment, the range of work available, and the level of wages and prices – was rather different. Much more work remains to be done on the historical context of service in the twentieth century but this chapter offers another small part of the story.

TWENTIETH-CENTURY SERVANT KEEPERS

Although it is still within living memory, the extent of which service persisted as the main employment for women into this century is often overlooked. Indeed, the number of servants increased in the depression years of the thirties. (See Table.)

Without going back to the enumerators' books which form the raw material of the published census figures it is difficult to know more about the typical sorts of households in which these women worked. This type of research has been done only for the nineteenth century and suggests that, at least in the middle of the century, the situation was complex. First there

TABLE. Female 'Indoor Domestic Servants', Scotland, 1901-31
Number and percentage of all 'occupied' women

1901	143 699	24.3
1911	131 084	22.1
1921	122 248	19.2
1931	138 679	21.0

Source: Census of Scotland 1901, 1911, 1921, 1931

was not a perfect match between servant keeping and upper-class status. Secondly, there is some evidence of the persistence of the 'old style' of service. Both these points are supported to some degree by the oral history work reported here.

Higgs' research on Rochdale, England[4] has shown that roughly one-sixth of servant-keeping households were 'working-class'. But Higgs also notes that a substantial minority of all the women recorded as servants were in fact related to the head of the household, suggesting that they were not domestic servants in the 'normal' sense of being employed for wages. In successive censuses it is likely that such women were eliminated as census enumerators focused on paid employment.[5] Michael Anderson's more extensive work on the British 1851 census[6] shows that about four-fifths of households headed by a professional, an upper manager or a large employer kept at least one domestic servant, although they employed only about a fifth of all servants, while about two-fifths of the much larger group of other non-manual workers, small employers and the self-employed accounted for about two-fifths of the servants.

A similarly imperfect fit in the early twentieth century between middle-class status and servant-keeping is suggested by oral history work reported here. Although the majority of middle-class informants did have servants, in some middle-class households all domestic work was done by the women of the family. In these cases it was taken for granted both that domestic work was women's work and that it would be done by family members if at all possible; there was no sense that middle-class women should be protected from the heavier or dirtier work. One elderly woman told me scornfully, 'There was no paid help when there were three girls in the family'.[7] Some middle-class daughters themselves came close to being servants when, often due to straitened circumstances, they took jobs as governesses.

With regard to those who did keep servants, it is not clear for what proportion this was automatically a part of being of a particular class and for what proportion it was also or exclusively related to the burden of housework. My interviews suggest that for some middle-class households the number of servants varied with the family life-cycle; if the norm for the household was one or two servants, this was supplemented by some form of nurse-maid or nanny during the child-rearing years. Similarly, a household might take on a single servant only for the duration of the child-rearing phase of the family life-cycle. Certainly, interviewees who worked as the sole general maid often had child-care duties.

Oral history work on the early twentieth century indicates that working-class households employing resident or daily servants were uncommon but not unheard of. Among my respondents, one woman talked of how her father employed a housekeeper when she herself could no longer keep up with running her own and her father's house. After her mother's death, Betty 'kept house' full-time from the age of thirteen until her own marriage and thereafter, persevering until her husband's objections and her own physical exhaustion forced her to stop. Her father's household contained four working coal merchants and therefore both a substantial burden of housework and a reasonable income.[8] It was more common, however, for working-class households to buy in help on a casual basis through neighbours and their children. For example, one respondent was sent once a week to scrub the floor and kitchen surfaces for the widower next door,[9] others regularly went to get 'the messages' (do the shopping) for elderly neighbours.[10] These jobs involved small payments.

Anderson's work on the 1851 census identifies farmers as having employed large numbers of servants. Anderson and Higgs both argue that the large number of servant-keeping farmers is a likely indicator of the persistence of the old style of service in which servants worked alongside householders and their families. The same argument is made with respect to the substantial number of retailers employing servants at this time. Higgs doubtingly asks, 'Were these domestic servants rigorously segregated from the productive activities of such households, that is from agricultural production and retailing?'[11] Moreover, he suggests that this more extensive role for servants persisted until the turn of the century. He cites work on servants in Edwardian Lincolnshire which demonstrates that they were expected to tend animals, milk cows, and make butter and cheese.[12]

The oral history work reported here includes two cases of residential workers whose mix of tasks blurred the boundaries between 'new' and 'old' service. Jane's first job, for example, involved paid domestic work but is not easily classified: 'I had to come to Edinburgh to get a job and I got a job in a fruit shop and I lived in and I helped the lady that owned the fruit shop in the house, and I used to go down and I used to have to help her in the shop after that... I was just like one of the family. I lived with them, And my wages was 12s a month. I had a little room of my own. She was an old lady and she had a married daughter. Oh they treated me very well'.[13] More interviews with women who worked as servants for Scottish farmers would be needed to clarify the situation there at this time.

RURAL WOMEN AND THE AVAILABILITY OF OTHER WORK

Domestic service was the main occupation for women in most of the counties of Scotland from the mid-nineteenth through the early twentieth century.[14] The exceptions were three rural counties less dominated by the big estates and shooting lodgings of the upper class, and the counties in which the main employment was textile manufacture. For example, in 1911 there were more women working in agriculture than in any form of domestic service in Orkney, Shetland and Caithness. In the same year there were more women in textiles than in domestic service in the following counties: Selkirk, Peebles and Clackmannan, where over half of employed women were engaged in woollen manufacture; Fife, where the main employment for women was flax and linen manufacture; and Renfrew, where thread manufacture employed more women than did domestic service. In these counties, then, rural women may have been less likely to be well disposed to service. For all other counties, service was the main employer, although the proportion of women employed in service varied from over forty per cent of all employed women in Aberdeen, Arygll, Elgin, Kincardine, Kircudbright, Nairn and Peebles to a mere twenty per cent in Lanark.

As they approached the age of fourteen working-class girls knew that they would have to get a job and had some idea of what work was available to them. For many rural young women domestic service was the only option. Moreover, the work was not typically approached with either loathing or excitement, but matter-of-factly, with little idea of what they were going to. The hurt expressed by Jean Rennie[15] at going away to service was absent from many households. She was acutely aware that she was ending up doing what her mother did, wearing 'the badge of servitude' – the cap and apron; despite a secondary-school education and winning a scholarship to go to Glasgow University. Many had not had her opportunity to be aware of other possibilities.

This was particularly so for women in rural areas. As a Moray woman born in 1917 said about leaving school and home to go 'into service', 'Ye just knew what yer job was'[16] or, as it was put by a woman from West Lothian, 'In those days girls had to go to service'.[17] Molly, who lived within what would would now be considered as easy travelling distance from the centre of Edinburgh, explained that she had to go into service rather than into a non-residential job such as shop-assisting because 'being in the country, we had to be [living] in the town because father couldn't come and meet us to bring us home at night if we were in shops.' What these women were referring to was the reality of their relationship to the local economy. If they had to leave home for employment, a living-in job was the most practical and respectable option. Indeed, it may be a mistake to call it an option, since in many areas what girls did was so much taken for granted. For nine of the twelve rural women who went into service, service was their first paid job. (Three had previously worked without pay cooking and cleaning in their family household.)

For some, farm work was an alternative to domestic service. Janet, who was brought up in Midlothian, said of her work prospects on leaving school, 'To tell you the truth there was really nothing we could do except go to the farm or go to service. So we [she and her sister] preferred the farm. If you went to service, well I was away from my people'.

The working hours and physical conditions of farm work were not necessarily better than those that prevailed 'in service'. Here, Alison describes her work as a dairy maid on the East Lothian farm where her father worked as a ploughman: 'We had three milkings a day… We were up at five o'clock in the morning and you'd all the cows' udders to wash… Then we started milking again at one o'clock and the last milking was at five o'clock at night. Nine shillings a week. We had a Sunday [off] every third Sunday'.[18]

Janet tried working away from home with her sister. They took jobs as relief maids in an Edinburgh hospital but returned because of homesickness and went back to farm work. One particularly cold morning she walked off the job: 'It was so cold this morning that the farmer said to us there is nothing else to do but shawing turnips. And it was too cold and, you know, the frost was on them and I said, 'Och we're going home'. So when we come down [the road towards home] we saw the pit head and I said to my friend that was with me, 'I think we'll go in and see if we can get a job there…' She spent the rest of her pre-married working life 'couping coal' and making bricks at the pithead. Clearly this, like agricultural work, was still very hard physical work but it was less exposed to the elements and, unlike domestic service, allowed her to live at home.

A couple of respondents who had the option of farm work went into 'inside service' because they believed it would be less physically demanding than 'working out' on the farm. May, a ploughman's daughter, explained that she went into service because her mother forbade her to work on the farm because of her health. In some ways this was ironic as her health had suffered doing domestic work. After leaving school May was an unpaid domestic worker in the family household while her mother worked out on the farm. By the time she was eighteen she wanted to be working for wages. But because she had suffered a serious bout of rheumatic fever her mother did not want her to do farm work. She went instead into domestic service.

Sarah, a coachman/gardener's daughter, also opted for service as an alternative to farm work. Her first job at age fourteen was as a resident farm servant not far from the farm on which her father and mother worked. She left for domestic service on the advice of the local doctor who said that the farm work was too heavy for her after she suffered a serious attack of jaundice. First she tried to be a hospital nurse but was turned down because of her lack of educational certificates. Sarah's occupational history is a good example of reluctant recruitment to service during the 1930s. It also demonstrates that once 'in service' women could find themselves trapped in it, at least during the inter-war period. Between 1931 and 1938 Sarah had five jobs. She first worked as a housemaid in the Edinburgh household of a colonel, then as maid in a two-servant farm household, then as a cook in the household of an Edinburgh University professor. She then ran a shop in Dunbar for the summer season, finally returning to service to work for another university professor. Running the shop was a welcome escape from service. Her brother-in-law did not like the idea of her being in service and fixed up the temporary job running the shop (situated by the side of an outside swimming pool) with a friend who ran the associated café. However, once the season was over, she had to return to service.

Not all girls who went 'into service' stayed there all their pre-married working life. About a quarter of those I interviewed who were first in 'private service' moved on to other work. Information about jobs was often passed on by personal contact with friends and siblings, since they too were often 'in service'. Discontent in one job might equally well be resolved by moving to another rather than leaving 'service' entirely. At age eighteen Molly traded private domestic service in the 'big house' for another form of paid domestic work for the Women's Army Auxiliary Corp:

> You could go as a waitress or a general domestic or a cook or else you could go in as clerical work, you see. Well me having trained as an under-house maid they advised me to go as a waitress, which I did. And I was very glad I did because as a general domestic you had all the huts and everything to keep [clean] and food [to prepare] and all that. Whereas I was drafted to the officers mess and I was very lucky I was there all the time.

Institutional service was an alternative to service in private households for young women from 'the country' who had to leave home for work. A number of people I interviewed moved between the two forms of service. Jane, for example, left her job working for the old woman who kept a fruit shop even though, by Jane's own account, her employer treated her very well: 'And then after that one of my sisters worked in a hospital... After I got older she [her sister] said she would get me a job as a nurses' maid. You know, setting the nurses' dining room and I'd have more money and it would probably be cheerier for me.'

The hours of work and other conditions were not necessarily better in institutions than in private service but, presumably, less depended on having 'nice people' for employers. Jane described her time off when she was a nurses' maid: 'We got a weekend off once a month. Well it was like a weekend. We would finish on Friday and we had to be back on Sunday night. We had to be in by ten. We could get a late pass if we wanted a late pass but we never wanted late passes. We didn't go to dances and things like that.'

The aetiology of 'the decline of service' was spontaneously commented on by a number of interviewees who had been brought up in servant-keeping households. Some believed that the First World War had struck service a body blow and that the Second World War put an end to it. Speaking of the First World War, Helen [19] said that maids left as soon as they were eighteen to go in to munitions. A couple of other respondents who were in their twenties during the First World War commented that this was the first time they had ever done any cooking – they had to cook during this period because of the lack of maids. As Irene[20] commented, 'Nobody had maids after the [first] war'. This was obviously not factually correct but was perhaps true for her own social circle (although it may have been bluster to disguise the fact that they could not afford a maid, money 'being tight' since the business to which her father was attached had gone bankrupt). Grace[21] talked of how they always had two maids until the First War 'reduced them' to one. Florence[22] talks of a similar reduction but she clearly attributed it not to the difficulty of getting servants but to their own reduced financial circumstances during the depression of the inter-war years.

URBAN WOMEN IN SERVICE

Given the presumption that service was a stigmatised occupation for urban women, it seems worth paying particular attention to the question of why these women were in service. Of the nine women in service who had wholly or partly urban backgrounds, only two went straight from school to private domestic service; for only one of these women, Kate, was this residential work. Rosie's first job was as a servant but she was a daily worker, not a resident maid. Two women went from school to a form of service which was not private service. Chrissie's first job was in institutional service as a laundry maid and Mary's was as a resident shop assistant with some domestic responsibilities. Of the remaining five, four left other jobs for some form of domestic work [23] and one, Tina, went into service when she was made redundant and could not find other work.

Rosie, a baker's daughter, actually chose to be employed doing domestic work and she knew that this was what she wanted before she left school. She was born and brought up in central Edinburgh at a time when there was plenty of local factory work, but because she liked housework she fancied a job in this line. This desire was based on experience of doing housework at home, not on an image of a uniformed maid in a genteel household. It was not residential work that she was seeking. She got notice of a vacancy through a bureau and like many girls went to her first job interview with her mother. The household was that of a blacksmith and his family. She was interviewed by the wife. There were five resident children. She was paid 8s for a five-and-a-half-day week as a daily maid; she was the only paid help.

Rosie was not treated as belonging to 'a class apart'. She was doing work alongside the woman of the house. For example, the wife did the laundry herself and Rosie had to wring it and hang it out. But Rosie very quickly came to hate the job. She was frightened of her employer – whom she de-

scribed as 'a big overbearing kind of woman' – and disturbed by the fact
that one of the children 'took fits' and that there was an additional child
who was institutionalised because he was deaf and dumb. Aspects of their
life style also slightly shocked her: 'Money didnae seem to be any object.
They had a big side of ham and he [the blacksmith] would just go through
for a breakfast and cut off slices.' She described how she came to leave:

> 'I was there for six or eight months and I was at the stage where I was
> crying because I didn't want to go. So my mother says, 'Right. We'll
> see. I'll go up and see what's going on that you don't want to go.' So
> we goes into the place, into this room and there was a basket full of
> long black stockings. I donno whether I was supposed to be gonnae
> [going to] mend them or no, but I never got round to that... Anyway
> mother went up and said to her, 'She's never home before four
> o'clock on a Saturday afternoon [her half day].' She says, 'But she
> goes the messages [shopping].'... So my mother says, 'Well I'm
> afraid she won't be coming back again. I can see there is gonnae be
> more in store for her.' Well I didnae know there was anything wrong
> with the woman. Here she was expecting again. She had twins a
> month after I left.'

After this episode Rosie set off with her mother down to the bureau to find
another job but on the way they passed a shoe wholesaler's and on a whim
(her mother's) went in there to ask for a job. That was the end of Rosie's
career in service.

Kate was from a more privileged background. Her route into domestic
service was different. She was encouraged to take up nannying as a
'suitable' career. Like Sarah she wanted to be a nurse. It was not lack of
qualifications which stopped her from nursing (she had gone to a high
school till the age of fifteen) but her mother's disapproval of the scheme.
Her mother had been brought up in a servant-employing household in
Dublin until she abruptly lost both her parents and moved to London,
eventually moving to Glasgow where she worked as a buyer for a glass and
china department. In Glasgow she married Kate's father, a steel-erecting
engineer with British Steel. Kate recounts:

> Actually I wanted to be a hospital nurse but my mother wouldn't
> consent to it. In those days, you know, nursing wasn't what it is now
> and she just didn't like the idea of me going into a hospital where I
> might be working with men and that kind of thing. She was very
> much against it and it was our family doctor who suggested that I go
> with the children. So that was how it came about.

The urban women were more likely than the rural women to have
worked in other jobs before entering domestic service. Tina, who had a
mixed rural and urban background, went into service after she had been
'laid off' from a Galashiels woollen mill. It could be argued that, living in
a textile town in a rural county, she was more rural than urban and hence
more open to domestic work. However, there were cases of Edinburgh-

based women moving into service, leaving other work to take up a particular opportunity which had presented itself. In three cases the work itself – which involved looking after children – seemed to be the attraction. For example, Peggy had a variety of jobs before settling down to work for a year and a half in a bias-binding factory. When she was eighteen, she was offered a position in service: 'We had a friend that had a villa in Davidson's Mains [just outside Edinburgh] and we visited quite regularly. Here a young couple came to live there and he was the manager of [city centre shop] and they had a baby. So one day she asked my friend if I would come and help her with the baby.' In most cases, however, entering service had more to do with leaving a set of living circumstances than with the attraction of the work.

DOMESTIC SERVICE AS A HOME FROM HOME

I interviewed three women, one urban and two rural, who turned to domestic service because they were seeking an alternative to their family-household. All came to domestic service after having done some other paid work.

Meg had moved into domestic service from factory work in response to her employer's efforts to look after her well-being. She had gone into digs to escape from an unhappy living situation. The illegitimate child of a domestic servant, she had been entrusted to an elderly couple who could barely provide for her because of their alcoholism. They lived in one scarcely furnished room. Enforced moves followed non-payment of rent. Any decent clothing Meg ever acquired was pawned. Meg's first job was in printing (she trained to be a lithograph operator) but she moved from this job to become a boiling-room worker in a sweetie factory in order to increase her wage from 4s 6d to 8s a week. After a failed attempt at concealing her wage increase from 'the old folks' (in order to buy a coat through a 'menage' a type of savings club), she found digs through the help of a girl at work. Obviously, word of her situation got around, as she was summoned to the office of the works' manager. After questioning her about her circumstances, he said that she was far too young to be in digs and that he had a friend who needed a maid as her maid had left. With assurances that she would be trained and continue to get 8s a week, Meg went to become a servant. She left at eighteen when she 'had to get married' to her boyfriend.

Jessie, whose mother had died when she was four, was the youngest of two brothers and a sister. Her grandmother kept house for the next six years until she died. Her older sister did domestic work in the house until her father's authoritarianism and the lack of rewards for the work drove her away: 'my sister did with [lodged with] my other aunt in town. She went away. She got browned off with the old fellow.' Jessie was to get 'browned off' in turn. Her father got her exempted from school at the age of thirteen so that she could keep house. Eventually she took paid work, still carrying responsibility for housework. Her first job was in a pottery packing dishes in straw for twelve hours a day (with two one-hour breaks for breakfast and dinner). Her second job was in a woodyard shifting props and checking deliveries. She was paid 15s a week, which she gave to her father who gave her pocket money in return. Her main interest was in going to dances but her father never approved of this and would often try to stop her. By the time she was seventeen she decided to leave, taking a job as a maid (the only servant) in the household of a local barrister. Her father was left alone in the house. Her sister and a brother were married. When she went into service her single brother went to live with his married sister.

Jessie decided in retrospect that service was better than her other jobs: 'If I had my days to begin again that's where I would go. I wouldnae work in neither wid yards nor potteries nor nothing else. I'd go right to service. Because you learned. You didnae get rough like they are.' Swearing and shouting was an everyday mode of communication, at least among men, in the woodyard. Ways of speaking in service were certainly genteel in comparison. But at the time the attraction was not the respectability in itself but a respectable way of leaving her father's household.

Netty reluctantly became a nanny when she was twenty because she did not feel able to keep a home of her own, on her own. She wanted to be a nurse when she left school but instead became a clerkess when a friend of the family who had his own business asked her mother and father if she could come and work for him doing his books. Netty stayed at this job until she was eighteen, when her mother died; she took over keeping the house for her father and siblings for the next two years.

> Well my father worked away from home. He only came home occasionally. [He was a woodturner for a large firm]. So then my sisters and brothers all got married. But I didn't at that time… then I felt I just couldn't do it any longer. So I just. I mean they were marrying and going away and leaving me on my own. I mean I couldn't live on my own. So I had to give up my home and I became a nanny. I went as an under-nurse and then I followed that up until I was married. Oh I missed my home very very much.

SNOBS, TYRANTS, DEMEANING CONDITIONS AND GOOD EMPLOYERS

Once in service not everybody disliked it. Whether it was liked or not had more to do with the experience itself than with any preconceived ideas derived from an urban or rural background. If employers were obviously unpleasant and/or created particularly demeaning conditions then the work was disliked. In the 'big house' it was not the employer who was the obvious boss to be hated or liked but the housekeeper, or cook, or butler. For the servants who entered the big houses in trainee positions, the working conditions and the inequalities between servants, and often their own lowly status within the hierarchy was more striking at first than the condescension of their employer. This world of domestic service was very different from that of the household with one, two, or even three or four servants.

Molly's first job was as an under-house maid during the First World War in the large household of an Edinburgh advocate. She counted out the staff for me: 'There was the head cook and the kitchen maid, and the table maid and the under-table maid. So that was four. And then the head-house maid and I trained under her. That was six. And then the ladies maid, seven and the laundry maid was eight... They'd had a footman as well but he was off. He was away to the war.' Then she went on to describe her work:

> I had quite a lot of work to do because I had to help in the laundry as well as [doing the work of] an under[-house maid]. I had to carry the coal from the basement right up to the drawing room flat and the under-table maid, she had the dining-room. I was right at the top flat too because I had the nursery as well. I had all that carrying and I was up early in the morning because of course the head maid she didn't do anything like that. And then in the afternoon I had to go and help in the laundry and it was all the sheets. I had to fold the sheets and then they were all mangled. That was my afternoon work. And I was only allowed out, being the under-housemaid... Of course things had changed by then because there wasn't the staff and I had to do the hall tea for all the staff. The cook was at the top of the table. The table maid was at the foot of the table... On her [the cook's] right hand there was the lady's maid, the head-house maid and the under-table maid. That was they three. On the other side there was the laundry maid, the kitchen maid and I was the sixth. I had to do the hall tea on my evening off and I hadn't to go out till that tea was finished and washed up which meant I wasn't out till after five o'clock. And that was only once a week.

The pleasantness (or lack of it) of the employer was a crucial element in the conditions of service for those who worked in more direct contact with him or her. There was of course more than one way of being unpleasant. Rosie had found her employer domineering and intimidating. Other employers made their servants feel that they were a lesser species of human being. Sarah was from a rural background but talked of how much she disliked service. She made this general observation: 'The fact that you were a servant [meant that, as far as your employer was concerned] you had neither feeling nor brains; you were just a servant.' Her first experience of working in the household of a university professor had been particularly trying: 'It was in Regent Terrace [New Town, Edinburgh] and your bedroom was in the area off the kitchen. I was the cook. I had to order all the things, the provisions but it [the order] had to go to her ladyship. And she called you by your second name, you know. And she would say, "And why do you need this? And why do you need that?" And I got 2s 6d a week to provide suppers for two of us.' The second time she worked in a professor's household she was much happier with her employers whom she described as 'really nice people'. She continued with them after she was married in 1938 (the professor encouraged her to marry and stay on) until she was pregnant with her first child in 1940.

Kate, who was from an urban background, did enjoy service but then she was in the 'labour aristocracy' of service and as a nanny did not ever expect to be at an employer's beck and call. She described the one employer who did order her about as displaying 'uppishness'. Her description of the layout of the house (and the use of the card table) helps build up this picture of 'uppishness' and illustrates the relative privilege of the nanny in comparison to the maid.

> One, only one job I was in, and it was out here [in Midlothian], did I ever find uppishness. I was only two months in it, because I just couldn't have stayed. I took the post with one little girl [under her care]... We had the day nursery which was really the dining room. If they [her employers, the little girls parents] had anyone in, they had to use the day nursery. My bedroom was upstairs... Beautifully furnished. There was the kitchen and there was a little bedroom off which was the maid's bedroom. My room, well, the child slept in my room. There was just the one room upstairs. It was the kind of bedroom that you just went up the stairs and you were into the bedroom. They had their bedroom downstairs to the front and they had the little sitting room. I used the diningroom, the day nursery, and I sat in there in the evening. They used to dress for dinner every night and they had their dinner off a card table.

She goes on to tell the details of the first of the offending incidents.

> Of course, when I went to the interview she says to me, 'Would you mind helping me with the washing up nanny when its the maid's day off.' I said, 'That's alright I don't mind helping you.' And the first week I was there... Of course, my supper at night was the only meal I got in peace, after the wee one was in bed, you know. And I usually thoroughly enjoyed it as all nannies probably do. And I used to sit and have a read while I was having my supper. And I heard this bell ringing. I didn't pay much attention to it because normally I didn't have anything to do with the door bells or anything and then it rang again louder. So I got up and went into the hall and looked out the front door and there was nobody there. So I knocked on the lounge door where they were and said, 'Did I hear a bell ringing? Was there a bell ringing?' 'Yes, nanny' she said, 'Would you mind bringing in the next course.' Now if she'd said to me in the beginning would I do it, I would have done it but the fact that she sat there and rang that bell. I said, 'I'm sorry Mrs MacIntosh I didn't promise to do that for you. This is the only meal I get in peace all day and I really want to enjoy it. I don't mind helping you with the washing up after you're finished but I'm not going to serve table for you.'

The final incident stemmed from Mrs MacIntosh asking her where she had been with the child.

Why she particularly asked me that day I don't know. She wasn't in the habit of asking where we went. I said, 'We just went through the village and I posted some letters and got some stamps.' She said, 'You mean to tell me that you took my child through the village and left her sitting [in the pram] outside the Post Office door?' I said, 'Yes'. Well she was furious. 'I have a father who has a title and I will not have my child mixing with the village children.' 'She was only at the door three minutes.' 'Never do that again.' 'Well I won't because I won't be there. You can take a month's notice from me.'

Kate presented this as very atypical of her general experience of relationships with her employers. Indeed, she claimed that she deliberately did not take jobs with the landed gentry or with 'titled' employers because she wanted to be treated *as one of the family*.

If you take a job like that your're a very lonely person because you're neither family nor staff. You're in your nursery and you've to stay there. You're not allowed to mix with the staff and you can't mix with the family. Well you see I didn't like this. In my type of job I was part of the family, you see which I preferred. You dined with them. You went holidays with them and went out with them. But you see if you're with these titled people you don't get that kind of treatment. You're in the nursery and you stay there.

It is also interesting to look at servant/employer relations from the viewpoint of the employing class. Respondents from servant-keeping households commented both defensively and guiltily on the working conditions of their domestic servants:

The maids then got up at four o'clock on a Monday morning to wash and washed till breakfast. But it was their home and they seemed quite happy, although they worked far too long hours.[24]

Everyone in those days had help. And the conditions they lived in were really terrible I think. It [their own maid's sleeping accommodation] was a dark room off the kitchen with no air [box room]. Nobody thought that was a terrible place to put somebody to live.[25]

But few commented on the servant/employer relationship more directly. A couple of interviewees from servant-keeping households remembered being taught to show respect for their 'help'. One of the few times Florence [26] was smacked by her parents was for 'cheeking' the cook. She was playing on the dining-room table and was rude to the cook when she wanted it cleared. Her mother told her to apologise and she refused. She was sent upstairs to await the smacking. Like many petit-bourgeois families, Dorothy's [27] did not have a resident maid. Her mother paid a local woman, a miner's wife, to come and do the laundry on Mondays; the same woman called in at lunch-time to look after the children if their mother had to go away for any reason. She was told how to address this woman: 'We were never allowed to call her "the washer woman". She was always called by her name.' As Davidoff and Hall note,[28] such strict instructions to treat others with respect only emphasise social distance.

A few of the servant-keeping respondents explained how their families had no trouble getting servants. They talked of a special relationship with either a particular servant or a servant-supplying family, suggesting that they were a 'good employer' to that individual or family.

> Mother had no trouble with maids because there was a big family and when the one left the other came. I think there was about half a dozen of them.[29]

> 'Well we had one – she must have come when she was quite young. We had her for fully ten years and when she left to get married her sister-in-law came and she was with us for about ten years till she got married.'[30]

Grace [31] explained how 'nurse' stayed with the family for her entire working life. Grace was the youngest of eight. Her nurse had looked after all of them and formed a very close bond with all the children. She left the family to look after her own father but was begged to come back when Grace's eldest sister had her first child. Grace and her spinster sisters in turn looked after nurse in her old age.

REDEEMING FEATURES OF THE WORK

One possible source of satisfaction in any job is a sense of learning something. Molly believed that if she had remained in the 'big house' she would have received a good training as she worked her way up the servant hierarchy. Her sense of receiving a training was not shared by many women who went into service in more middle-class households. If they learned new skills, typically they learned by themselves on the job and they were often forced back on whatever resources they brought with them. Meg, who arrived in domestic service with very little experience of the type of housework that was expected of her, was allowed to learn by her mistakes despite the cost to her employer. For example, she whitened the polished floors and boiled the woollens. After the latter episode a washerwoman came in to help her to wash. Otherwise, Meg was the only paid help employed by an Edinburgh accountant and his wife who lived with their two-year-old daughter. Meg took the little girl out in the afternoon. The type of training which Meg got was more akin to the way girls typically learned housework at home. They learned when they had to, when a task was thrust upon them. Training of servants was more programmatic in the 'big house', where servants trained each other and progressed through a hierarchy.

The amount of responsibility given to the maid in the one-servant household might also have been a source of satisfaction for some. This was most notably responsibility for children. Molly's sister Dot went from school to such a position in a household where four boys were being looked after by their aunt while their mother was in India. She had to do some housework but her main duties were keeping the boys occupied: 'I used to teach them all to dance. I do'know if I was suppose to. I was certainly supposed to sit in the room to see that they got on with their homework but when they were finished I used to teach them to dance the Highland Scottish and the Highland Fling and all the dances that I got at school... I often think what a daft thing to do teaching them all to dance.' Dot was only three years older than the eldest of her charges but was left to get on with the job. By her own testimony she enjoyed being able to boss the boys around.

In servant-keeping households with children, a servant invariably had some responsibility for child care. With young children the afternoon outing was a standard procedure. When a full-time nursery nurse or nanny was employed, children were primarily brought up by the nanny or nurse. The following story illustrates the extent to which authority was delegated. Grace [32] and her sister discovered what a 'wonderful noise' could be made by sliding flower pots down the coal shoot into the coal cellar. They smashed their way through a new delivery of flower pots. The gardener (nurse's father) reported them to nurse. Nurse thought this was so serious that their father should be told. However, when she led them by the hand to see their father and told him the facts, his response was to burst out laughing. Nurse took them back to the nursery and smacked them herself.

A successful career in service involved moving to more responsible and better-paid positions such as cook and housekeeper. But, of all the positions, that of the nanny was perhaps the most privileged. The full-blown nanny of the multi-servant household had total and exclusive charge of the children and no other responsibilities. The other servants cooked her meals and cleaned her nursery.

Kate started her career as a nurse and nanny in the household of a gentleman-farmer in East Lothian. Other than herself on the staff, there was a cook and a house-table maid. There were two children in the family and a third expected shortly. Her only training was given by the Maternity Nurse, a state-registered nurse who was hired six weeks before the baby was born until the baby was six weeks old. Kate left this job at nineteen to go onto a series of jobs in which she was in sole charge of other people's children. She stopped being a nanny at twenty-four when she got married. By this time, 1932, she was earning forty-eight pounds a year (the same as Sarah in 1938), double her starting salary. Unlike Sarah, whose position was closely supervised, Kate talks of how she was 'her own boss'.

CONCLUSION

Most of the data presented in the chapter is suggestive rather than conclusive. It in no way challenges the view that rural women were more likely to go into service than urban women were. But it does indicate that service was a heterogeneous occupation which could attract urban women in certain circumstances. 'Looking after children' had its attractions for women who with better access to education and employment might have been nurses or teachers. Going into service could also provide a respectable way of living for the single woman who had no family-household, or who wished to escape from one.

The combination of this material with other published sources is not sufficient to tell us what proportion of the Scottish servant-keeping population treated their servants unashamedly as less than human. But clearly not all did so, just as not all who entered service hated it. Many could not afford to hate it. They entered it matter-of-factly. When they felt ill-used or in need of more pay they found alternative positions. With the exception of those who came to vehemently hate service because of early or repeated bad experiences, only those who could readily see alternative forms of work were likely to dwell on the fact that service was not what they really wanted. Moreover, there were a few pockets of 'old-style' service left and a portion of the Scottish middle-class continued to do their own housework without paid help.

Some, perhaps even many, servants enjoyed aspects of their work. First, it is important to remember that conditions and tasks varied from position to position. For those working as children's nurses and nannies the job often had better living conditions, more autonomy, a greater sense of skill and responsibility, and sometimes higher pay, as well as the rewards of the relationship with the children themselves. Some of these sources of potential satisfaction were found in smaller measure in the work of the general servant, at least in households with children. Taking the young child out for the afternoon walk was a routine, albeit relatively brief, escape from the household. Many general servants had as much to do with the children as did the children's own parents. While one would not wish to romanticise child-care, it seems clear that it was often more fun than heavy cleaning.

It is also possible that some servants gained satisfaction in developing skills. Even in a modest middle-class home at the beginning of the century, some of the materials of the job were more elaborate than could be afforded in most working-class homes. This could be experienced in a variety of ways. Young girls entering service were perhaps as likely to be intimidated or intrigued by the life style of others as they were to be scornful of unnecessary frills. In some areas of work, differences in domestic apparel and technology amounted to having more to do and nothing better to do it with (cleaning brasses, fire grates and china, for example). But in other areas this was not necessarily the case. Cooking with a wider range of ingredients and utensils than in the average working-class home might have had its compensations, although this was the work of only a minority of servants.

How much people 'liked' service often came down to how they felt about their employer. It seems that there were 'nice people'. This does not mean that 'nice people' treated their servants as equals. The employer/servant relationship is one in which the servant is structurally subordinate. This was as true in the early twentieth century as it was in the nineteenth.

The 'nice' employer was sufficiently decent and tactful to minimise his or her displays of superordination while still managing the relationship such that the required service was obtained. 'Nice employers' were not necessarily those who treated their servants like daughters. The 'domineering' woman who worked alongside the daily maid may not have treated her daughter very differently but she was not experienced as 'nice'. And the upper-middle-class woman who was 'nice' would probably never have asked her daughters to do the work she demanded of her servants.

As Davidoff has argued, many working-class girls were subordinate all of their lives – as daughters, servants and wives.[33] Almost all working-class women in service would have had housework demanded of them while they were living in their parents' house. Some had spent a year or more as an unpaid full-time housekeeper for their family-household before going into service. With this 'training', being paid for being at the constant beck and call of others could be regarded as an improvement even if it was also recognised as a result of class inequality. Moreover, if the employers were perceived as 'nice people' the job was likely to be experienced as a good one. Again, this need not mean that women were blind to their subordinate position. The 'good employers, were like 'good parents'; they still expected the work but asked you 'in a nice way'.

NOTES

1 Explanations of the decline of domestic service often emphasise 'demand' factors as well as 'supply'. See Joseph Banks, *Prosperity and Parenthood* (London, Routledge and Kegan Paul, 1954); Pamela Horn, *The Rise and Fall of the Victorian Servant* (London, Gill and Macmillan 1975) and Theresa McBride, *The Domestic Revolution* (London, Croom Helm, 1976). The debate concerning the causes of decline is reviewed by Edward Higgs, 'Domestic service and household production' in *Unequal Opportunities: Women's Employment in England, 1800–1918*, ed. Angela John (Oxford, Basil Blackwell, 1986).

2 See John Burnett, *Useful Toil* (Harmondsworth, Penguin, 1974); Edward Higgs, 'Domestic service and household production', op. cit.

3 Ibid., 142-3.

4 Higgs, op. cit., and 'Domestic Servants and households in Victorian England', *Social History* 8, no. 2 (1983), 201–10.

5 The 1861 Scottish Census listed separately wives, widows, children and relatives at home 'not otherwise described' under the heading of 'Domestic Class'. They were distinguished from 'Persons engaged in entertaining and performing the Personal Offices for Man' either in 'Board and Lodgings' or 'Attendance'. The census definitions changed over the decades of the late nineteenth and early twentieth centuries as notions about which women doing domestic work should be classified as 'occupied' resulted in the exclusion of most but not all women who did the work as 'wives'.

The specific occupations which the 1861 enumerators used to

itemise women in 'Attendance' were General domestic servant, Housekeeper, Cook, Housemaid, Nurse, Laundrymaid, Inn Servant, Hospital and Lunatic Asylum attendant nurse, Nurse (not domestic servant), Charwoman, Office keeper etc., Parkgate and lodgekeeper. General domestic servant was overwhelmingly the largest category of 'Persons engaged in entertaining and performing the Personal Offices for Man' (111 377 women in 1861 compared with 8261 working in hotels, inns or otherwise 'in board and lodgings', or compared with the next largest categories of those women 'in attendance', 7250 housemaids and 5884 cooks).

The subsequent censuses further refined the distinctions between those working in private households and those working in more specific institutions like inns, hospitals and laundries. By 1911 all working in private households were assigned to a single occupation, 'Other Domestic Indoor Servant'. Wives had by now disappeared as a category in the list of 'Occupations'. Although it is possible that enumerators may sometimes have listed women working as unwaged housekeepers (usually for relatives) under this heading, it can be assumed that the bulk of women listed worked for wages not love.

6   Michael Anderson, 'Households, families and individuals: some preliminary results from the national sample from the 1851 census of Great Britain', *Continuity and Change* 3, (1988), 421–38.

7   Claire, born 1891, auctioneer's daughter brought up in a Perthshire town.

8   Betty, born 1905, brought up in Falkirk and Edinburgh, miner's daughter, father started coal business with compensation money following serious accident.

9   Belle, born 1900, shoemaker's daughter brought up in Edinburgh.

10 For example, Amy born 1894 in Leith, a foreman-bookbinder's daughter, had the job of going to get other people's messages while her sister helped her mother do the housework.

11 Higgs in Angela John (ed.) op. cit. 135.

12 J. A. S. Green 'A survey of domestic service', *Lincolnshire History and Archaeology* 17 (1982), 65–9; Higgs, op. cit., 135.

13 See Appendix for details of Jane and subsequent respondents who were in service. One other respondent, Mary, was a resident shop assistant. She no doubt also helped with domestic chores. She shared the room above the shop with the woman shopkeeper. Their domestic life was marginalised by the shop as they served customers until 10 p.m. every week-night and until 11 p.m. on a Saturday.

14 It would be a mistake to think of servants as solely a city phenomenon. Servants were to be found throughout Scotland. Of the Scottish cities Edinburgh contained the highest proportion of servants throughout the period. In 1901 domestic servants were 5.7 per cent of the Edinburgh population, approaching twice the equivalent figure for Aberdeen (2.7 per cent) which in turn had a proportionately larger servant population than Glasgow (2.1 per cent) and twice the servant population of Dundee (1.2 per cent). The unequal distribution of the middle-class and upper-middle-class population among the Scottish cities is the most likely explanation for much of this difference.

15 Born 1906, Greenock, riveter's daughter; see Jean Rennie *Every Other Sunday* (Arthur Barker Ltd., 1955) quoted in Burnett, op. cit.,

234–45.
16 Ailie Currie, interviewed by Claire Toynbee in 1987.
17 Denise Scott. See Appendix for details of this and subsequent respondents who were employed as domestic servants.
18 Alison, born 1900, brought up near Gogarburn, near Edinburgh; became a dairy maid at age 13.
19 Helen, born 1896 Glasgow; her father was owner/manager of an engineering and crane-making business.
20 Irene, born 1903 Corstorphine, Edinburgh; accountant's daughter.
21 Grace, born 1890s, Edinburgh; chemist's daughter.
22 Florence, born 1902, Paisley; accountant's daughter.
23 Meg, Nina, Pat, Peggy. See (Appendix) for these and other respondents who were 'in service'.
24 Fiona, born 1901, Edinburgh; merchant's daughter.
25 Elizabeth, born 1897, Edinburgh; commercial traveller's daughter.
26 See note 22.
27 Dorothy, born 1905, near Hamilton; butcher's daughter.
28 Leonore Davidoff and Catherine Hall, *Family Fortunes* (London, Hutchinson, 1987), 394–5.
29 Fiona; see note 24.
30 Catherine, born 1902, Lanarkshire; commercial traveller's daughter.
31 Grace; see note 2.
32 Ibid.
33 Leonore Davidoff, 'Mastered for Life: Servant and Wife in Victorian and Edwardian England' in A Sutcliffe and P. Thane (eds), *Essays in Social History* (Oxford, 1986).

ACKNOWLEDGEMENTS

Thanks to Claire Toynbee of Victoria University, Wellington, New Zealand for sharing material and to Michael Anderson and the editors for comments on an earlier draft.

Appendix

My data are a subset drawn from semi-structured interviews with working-class and middle-class men and women brought up in towns or industrial villages of lowland Scotland in the early 1900s. Most of these interviews, 64 with working class people and 24 with middle-class people, are itemised in my unpublished PhD thesis, 'A case study in the development of the modern family: urban Scotland in the early twentieth century', Edinburgh University, 1983. The interview was primarily concerned with 'growing-up' and included detailed questions about family life and early work-history. Sixteen of the women itemised there entered some form of residential service – in three cases this was not private domestic service as it is normally understood. All these interviews are used for this article. At the time of doing these interviews I also collected histories from a small number of other rural respondents. Six of these interviews are also referred to in this paper and five of these women entered service. All the respondents who went 'into service' are itemised below.

Rural women who went into service

    Abigail born 1892, brought up in Lanark, was a housemaid at age 14.

    Dot, born 1904, railway linesman's daughter, brought up in Cramond, near Edinburgh, became a children's nurse/general servant, at age 14.

    Denise Scott, born 1907, brought up on farms near Stonyburn, near Edinburgh, kept house for her mother and then became a domestic servant.

    Janet, born 1906, Stobhill near Edinburgh, miner's daughter, was a hospital maid, then a field worker, then a brick setter and coal couper.

    Jane, born 1899, Broxburn, Linlithgow, engine driver's daughter, was a resident shop assistant and then a maid in a nurses' home.

    Jessie, born 1897, Boness, Linlithgow, ironmoulder/miner's daughter, kept house, was a packer in a pottery, then a woodyard checker and labourer, then a domestic servant.

    Martha, born 1904, Seafield Linlithgow, soldier/labourer's daughter, was a children's nurse and then an assistant cook.

    May Carruthers, born 1905, Caithness, ploughman's daughter, kept house for her mother and then went into service.

    Molly, Dot's sister, born 1898, Cramond, was an under-housemaid from age 14 until she joined the WAAC.

    Netty born 1898, Davidson's Mains, near Edinburgh, woodturner's daughter, was a book-keeper for a small business, then an under-nurse, then a nanny.

    Olive, born 1898, Berwickshire, groom and gardener's daughter, servant under supervision of the housekeeper at age 14, then between-maid, hospital maid, children's nurse.

    Sarah, 1913, near Dunbar, coachman/gardener's daughter, kept house for her mother for a year, worked on the farm, then became a domestic servant.

Urban women and women from mixed urban and rural backgrounds who went into service

    Chrissie, born 1905, brought up in Edinburgh, roadmender's daughter, resident laundry maid at age 12.

    Kate, born 1908, brought up in Wishaw, steel erecting engineers' daughter, became a children's nurse on leaving school at 15.

    Mary born 1897, brought up in Edinburgh, mason/bricklayer's daughter, at 14 became a shop-girl and resident servant to friend of her mother's, then hospital maid.

    Meg, born 1896, brought up in Edinburgh by foster parents, first job was learning to operate lithographic machine; left to work in boiling room in sweetie factory; left to be a maid.

    Nina, born 1903, brought up in Edinburgh, plumber's daughter, apprentice printer at 14 but left to be a children's nurse.

Pat, born 1903, brought up in Edinburgh but went to live with her grandmother on a farm near Edinburgh when 13, worked in the fields, then became a domestic servant and then went back to living with her mother and worked in a biscuit factory.

Peggy, born 1906, brought up in Edinburgh by her mother's ex-land-lady, worked as seamstress at 14, then printing works, then biscuit factory making tin boxes, then in bias binding factory, then children's nurse.

Rosie, born 1908, brought up in Edinburgh, daily maid at 14, then assistant in wholesale shoe shop.

Tina, born 1908, brought up in mining towns and villages near Glasgow until she was ten when they moved to Galashiels, worked in the mill at 14, went in to service when paid off.

8

FIT WORK FOR WOMEN:
SWEATED HOME-WORKERS IN GLASGOW, *c.* 1875–1914.

ALICE J. ALBERT

There is no industry in which women are employed where
they are so much victimised, so hard wrought, so poorly paid
as that in which they earn their living with their needle.[1]

INTRODUCTION

'Sweated' work and 'home-work' were two sides of the same coin in the
context of women's work in turn-of-the-century Glasgow. Contemporaries defined 'sweated work' as any work that was low paid and executed
under poor working conditions.[2] 'Home-work' referred to piece-work distributed either by management from the factory or workshop door, or by
a subcontractor serving as an intermediary between workers and management. This type of work presented an example of casual labour and its main
features; which included ineffective regulation, lack of security and rights,
and low pay. In these respects, home-work mirrored the larger labour
market for women.

Studies of women's work from the onset of industrialisation have
tended to concentrate on the concept of the separation of home and work.
This has taken hold of the imagination of scholars and has tended to be their
main focus when they address the subject of the labour market for women.
Home-workers for whom this separation did not apply, have remained an
obscure subject for study. Even the 'feminist challenge' to the way women's
labour history has been studied has, until recently, tended to overlook this
aspect of women's paid labour.[3] While home-work represented a form of
casual and marginal employment, it was still waged labour, and any study
of the labour market and of the participation of women in it must include
home-workers.

In the nineteenth and early twentieth centuries most women worked
long hours for low wages under conditions that were intolerable by any
standard. Insecurity of employment was a feature of the majority of
occupations employing women, particularly in the sweated and home-
work trades. In Glasgow, a trade crisis in 1892–3, the coal strike of 1894, and
the depression of 1903-5 and 1907–10 accounted for lengthy bouts of

underemployment and unemployment. Seasonal patterns of employment also caused lay-offs. This situation prevailed in trades such as tailoring, dressmaking, brushmaking, and umbrella covering. Overstocking, fluctuations in demand due to changes in fashion and weather, and the capricious nature of foreign markets also resulted in massive lay-offs in some of the same trades.

Large numbers of women were, therefore, displaced during 'seasonal troughs' and/or interruptions to trade. Some of these women – mainly the unskilled – competed with home-workers for any available work. In tailoring, for example, where a number of home-workers were engaged in finishing, any surplus labour put pressure on the amount of work available. One contemporary stated that any unemployment in factories and workshops meant that 'many in-workers were relegated to out-work as casuals doing surplus.'[4] A similar situation might have existed in other 'seasonal' trades such as umbrella covering, thereby intermittently swelling the ranks of home-workers.

According to the 1911 census, Glasgow's female labour force included 7047 married women. Of these, 2460 (or 34.9 per cent) were described as home-workers. However, many home-workers were omitted from the census data because of the casual and seasonal nature of their work.[5] Therefore it is impossible to determine the precise number of home-workers, although the official figure was sufficiently high for Glasgow to be considered the Scottish 'centre' for home-work. A 'home-worker' (the term apparently dated from the nineteenth century) received the following rather prolix definition by the Outworkers Committee:

> a person to whom articles or materials are given out to be made up, cleaned, washed, altered, ornamented, finished, or repaired, or adapted for sale in his [sic] home or on other premises not under the control or management of the person who gave out the articles or materials for the purposes of the trade or business of the last-mentioned person.[6]

This arrangement, sometimes also referred to as out-work, was derived from the pre-industrial putting-out system. It survived because in some trades it offered owners the chance of considerable cost-savings, but in its later form it differed from its predecessor in two important ways: it became entirely urban; and it co-existed with factory production. In most respects the actual organisation of the system remained the same. As defined by Duncan Bythel, its main features were that: the work was carried on in the home; the value of goods was low; the processes used required few skills and were performed on simple equipment; and the finished products were 'consumer goods' destined for the mass market.[7] The entrepreneur or manufacturer provided the capital in two ways: the actual goods to be worked on, and money wages. If a middle-person acted as the 'go-between', she/he provided the wages. The worker herself provided the fixed capital, i.e. the workplace and the necessary equipment, in order to turn out the finished product. In these respects there was nothing unique about Glasgow's home-workers, whether they were employed in needle-work (the biggest sector), the washing service, or hand-work trades such as paper bag or box making. In all cases, they plied their trade in much the same way as did, for example, their counterparts in the east end of London. But, unlike its English counterpart, the conjugal family in Scotland ceased to be the focus for domestic production, particularly in Glasgow. Women tended to work alone, or in small groups, depending upon the type of work.

For the small entrepreneur, the home-work system had many advantages, one of which was the ability to keep overhead costs low. Giving evidence to the Report on the Poor Laws, 1909, one local industrialist commented that home-workers 'do not add to capital expenditure ... and do not make inroads on space' at a time when rates on properties in Glasgow were on the rise.[8] Capital expenditures on equipment were passed on to the worker, who would either buy or rent items such as sewing machines from the firm. Fluctuations in trade from one season to the next, or during a trough in the trade cycle, would then not result in a great loss to the employer. Workers could be hired as needed and their services dispensed with easily; thus there was a ready supply of labour to be tapped. Commenting on this situation, the Glasgow Commissioners to the Royal Commission on the Poor Laws and Relief of Distress, 1909, stated that ... the employer's responsibility lies in his frequently doling out work as people dole out indiscriminate charity, and in his desire to have a reserve of labour, which costs nothing for upkeep, and which he can count on for a few hours, or days, or weeks as it suits his convenience.'[9]

Tailors, on the other hand, reported that they had resorted to the employment of home-workers because of the 'scarcity of regular tailoring workers.'[10] The number of firms which operated in this way is unknown, and the absence of business records makes it impossible to establish either the value of the materials put out or the savings realised. The wages paid to home-workers, however, suggest that the materials worked on were of extremely low value and quality. Glasgow women finishing cuffs and collars, for example, received an average wage of 5s 3d for approximately fifty hours' work; an umbrella coverer might earn 7s 2d to 13s 3d for a similarly lengthy work-week. A number of problems arise when we try to ascertain an 'average' wage. Quality of material, age of the individual, and type of work all bear consideration. Home-work did appear to be beneficial in two ways to the supplier. As has been noted, a surplus body of labour could be tapped upon demand. The dilution of labour skills that followed upon mechanisation and technological advances resulted in an expansion of the surplus of labour. These had important implications for wages and the type of employee – usually female – preferred. The main implication was the second main benefit of home-work to the employer:[11] the ability to pay very low wages. In order to better represent the nature of the home-work trades and the experiences of home-workers, a fuller discussion follows.

THE HOME-WORK TRADES AND HOME-WORKERS

As has been argued, official figures underestimate the true number of home-workers and represent only the core of a considerably larger body of women. (See Figure 1 for a breakdown of the main home-work trades.) Whatever the numbers involved, however, home-work was clearly a stagnating, but not necessarily dying, sector of the labour market. This contrasts with Marx's view in the nineteenth century, and with Bythel's in this, of the decline of home-work as an inevitable result of the capitalist mode of production.[12]

Generally speaking, home-work lost ground in practically all the industries and trades that put out work, but declined more dramatically in some sectors than in others. Since home-work was not enumerated separately until 1901, only two censuses plot this trend. Nevertheless, some generalisations about the changing structure of home-work can be made.[13] Several factors which help to explain the loss of opportunities in traditional homework trades are: competition, mechanisation (and the concomitant move to larger business organisations) and politico-social considerations. Competition from Lancashire and abroad had an impact on brushmaking and the once lucrative umbrella export trade. Mechanisation spread to the needlework trades and laundry service. The ubiquitous sewing machine made inroads in tailoring and dressmaking, and allowed for the growth of the ready-made market. This development was particularly disastrous to the following groups: milliners, staymakers, buttonholers, gusset finishers, boot and shoe makers, cap and hat makers, shawl fringers, and underclothing workers. Underclothing in particular had once been the preserve of the home-worker and an important source of work. As opportunities in factories and workshops opened up for paper bag and box making and for umbrella covering, home-workers in these trades witnessed a decline in the supply of work. The introduction of steam increased opportunities for work in laundries but depleted the numbers employed (the manglekeepers especially) in the domestic laundry. Another factor was the relocation of business to other parts of Britain. For example, Mr Lipton, the grocery entrepreneur, moved his business to London, throwing a number of home-workers out of work.[14]

Several politico-social considerations fostered the decay of the homework trades. Some employers, in reaction to business, social and public pressure, phased out home-work. There seems to have been an almost universal acceptance amongst the 'better employers' that home-work should be abolished. Home-workers worked in insanitary conditions and the public outcry concerning the effects of 'sweating,' influenced other employers to dispense with their home-workers.[15] Most employers apparently now preferred a supervised staff, under one roof, where the output

HOME-WORKERS
1901
total employed 3642

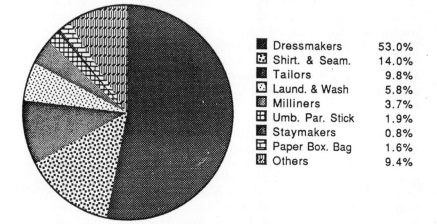

■	Dressmakers	53.0%
⊞	Shirt. & Seam.	14.0%
■	Tailors	9.8%
▣	Laund. & Wash	5.8%
▩	Milliners	3.7%
⊞	Umb. Par. Stick	1.9%
▧	Staymakers	0.8%
▤	Paper Box. Bag	1.6%
▥	Others	9.4%

1911
total employed 2460

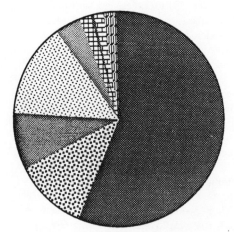

■	Dressmakers	56.6%
⊞	Shirt. & Seam.	11.1%
■	Tailors	8.7%
▣	Laund. & Wash.	14.1%
▩	Milliners	4.0%
⊞	Umb. Par. Stick	1.6%
▧	Staymakers	0.6%
▤	Paper Box & Bag	1.4%
▥	Others	1.8%

FIGURE 1. Proportional breakdown into trades and the total number of home-workers in Glasgow at 1901 and 1911
Source: B.P.P., Census of Scotland, 1901, 1911

TABLE 1. The marital status of women pauper home-workers in Glasgow, at 1900 and 1907

Status	1900 (1)	1907 (2)
Married	11	300
Widowed	119	176
Single	11	184

Source: 1. Margaret Irwin, *Report for the S.C.W.T. of an Enquiry into Home-Work Amongst Women (1 Shirtmaking, Shirtfinishing and Kindred Trades) 1900*, Appendix II, xiii. 2. British Parliamentary Paper, *Report, 1909*, Royal Commission on the Poor Laws and Relief of distress. Report of Miss Constance Williams and Mr Thomas Jones on the Effects of Outdoor Relief on Wages and the Conditions of Employment, (C. 4690), 248.

could be regulated. One Glasgow firm, for instance, had three home-workers in 1907, whereas eighteen years previously it had hired about two hundred. However, employers allowed those women who were family breadwinners to stay on, knowing that they and their families, would otherwise starve.[16]

The majority of home-workers was said to come from the ranks of married women. Difficulties as to the precise numbers of married women engaged in home-work arise from the fact that the census figures do not differentiate between married, widowed, or single women. Two samples dating from 1900 and 1907 do, however, attempt such a breakdown amongst pauper women. Table 1 shows the marital status for 'needle-women' in receipt of parish relief from the City Parish of Glasgow at 1900. The second column of figures is taken from the evidence of 660 home-workers visited by Peter Fyfe in his capacity as Commissioner to the Royal Commission on the Poor Laws and Relief of Distress, 1909. Neither of these tables can be considered as giving representative samples. The returns for 1900 underestimate the role of married women. The figures for 1907, however, appear to correlate fairly closely with the broad trend, and show that married women made up the greatest numbers of the three groups.

Miss Weatherspoon, a forewoman in a Glasgow manufacturing firm who gave evidence to an enquiry into home-workers and the insurance system in 1912, declared that 'most of them [home-workers] are married. Some of them are single, and some of them are widowed.'[17] She was also of the opinion that most of these women entered into the work at age thirty-five, though some of them started up to five years earlier. Given that, traditionally, married women in Glasgow did not seek work until 'necessity drove them,' an examination of the reasons for seeking work in the home-work trades would aid our understanding of the importance of this form of casual work.

In Glasgow a large body of labourers was required in construction,

TABLE 2. The number of home-workers in several districts in
Glasgow, at 1st May 1907

Districts	Home-Workers
Central	139
East	154
West	74
South	289
North	255
North-West	33
South-suburban	69
Kinning Park	10

Source: British Parliamentary Paper, Report, 1909, Royal Commission on
the Poor Laws and Relief of Distress. Report of Miss Contance Williams
and Mr Thomas Jones on the Effects of Outdoor Relief on Wages and the
Conditions of Employment, (C. 4690), 568.

shipbuilding, engineering works, and the docks. These industries and
trades tended to establish themselves in specific geographical areas.
Generally speaking, the major industries of the north and south of the city
were locomotive building and other heavy engineering, shipbuilding,
engineering and dockwork. The east end of the city was dominated by
foundries, chemical works, potteries and brick works, while the central
area's economic base rested on services, retail outlets, railway termini, and
small manufacturing works. Here, textiles, light engineering, and tailoring
establishments co-existed with insurance firms, shipping companies, banks
and local government offices. Table 2 breaks down the general areas
inhabited by home-workers at one point in time, and, while not very
specific, it indicates the broad locational patterns of home-workers in
Glasgow. Particularly noticeable is the concentration of home-workers in
the two areas of the city most dominated by the 'male' industries: shipbuilding, locomotive construction, dock work and heavy engineering.
Since married women were dependent upon their partners for economic
support, the family home was likely to be near the husband's place of work.
Whether or not the wives' own or potential work outlets would be
accessible did not figure in the decision of where to locate.[18] One case in
point is Mrs Brophy, a paper-bag maker. Mrs Brophy lived near the
dockyards because of her husband's work. Her work was not incompatible
with her duties as mother and wife and did not necessitate a long journey
for either the collection of the raw materials or the return of the finished
product. Mrs Brophy's situation and that of others like her demonstrate
that working from the home and, at the same time, being a mother and
housewife were not mutually exclusive occupations. There were few other
opportunities for work outside the home for married women in Glasgow.

Domestic responsibilities prevented these women from working in the 'regular' labour force. In this context, home-work, although viewed as an outdated mode of production, complemented the reality of married, deserted and widowed women desperately in need of wages.[19] An example of a desperate situation was highlighted by a Glasgow Herald report into poverty in the Broomielaw. One deserted mother of three, a washer, when asked about her situation could only repeatedly reply, 'I'm that weary'.[20]

Margaret Irwin observed two distinct categories of home-workers. At the top end was the 'prosperous married woman' – Irwin does not define her further, – who supplemented her husband's income; at the bottom end were women dependent upon home-work for their livelihood. A third category should also be included: married women ('with husbands present') whose work provided the family's chief, and sometimes only, source of income.[21] One Broomielaw couple, for example, depended upon the earnings of the woman, a rag-picker, since her husband 'couldn't work'; they were destitute.[22] On the other hand, some of these women earned a fairly regular income from home-work and their husband's earnings supplemented the family income. On the whole, single women sought higher wages in factories and workshops, and only worked at home if they were handicapped or psychologically unfit for factory work. A statistical description of the three categories of home-workers is impossible, and comparative inferences from other studies (for example, Bulkley's examination of London home-workers in the box making trade) can only be very approximate. Bulkley found that about one-third depended upon the income from making boxes in the home; just over one-third were 'partly dependent' due to the irregularity or insufficiency of the husband's wage; and the same proportion performed such work 'to obtain extras or to pass the time.'[23] Bulkley gave no indication as to how he had reached his conclusions, however, and their relevance to Glasgow's box makers or to the city's home-workers in general is impossible to assess. The most that can be said is that a significant proportion of women depended upon the income earned from home-work to either supplement the family income or, more importantly, to maintain their families. Sir Ernest Hatch, reporting to the Outworkers Committee, 1912, stated that he had 'considerable evidence as to why the women work for these small sums of money, and many varied reasons were given. I believe, however, that even these small earnings form, in many cases, an important [part] of the household income.'[24]

WAGES FOR HOME-WORK AND THE QUESTION OF A 'LIVING WAGE'

Wages for women's labour were low. Home-workers earned even less than in-workers in the same trades, and even this minimal income was neces-

sary for survival. Nevertheless, not every woman was successful at securing work, not unheard of was the 'very respectable woman who through
the pinch of poverty was selling up her home for food, having tried every
possible place to get work, but failed.'[25]

Those women who did secure work in the home-work trades were
guaranteed low wages for several reasons. Apart from the actual low
wages offered, fluctuations in trade, periods of idle-time and competition
help explain the very low rates of pay. Married women themselves were
accused of ensuring that rates of pay remained low. Poverty remained a
feature of daily life. The concept of a 'living wage' and the establishment
of minimum rates of pay figured prominently in attempts by contemporaries to end the cycle of poverty amongst home-workers, indeed amongst all
working women.

Home-work was subject to seasonal fluctuations for two chief reasons.
On the demand side, the availability of women for work depended upon
the security of their husband's work. When husbands were laid off, became
ill, or worked irregularly, the wives sought work in the home-work trades.
With respect to the supply of home-work, many of the trades employing
home-workers were seasonal – for example, tailoring, mangle-keeping
and umbrella covering. Umbrella coverers, for example, were often idle
from four to six months of the year. In the needlework trades, 'idle-set'
fluctuated with the season and the change in fashion. Home-workers
employed at making 'cheap shirts' and shawls for the export market also
suffered slack periods as a result of the capriciousness of the demand for
these products. A few women, however, could be employed throughout
the year, for example in sewing sacks or underclothing. Their dependence
not only on the whims of their social superiors but also on the limited
prosperity enjoyed by the working-class community itself is well illustrated by the plight of the mangle-keepers. Mangle-keepers working for
more prosperous clientele were unemployed or underemployed during
the summer when their employers left for their holidays. However, women
working for the poorer classes considered that they had a more steady
trade, as the working classes took short holidays. They were, on the other
hand, subject to depressions in the trade cycle 'as the mangling of clothes
is a luxury with poor folk and can be dispensed with when times are
hard.'[26]

In general, home-workers were the first to feel any contraction in work.
But with respect to employment overall it was reported: '... there is never
enough home-work of any kind to go around. It just means that many
women go without ... There are always people to do the work but a very
large proportion of the women are unemployed and cannot get work.'[27]

Competition – a major contributor to unemployment and underemployment amongst home-workers – put pressure on the home-work
trades. Competition manifested itself in various ways. The introduction of
the sewing machine, for example, reduced the amount of work available to

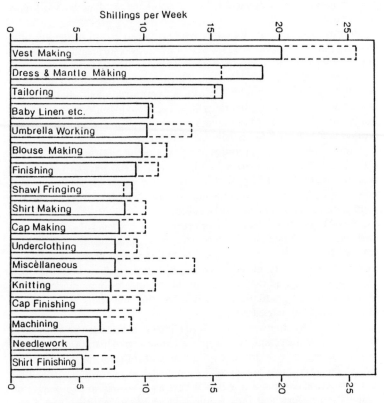

Shillings per Week

Vest Making
Dress & Mantle Making
Tailoring
Baby Linen etc.
Umbrella Working
Blouse Making
Finishing
Shawl Fringing
Shirt Making
Cap Making
Underclothing
Miscellaneous
Knitting
Cap Finishing
Machining
Needlework
Shirt Finishing

FIGURE 2. Rates paid to in-workers and home-workers
Source: B.P.P., 1909, Report, (C. 4690), Royal Commission on
the Poor Laws, 263.

shirt finishers, paper bag makers and sack sewers. Increasingly, this work
was done in workshops and factories; thus, the home-worker competed
with the in-worker. As early as 1893-4, the Commissioners to the Royal
Commission on Labour were of the opinion that: 'the more mechanistic,
efficient methods and production in factories and organisation of work, the
more hopeless becomes the lot of the home-worker' [*sic.*].[28]

However, it was not only competition from machinery that placed the
home-worker in an increasingly precarious position. Competition from
other parts of Britain, from abroad, and from institutions – employing even
cheaper, boy labour – had an impact on the Glasgow market. Two trades
specifically affected were umbrella making for the export market and
paper bag making. Local firms also competed with each other, which often
resulted in underbidding 'in some of the worst sweated trades.[29] Competition amongst subcontractors made possible a situation in which individ-

ual home-workers competed with one another for whatever work was available.[30]

In order to compete, the home-worker had to accept the going rate. Rates of pay were as diverse as the classifications of jobs, and varied from shop to shop. As one worker remarked, 'it (rates of pay] a' depends on the conscience o' the maister.'[31] Margaret Irwin was of the opinion that there was no 'standard rate' and this 'comes out very strikingly ... in the home-work trades.'[32] (Figure 2 illustrates the wages paid to in-door workers and home-workers for a few home-work trades and shows overall that the in-worker was better off financially than the home-worker.)

Home-workers in most trades were paid by the piece or dozen. On the other hand, the home-worker had her overheads to pay, as well as her working materials to buy, such as paste (for paper bags), thread and needles. The quality of available material, the skill of the worker, and the conditions under which she worked all affected her ability to earn a regular income. Although much of the work required a low level of skill, 'considerable time and practice' was necessary to do 'rapid production', which was particularly vital when work was abundant.[33] Skill was required in mangle-keeping and umbrella covering, the latter requiring seven months' training. Over the period under consideration, the demand for cheap products created a situation in which 'inferior' materials were used in order to meet the market demand.

Consequently, there was an adverse effect on the rates paid; in turn, speed and output became more important than ever in maintaining a given level of income. By working 'early and late' at a rapid rate, declared one bag maker, she could earn 7s per week.[34] Home-workers were thought of either as housewives earning a few bob for extras or as women who were so desperate for work that they would take anything that they could get. Women factory and workshop workers accused married women of holding down wage rates. They failed to see the role played by the employer and those ubiquitous 'market forces'. Women working for money wages in their homes were not so very different from women working outside of the home for money wages: their needs and circumstances as workers were the same. They needed the money for their own and their families' survival. Even those women who worked for so called 'pin money' at the 'quality' end might find themselves seeking work of any kind after a sudden downturn in the labour market. Their well-paid and skilled husbands might find themselves under or unemployed.[35] Mrs Brophy, a highly skilled and apparently secure home-worker with a 'very skilled husband', feared any loss to her family's income and needed those few bob per week that she earned. She did not consider that she should not do home-work because her husband earned a 'good' wage: he might be out of work at any moment.

Home-work, according to Walkowitz and Allen, 'represents women's position in the labour market', it does not stand in marked contrast to it.[36]

The perpetuation of low rates, contemporaries argued, stemmed from the casual nature of the work, and from the fact that it was considered supplementary. Home-work was said to be undertaken to supplement the family income and it was falsely assumed that 'supplementary workers' determined the 'standard rate paid to self-supporting women'.[37] Home-work was also said to supplement parish and charity relief, a situation which further served to perpetuate low wages. From a slightly different perspective, however, it would appear that such relief supplemented the meagre earnings made at home-work, especially by widows and elderly women. Thus, the Commissioners reporting to the Royal Commission on the Poor Laws, 1909 stated in their conclusion to the Glasgow evidence that: 'this reserve of labour is partly maintained by the Poor Law, but exists to a far greater degree outside its area. The great majority of woman paupers are not in the arena of labour at all; for the few who are in it the strain is eased a little by out-relief and these are the feeblest and most heavily handicapped among the workers.'[38]

Peter Fyfe estimated, in 1907, that the average weekly earnings of home-workers on relief was 6s $2^1/_2d$ with an out-relief allowance of 3s.8d.[39] The Report of the Select Committee into Home-Work, 1907, suggested that if sweating 'means a wage that is insufficient as a "living wage," then home-work comes within this definition'.[40] Contemporaries, including Irwin and Fyfe, attempted to find a standard daily or weekly wage in an attempt to determine how far home-workers fell above or below a 'living wage.' Margaret Irwin indicated that many women 'usually' received less than 7s or 8s per week, significantly below Peter Fyfe's estimated minimum weekly rate of 10s.1d. 'under which, if we find the average worker at any trade being paid for her 51 hour week, we agree to condemn it as a sweated trade.'[41] (Figure 2 also shows, based on the evidence collected by Peter Fyfe, those trades which fell below his concept of a minimum 'living wage'; typically these were the worst of the 'sweated' trades.) One fairly evident trend over the period of this study was a decline in wages. Both workers giving evidence to Margaret Irwin and Peter Fyfe, and those testifying before official investigations, asserted that the rates paid to them had been falling and were continuing to do so. Employers declared themselves powerless to prevent this trend, due to the extent of competition and the demand for cheap products. Some employers who 'admitted that rates were falling' attributed this to the increasing use of machinery; but suggested that workers were in fact 'better off, since they could increase their output, thereby raising their earnings.[42] All the evidence thus far suggest that this was not the true situation.

Co-operation amongst home-workers was thought of as one solution to the wage situation, but for reasons already indicated, this course of action was unlikely. Thus attention was increasingly devoted to legislative proposals. Trades Boards were suggested as one answer. By fixing minimum wage rates it was argued that the practice of maintaining great variations in rates as well as the arbitrary fixing of rates would be eliminated. The Scottish Council for Women's Trades backed this idea whole-heartedly, although Margaret Irwin had some reservations as to the effectiveness of fixing minimum rates.

Trades Boards were in operation from 1909 on, but were only applicable to tailoring, the ready-made and wholesale bespoke sectors, cardboard box-making, machine-made lace and net finishing, and ready-made blouse making.

These sectors constituted the testing ground although, at the time, Parliament felt that other trades would gradually be incorporated. 'Home-workers' were 'to be represented as well as workers in factories and workshops' on these trade boards.[43] Meanwhile, the Sweated Industries Bill, 1909, was to fix minimum wages through a wages board for tailoring, dressmakng and shirt-finishing. However, it was not until 1912 that the Trades Boards' fixed wages went into operation. There was no attempt to provide equal pay for men and women. In the tailoring trade, men's rates were fixed at 6d per hour while the women's rate was being 're-appraised' at $3^1/_4d$ per hour. One ultimate effect of these Trades Boards was the elimination of the 'small employer who can only stay in business by paying out small sums to home-workers.'[44]

The effect of a fixed minimum wage was a decrease in the differential between the skilled and less skilled worker. Mrs Brophy, interviewed by the 1908 Select Committee, asserted that because of fixed minimum wages women like herself, the very skilled, would be placed at a disadvantage, for the less efficient worker could earn as much as the skillful. She stated: 'I should not like to kill myself when other people not half as quick as me would get as much money as I do.'[45] Her greatest fear was that her work would be taken away and women like herself and her sister, who had six children, would suffer as a result. Nevertheless, the work, and the demand for it persisted, and the few shillings that were earned demanded long hours under poor working conditions.

HOURS OF WORK AND CONDITIONS OF WORK

Home-working, 'instead of acting as a liberating influence', by releasing women from domestic duties or even reducing the burden of the 'double day', in fact 'intensified the pressures of both waged work and unpaid domestic labour'.[46] One trouser-maker finisher, whose husband was in-temperate, worked about six hours a day at her trade; she did not feel that she could leave her family to go and take work in a workshop where she knew she could earn more.[47] An umbrella coverer could do only three dozen a day 'by working very hard' owing to the necessity of doing her housework.[48] A mother of two young children complained of being unable to earn much, the pay was that poor, and of the fact that her domestic duties prevented her from doing more.[49] Another trouser finisher, whose la-bourer husband was often out of work, declared that 'times are hard and it's ill to keep the hoose an' the bairns whiles.'[50]

All home-workers, including the above-mentioned few, indicated to investigators that they worked long and interrupted hours – 'by far too long for any woman', charged one mangler.[51] Margaret Irwin wrote that: 'there is unquestionable evidence that home-work is carried on with extremely long and irregular hours and that hard work and the work is necessary to earn even the very low wages quoted.' [*sic.*].[52]

One paper bag maker declared that all she could earn was 12s per week even though she worked until two and three in the morning.[53] This woman also expressed the view that home-work was bad for one's health due to the late hours worked. During the 'busy season' 'excessively' long hours were spent over the needle – sometimes up to sixteen hours a day. The length of the working day or week was also influenced by the skill of the worker and the quality of the material being worked on. Many women, however, worked interrupted hours according to their family duties and social activities. Mrs Brophy, for example, worked about six hours each day, broken by social and 'family duties.'[54]

It was asserted that even during a busy period, women might not have enough work to keep them fully occupied each day. It was common to work only during the week and sometimes a half day on Saturday. Some types of work lent themselves to particularly long hours. Mangle-keepers held this to be a distinctive feature of their work. Umbrella coverers also spoke of working 'early and late' hours during the busy season, and the only limit to the amount of work undertaken was the amount that could be carried to and from the workshop or factory. Health and age would also determine the length of the working day or week, as would the time required in transporting the products to and from the employer. It would not have been possible to check or regulate the hours worked, even if there were some form of legislation. As one Inspector of the Poor explained, 'when the work is done at home the employer has no control over the hours the employee chooses to work.'[55] Hours worked varied widely from trade to trade. Women worked anywhere from one hour per day to a maximum of sixteen hours per day.[56] The irregularity of the work, reflected in the number of hours worked per day, clearly demonstrates how hard it was for these women to be sure of a secure or regular income since they had little or no control over the supply of work as well as the rates paid. And no matter how few or many hours they spent occupied at home-work, these women still had their domestic duties to fulfil. Home-work, therefore, enslaved women even further to their domestic responsibilities as well as to the necessity of earning some money in order to support their families.

Earning some income from the confines of the home while fulfilling family duties, could place a burden on the conditions of the women's living quarters. Several assumptions were made of home-workers: they were recruited primarily from the ranks of the lowest classes; they had no sense of cleanliness; and they lived in the worst slums of the city. A full breakdown of the areas inhabited by home-workers would be of some interest. The only data available, however, is a table compiled by Peter Fyfe at 1 May 1907 from lists of home-workers, (illustrated in Table 2.) Although the districts are general areas, the table does give an idea of the numbers in a given area at a given time.

During the course of her investigations into home-work from the early 1890s, Margaret Irwin found that home-workers frequently lived in the attics of five-storied buildings, reached by 'dark and dilapidated staircases with effluvia emitting from a "common" sink on every landing.'[57] She also concluded in 1907 that 'a very large proportion of home-workers inhabit these ticketed houses.'[58] Irwin further asserted that the rooms were sparsely furnished. This might corroborate two assumptions: that home-workers lived in the worst slums, and came from the lowest classes. Peter Fyfe, writing in 1907 on cleanliness, observed that fifty per cent of the houses were scrupulously clean', although he indicated that those houses in which women were engaged in tailoring and sack-making 'were characterised by dirt and a few articles of furniture'.[59] Margaret Irwin went to great pains to explain that not all homes were 'dens of dirt and disorder.'[60] Besides, it was quite understandable that in some cases dirt and disorder would be prevalent, for, as Irwin reasoned, any attempt at cleanliness and 'every half hour given to carrying water and "reddying up" the houses "hinders needle and thread" and may mean the loss of a meal to the worker.'[61]

Since home-workers did not come under the Factory and Workshop Act, regulations could not be imposed. Medical Officers of Health, however, in February of 1903 were instructed by the Home Office to keep a list of home-workers 'as furnished by the employer' and also 'a register of workshops.'[62] This was to try to prevent 'said work being carried on in dwellings that are injurious and dangerous to the health of the workers through overcrowding, want of ventilation, or other sanitary defects, or in dwellings in which infectious disease exists.'[63]

Overcrowding could be regulated by law.[64] Sanitary Inspectors had the power to bring charges and exact fines from any home-workers failing to meet the established criteria. Data is available showing the number of inspections to premises of home-workers and the numbers found maintaining a 'dirty house.'[65] In 1904, for example, of 2502 visits 42 homes were found 'dirty'. Hardly a significant number. In any case, home-workers went 'underground' to avoid the inspectors. Furthermore, no data is readily available at this point by which we may discern how and if working in her home was more harmful to a woman's health than working in factories and workshops where accidents frequently occurred, and where lack of lighting, ventilation and toilet facilities, for example, contributed to illness and death.

Generally speaking, the working conditions for home-workers depended upon several factors: the amount of work supplied to them, often a consequence of the time of year or season; the limitations of their living quarters; the type of work – for example, whether or not it involved working with materials that were considered 'dirty'; family commitments that lengthened the work day; and the pressures of meeting legislated standards of sanitation. Earning a living while working in her own home did not appear to be an ideal way for a woman to provide a regular source of income over the long term. Nevertheless, many married women sought out the work for reasons more to do with survival than with whiling away a few spare hours.

CONCLUDING REMARKS

Details have been presented concerning the organisation of home-work, structural changes to the demand for it, rates of pay, hours of work and working conditions in order to provide as full a picture as possible of a small, but often neglected sector of the industrial labour force. It would seem that the situation for home-workers worsened as rates fell, and that the amount of work available decreased as a result of structural and social changes. The situation may also have been adversely affected by a worsening of the economic climate, particularly during the two depressions in the first decade of the twentieth century. Apart from the few married women regularly employed in the home-work trades, most married women entered the labour market when their partners lost their jobs or when demand for their own services escalated. These home-work trades tended to be cyclical and seasonal or both, and those engaged in home-work, on the whole, formed a casual supply of labour. Ironically, technological developments in industry, mechanisation, and the expansion of the factory system often created a demand for home-work which is usually viewed as a relic of a more backward production system.[66] One of its major attractions for employers, of course, was the availability of a supply of cheap labour. This, in large part, explains the persistence of home-work. However, while recognising the need to have a residual labour force in times of heavy demand, many employers preferred to bow to public opinion and condemn the practice. Employees in factories and workshops considered that home-work was used as a mechanism to keep wages low. Investigators deplored the use of home-workers on moral and economic grounds. Yet there was a tacit understanding that without home-work many women 'would starve.' Home-workers themselves would have preferred to improve their situation but were powerless to do so. Lack of organisation, fear of the unknown, the nature of their work, and, of course, their poverty worked against them.

During the period under discussion, structural changes in the economy and to industries and trades employing home-workers resulted in a contraction of work. It seems likely that personal circumstances would have prevented all but a few home-workers from seeking work outside their homes; those who did seek outside employment would most likely compete in a shrinking labour market. In any case, few opportunities existed for married women in the 'regular' work force. Legislation to improve a worsening wage structure and conditions of work did not solve this problem. In the final analysis, home-workers such as Mrs Brophy wanted to be left alone to ply their trade for, ' … it would be awful cruel to interfere with us, because it means poverty for a good few of us if we are not able to earn something to help the husband.'[67]

NOTES

1. Mr Dicksons's Speech, 18 November 1895. Labour League Correspondence.
2. Sweated labour, as defined by the House of Lords Committee on the Sweating System, 1888–89, refers 'to any work that is characterised by excessive hours of work, low rates of pay and conducted under insanitary conditions.' B.P.P., *Fourth Report*(331), viii. Sweated work was, however, most often associated with home-work. In 1907 the Select Committee on Home-Work defined the term more precisely: it was any work that was 'insufficient as a "living wage".' 'Super-sweating' was one contemporary term used for anyone working as cheap labour at cheap products for working-class consumption. *FORWARD*, 14 November 1908.
3. Sheila Allen and Carol Wolkowitz, *Homeworking Myths and Realities* (MacMillan Education, Houndmills, Basingstoke, Hampshire, and London, 1987), 28.
4. Report of an Enquiry by Margaret Irwin, *Women's Work in Tailoring and Dressmaking*, Scottish Council for Women's Trades, 1900, 16.
5. See E. Gordon, '*The Scottish Trade Union Movement: Class and Gender 1850–1914' Journal of the Scottish Labour History Society*, no. 23 (1988), for a discussion of the under-representation of women workers in the census.
6. B.P.P. 1912 Vol. 1, *Report*, (Cd. 6178 - XLII), Outworkers Committee, Report of the Committee Appointed to Consider and Advise with Regard to the Application of the National Insurance Act to Outworkers. 6.
7. Duncan Bythel, *The Sweated Trades: Outwork in Nineteenth Century Britain* (Batsford Academic, 1978), London, 16.
8. B.P.P., 1909, *Report*, (Cd. 4690), 247.
9. Ibid.
10. *FORWARD*, 13 April 1912.
11. See Jenny Morris' discussion in *Women Workers and the Sweated Trades: the Origins of Minimum Wage Legislation* (Hants and Vermont: Gower Publishing Company Limited, 1986), 20-23.
12. Quoted in Allen and Wolkowitz, op.cit., 19, Bythel, op.cit., 254.
13. A. Albert, 'Patterns of Employment of Working Class Women in Glasgow 1890–1914, unpublished M.A. Thesis, University of Victoria, 1985; see Chapter 3 section 3 for a fuller discussion.
14. S.R.A. C3/2/128, Report of an Enquiry by Margaret Irwin on *Home Work Amongst Women (II Miscellaneous and Minor Trades)*, S.C.W.T., 1900, 17.
15. The agitation had encouraged consumers, businessmen, and the women themselves to contact the Glasgow Council for Women's Trades (later the S.C.W.T.) and reports of their findings were posted to the Continent, Canada and the U.S.A. S.R.A. C3/2/29

4th Annual Report, 1898–9, 9.

16. Irwin, *Women's Work in Tailoring and Dressmaking*, 18.

17. B.P.P., 1912 Vol. 1, *Evidence and Appendices*, (Cd.6179), Outworkers Committee, q. 5295.

18. Dr James Treble, however, states that apart from the cost factor and availability of surplus labouring work outlets, living near the central areas of Glasgow allowed the children of the families of unskilled males to find work as newsboys and milk boys. But in addition, their wives 'who were working in the sweated trades would then be within easy reach of most of the large wholesale warehouses and firms involved in the domestic system of production.' 'The Market for Unskilled Male Labour in Glasgow, 1890–1914', in *Essays in Scottish Labour History*, ed. Ian MacDougall (Glasgow, Collins, 1978), 131.

19. Allen and Walkowitz, op.cit., 98.

20. 15 November 1907.

21. The man's irregularity of employment, due to the casual or seasonal nature of their work, or to illness, or physical disability, resulted in this situation.

22. *Glasgow Herald*, 15 November 1907.

23. M. E. Bulkley, *The Establishment of Legal Minimum Rates in the Box-Making Industry under the Trade Boards Act of 1909* The Ratan Tata Foundation University of London, Studies in the Minimum Wage 11, (G. Bell & Sons Ltd., 1915), 67. Jenny Morris has similarly identified three categories of home-workers similar to Bulkley's, but derived from the Select Committee on Homework of 1908. These categories differ in some respects from my own inasmuch as they attempt a breakdown among full-time home-workers, casual worker and part-time workers. Whatever the category, few working-class women were in a position to be supported! op.cit., 14.

24. B.P.P., *Report on Married Women Outworkers*, (Cd.6600–LXXXVIII), 6.

25. *Glasgow Herald*, 19 February 1895.

26. Great Britain, Parliament, *Parliamentary Papers, Report of the Select Committee into Home-Work* (290), 1907, evidence of Margaret Irwin, q. 2320.

27. Irwin, *Home-Work* II, 36.

28. B.P.P., 1893, *Report*, (C.6894 – XXIII), Elizabeth Orme, 277.

29. B.P.P., 1908, *Evidence*, (246-VIII), Select Committee into Home-Work, p. viii.

30. B.P.P., 1909, *Report*, (Cd.4690), Royal Commission on the Poor Laws, p. 250. By 1907, Margaret Irwin was of the opinion that the numbers of sub-contractors was on the decline, and work was distributed directly by the factories and workshops, B.P.P., 1908, Evidence, (246-VIII), Select Committee into Home-Work, q. 2238. According to returns to the M.O.H., Glasgow, the number of sub-contractors fell from just over one thousand in 1906 to about seven hundred in 1913. A.R.M.O.H., 1906, P. 1906 AND 1913, P. 158.

31. *Glasgow Sweated Conference*, 1907, 384.

32. B.P.P., 1907, *Report*, (290-VI), Select Committee into Home-Work, q. 2115.

33. Irwin, *Home-Work* II, p. 17.

34. *Glasgow Herald*, 15 November, 1907.

35. See Treble, op.cit., 123–5 and also his 'The Seasonal Demand for

176   ALICE J. ALBERT

Adult Labour in Glasgow, 1890–1914', in (*Social History*, 7 Jan. 1978): 46–8.

36. Op.cit., 85. Morris also makes this point when she talks about the problems of women as a cheap supply of labour. Op.cit., pp 11-22 in passim, p. 67.
37. S.R.A. C3/2/18 Evidence of Margaret Irwin, *Glasgow Municipal Commission on the Housing of the Poor* (190-2-3), 532.
38. B.P.P., 1909, *Report*, (C.4690), Royal Commission on the Poor Laws, 257. Margaret Irwin expressed the opinion that 'in so many cases, wages have sunk below the actual "starvation level",' and therefore charity and parish relief supplemented wages. *Home-Work II*, 8.
39. B.P.P., 1909, *Report*, (C.4690), Royal Commission on the Poor Laws, 271.
40. B.P.P., 1907, *Report*, (290-VI), iii. Although the Select Committee into Home-Work never defined their concept of a 'living wage.'
41. B.P.P., 1909, *Report*, (C.4690), Royal Commission on the Poor Laws, 265–6.
42. B.P.P., 1909, *Report*, (C.4690), Royal Commission on the Poor Laws, 251.
43. *Glasgow Herald*, 27 March 1909.
44. Ibid., 27 March 1912.
45. B.P.P., 1908, *Report*, (246-VIII), Select Committee into Home-Work, q. 2907.
46. Allen and Walkowitz, op.cit., 134.
47. Irwin, *Women in Tailoring and Dressmaking*, 32.
48. Irwin, *Home-Work Amongst Women (I shirtmaking, Shirtfinishing and Kindred Trades)* S.C.W.T., 1900, 10.
49. Ibid., 25.
50. Ibid.,
51. Irwin, *Home-Work II*, 37.
52. *Women in Tailoring and Dressmaking*, 9.
53. Irwin, *Home-Work II*, 18.
54. B.P.P., 1908, *Report*, (246-VIII), Select Committee into Home-Work q. 2900.
55. Irwin, *Home-Work I*, 10.
56. See M.A. thesis for a fuller treatment, especially Chapter 4, section 2.2.
57. Irwin, *Home-Work I*, 10.
58. 'Ticketed' refers to the process used by Inspectors of Health who visited slum dwellings affixing the number of residents permitted by law to reside in each tenement house. B.P.P., 1907, *Report* (290-VI0), Select Committee into Home-Work, q. 2141.
59. B.P.P., 1909, *Report*, (C.4690), Royal Commission on the Poor Laws, 246.
60. *Home-Work I*, 10.
61. Ibid..
62. *Municipal Commissions*, 533.
63. *ANNUAL REPORT of the MINISTRY OF HEALTH*, 1903, 113.
64. By law, 400 cubic feet per person was the measurement used to determine overcrowding. When such conditions were found to exist, those responsible were to be punished. In 1903 three tailors, one underclothing maker and two dressmakers were found guilty of working in overcrowded conditions. Ibid., 114. Moral persuasion apparently worked as an effective method of encouraging

women to keep cleaner houses!

65. *ANNUAL REPORT of the MINISTRY OF HEALTH*, 1904, 133.
66. Morris, op.cit., 221.
67. B.P.P., 1908, *Report*, (246-VIII), Select Committee into Home-Work, q. 2910.

SELECT BIBLIOGRAPHY

Allen, Sheila and Carol Wolkowitz, *Homeworking Myths and Realities*, Hampshire and London, Macmillan Education, 1987.

Bythel, Duncan. *The Sweated Trades: Outwork in Nineteenth Century Britain*, London, Batsford Academic, 1978.

Irwin, Margaret. *Women's Work in Tailoring and Dressmaking*, Scottish Council for Women's Trades, 1900.

Irwin, Margaret. *Home-work Amongst Women (I Shirtmaking, shirtfinishing and Kindred Trades*, Scottish Council for Women's Trades, 1900.

Morris, Jenny. *Women Workers and the Sweated Trades: the Origins of Minimum Wage Legislation*. Hants and Vermont, Gower, 1986.

INDEX